SHIVAJI THE GREAT

SHIVAJI THE GREAT

BY

BAL KRISHNA, M. A., Ph. D.

IN TWO VOLUMES
VOL. I

Published by

Gyan Publishing House
5, Ansari Road
Daryaganj, New Delhi-110002
Phone: 011-47034999, 9811692060
E-mail: books@gyanbooks.com

Distribution Network
gyanbooks.com
India, USA, Canada, UK, Australia

ISBN: 978-93-6433-051-0 (Set)
978-93-6433-162-3 (HB)
First Published, 1932

2nd Impression 2024

Printed at: Gyan Press, Delhi.

SHIVAJI THE GREAT, (VOL. I)
Author: BAL KRISHNA

SHIVAJI THE GREAT

BY

BAL KRISHNA, M. A., Ph. D.

Fellow of the Royal Historical Society, the Royal
Statistical Society, the Royal Economic Society, London;
Professor of Economics and Principal, Rajaram College,
Kolhapur, India

Vol. I

BOMBAY:

D. B. TARAPOREVALA Sons & Co.
" Kitab Mahal," Hornby Road

To

HIS HIGHNESS

LT. COL. SIR RAJARAM, G. C. I. E., G. C. S. I.,

CHHATRAPATI MAHARAJASAHED OF KOLHAPUR,

the only ruling representative of

the noble house of

SHIVAJI THE GREAT

FOR

HIS KIND PATRONAGE.

FOREWORD

A vast literature has grown up in Marathi on the romantic career of Shivaji. He is hailed by his admirers as the maker of Maharashtra, the founder of the Maratha Empire, the liberator of the Hindus, the destroyer of Muslim sovereignty in India, the prophet of patriotism, the apostle of Hindu culture. His military achievements have undoubtedly placed him in the galaxy of the world–famous conquerors like Alexander, Cæsar, Hannibal, and Napoleon. The Great Shivaji underwent an apotheosis even in his life time, and was looked upon as God Shiva who had incarnated Himself for saving His devotees from the inhuman oppressions of their alien rulers. It is indisputable that in him the national spirit of Hindu India took a visible form. He is one of the immortals of the world and has so thoroughly captivated the imagination of Indians with his burning patriotism that he has become the pole-star of Indian Swarajya. It was natural that myths and legends should have fast multiplied on the life of this superman, so that it has now become difficult to distinguish facts from fables. In truth, there is scarcely an event in his brilliant career, the veracity of whose details recorded in the Marathi chronicles cannot be challenged. Hence I considered it necessary to turn the torch-light of foreign contemporary writings and records on the vernacular literature to pick up the grains of truth lying scattered here and there.

The archives in London, at Batavia and the Hague, in Bombay, Goa, Pondichery, Madras, Tanjore, Satara and Poona have been ransacked to secure every scrap of information on the life of the hero.

The material of this book has been in process of collection and preparation by the author for more than seven years. During this period many difficulties were encountered in securing documents, paintings, pictures, and plans, in getting authentic translation of the Dutch, Portuguese and Persian extracts, and in the printing of the three volumes from an out-of-the way place like Kolhapur. Thus the book is the outcome of an intensive study of the historical literature on the life of Shivaji and of the personal knowledge of many parts of the country which was the scene of his manifold activities. Since nothing is more eloquent than facts, I have given foreign

❡ 1

documents in extenso even at the risk of overburdening the book with details, so that the reader may have the account of the events in the very words of the contemporary writers themselves. I am conscious of the difficulty which some readers will experience in going through 17th century English, but care has been taken to break the monotony of long letters by marginal headlines and to make the topics dealt therein easy to understand.

My aim has been to construct the history of Shivaji and his forefathers with original materials obtained through earnest and scrupulous research, cautiously sifted and impartially used. For the realization of this object, I have discarded anecdotic and fragmentary history, and mainly relied on the genuine and well-authenticated facts met with in the Indian and European records. Being fully equipped with stern facts, the reader will be able to judge for himself the validity of my conclusions and will correct the assertions of various historians, if these should seem unduly categorical.

I wish to express my deep sense of obligation to Their Highnesses, the Maharajas of Baroda, Indore, Kolhapur, and the Rajasaheb of Mudhol for their kind patronage. It gives me much pleasure to acknowledge with gratitude the valuable assistance received from the Superintendent of Records, India Office, London; Directors of the Archives at Batavia and the Hague; the Superintendent of the Record Office, Bombay; the Secretaries of the Shrishiva Charitra Office and Bharat Itihas Sanshodhak Mandal, Poona; and the Rajasaheb of Mudhol who gave me access to all the published and unpublished material and permission to reproduce the same. My cordial thanks are also due to Prof. E. C. Godce Molesbergen, Archivist at Batavia, Mr. C. C. Rammerswaal of the Hague, and Prof. Brij Narain of Lahore for their translation of the Dutch documents, to Mr. P. Pissurlencar of Goa, Prof. A. X. Soares of Baroda and Rev. S. Cotta of the Catholic Mission at Miraj for the translation of the Portuguese extracts, to Rev. H. Heras, S. J. of Bombay, for lending me the English translation of the Dagh-Register, and to several friends who have assisted me in the publication of these volumes.

Kolhapur,

5-5-32.　　　　　　　　　　　　　　　**BALKRISHNA.**

BIBLIOGRAPHY

India Office Manuscript Records

Factory Records:

Bombay. Vols. 1, 2, 3, 6, 8, 19, 105, 106.
Fort St. George. Vols. 1, 18, 27, 28.
Master Papers No. 10.
Masulipatam. Vol. 10.
Miscellaneous. Vols. 2, 4, 11.
O. C.–Original Correspondence. Vols. 21, 28, 29, 30,
     31, 32, 33, 34, 35, 36, 37, 38, 39, 40.
Orme Mss. Vols. 1, 114, 116, 155, 174, 263, 331.
Rajapur Vol. I.
Surat. Vols. 2, 3, 4, 19, 66, 69, 85, 86, 87, 88, 89,
    90, 91, 103, 104, 105, 106, 107, 108, 166.
Finch Mss. Vol. I.
Letter Books. Vols. 1-6.
Mackenzie Mss. Vol. 201.

Public Record Office, London

C. O.— Original Correspondence. Vols. 77 IX; 77X;
         77 XIII; 107 XII.
State Papers for Turkey. Vol. 18.

Bombay Record Office

Papers Unavailable. Vols. I–VII.
Surat Factory Diary No. I.
Surat Factory Outwards Nos. 1, 1 A, 1, 2 3.

Dutch Records

The Hague:

Dagh–Register–All Vols. up to 1680 A. D.
Kol. Archives. Vols. 1122, 1123, 1124, 1132, 1133, 1136,
  1137, 1142, 1143, 1144, 1145, 1146, 1152, 1156,
  1159, 1160.

Batavia:

Letter Books. Vols. 1660–1, 1661–2, 1663–4, 1664–5,
  1665–6, 1668–9, 1670–1, 1671–2, 1672–3, 1673–4,
  1674–5, 1675–6, 1676–7, 1677–8, 1680–1, 1681–2,
  1682–3.

India Office, London:
  Hague Transcripts. Series I. Vols. 15, 17, 18, 23, 24, 27, 28, 29, 31,32.

Saraswati Mahal Library, Tanjore
Bhosal Vanshavali in Sanskrit No. 5021.
Raj Ranjan Puran No. 1430.
Sangita Makranda or Shahi Makaranda by Veda. No. 662.3.
Sangita Saramritam by Tulaja Raja. No. 6629.
Shahendra Vilasa by Shridhara Venkatesa. No. 10261.
Bundle No. 117/595

Rajasaheb of Mudhol
Chronicle of Mudhol in Marathi.
Persian Sanads

Published Records
Court Minutes. All the Vols.
English Factories. Vols. 1–13 for the years 1619–1669.
F. R. Fort St. George-Diary and Consultation Bk. 1672–78; 1678-9.
Sir G. Forrest, Home Series. Vol. I.
Sir G. Forrest, Maratha Series. Vol. I.

Publications of the Hakluyt Society
First Series:
  70–71. The Voyage of John Huyghen van Linschoten to the East Indies.
  74–75. The Diary of William Hedges, Esq.
  84–85. The Travels of Pietro della Valle to India.
Second Series:
  1—2. The Embassy of Sir Thomas Roe to the Court of the Great Mogul.
  17, 35, 45. The Travels of Peter Mundy in Europe and Asia.

List of Books
English
  Ackworth, H. A. Ballads of the Marathas. London 1894.
  Aiyar, R. Satyanatha. History of the Nayaks of Mudura. Madras. 1924.

Aiyangar, S. K.   Sources of Vijayanagar History. Madras.

Anderson, P. The English in Western India. Bom. 1854.

Apte and Paranjpe.   Birthdate of Shivaji.

Baldaeus, Philip.   A true and exact Description of the East India Coasts of Malabar, Coromandel and Ceylon.

Balkrishna, Dr.   Commercial Relations between India and England. London 1924.

Ball, V.   Tavernier's Travels in India.   2 Vols.

Beni Prasad. History of Jahangir. 1922.

Bernier, F. Travels in the Mogul Empire, ed. by Constable.

Bhandarkar, Dr. Sir R. G. Commemoration Vol. Poona.

Bharat I. S. Mandal, Poona. Varshik Itivritta; Sammelan Vritta; Ahaval.

Briggs, John.   History of the Rise of the Mahomedan Power in India. 4 Vols. London 1829.

Brown, Sir Thomas. The Works. 4 Vols. London 1846.

Bruce, J.   Annals of the E. I. Co. 3 Vols. London 1810.

Buchanan, F.   Mysore, Canara and Malabar. 2 Vols.

Cambridge, R. O.   Account of the War etc. Lond. 1761.

Careri, G. F. Gmelli.   A Voyage round the world.

Clunes, Capt. John.   Historical Sketch of the Princes of India. London 1815.

Courtney, W.   Memoir on the Sawantwaree State.

Cousens, H.   Bijapur and its Architectural Remains.

Dampier, Capt. William.   A new Voyage round the World. London 1699.

Danvers, F. C.   The Portuguese in India. 2 Vols.

Dellon, M. D.   A Voyage to the East Indies. London 1698.

Diary of Strenshyam Master.   3 Vols.

Douglas, J.   Bombay and Western India, 2 Vols. London.

Dow, Alexander. History of Hindustan. 3 Vols.

Du Jarric, Pierre S. J.   Histoire des choses plus memorables advenues tant es Indes, etc.

Duff, J. Grant.   History of the Mahrattas. Bombay 1873.

Elliot, H. M. and Dowson, John. The History of India as told by its own Historians. 8 Vols. London.

Elphinstone, M.   History of India.

English Records on Shivaji. Shiva Charitra Karyalaya. Poona 1931.

Forbes, James. Oriental Memoires. 2 Vols. London 1834.

Forrest, George W.   Selections from the letters, despatches, and other state papers. Maratha Series. Vol. I.

Foster, Sir William. The English Factories in India.

Fryer, Dr. John. A new account of the East Indies and Persia. London 1698 and 3 Vols. London 1909-12.

Gazetteers of the Bombay Presidency. Vols. X to XXIV.

Grose, J. H. A Voyage to the East Indies. 2 Vols. London 1772.

Harmilton, Capt. A. A New Account of the E. I. Lond. 1744.

Hedges, Sir W. Diary during his Agency in Bengal. 3 Vols. London. 1887-89.

Heras, Rev. H. Beginnings of Vijayanagar History. Bombay 1929.

Indian Antiquary, a Journal of Oriental Research.

Indian Historical Records Commission—Proceedings. Vols. IX-X.

Indian Journal of Economics. Vol. XI. Part II.

Irwine, W. Storia Do Mogor (Travels of Manucci' 4 Vols. Army of the Indian Moguls. London 1903.

Jervis, Major T. B. Geographical and Statistical Memoir of the Konkan. Calcutta 1840.

Journal of the Bombay Historical Society. Vols. II, III.

Khan, Dr. S. A. Anglo-Portuguese Negotiations.

Kincaid and Parasnis. History of the Maratha People. Vol. I.

Lane-Poole, Stanley. Aurangzeb. 1908.

Malleson, Col. G. B. Historical Sketch of the Native States of India. London 1875.

Mandelslo, J. Albert de. The Voyages and Travels into the East Indies. London 1669.

Manker, J. L. Life and Exploits of Shivaji.

Manrique, Fray Sebastien. Travels of F. S. Manrique 1629–43. 2 Vols.

Manucci. See Irvine.

Marco Polo. Travels. 2 Vols. 1903.

Martin, R. Montgomery. The Indian Empire Vol. III.

Modern Review, 1907, 1908, 1917, 1924, 1929.

Mundy. See Hakluyt Society.

Nieuhoff, John. Travels of– London 1704.

Orme, Robert. Historical Fragments of the Mogul Empire. London 1825.

Ovington, J. A Voyage to Suratt in the year 1689.

Owen, S. J. India on the Eve of the British Conquest. Fall of the Mogul Empire.

Parasnis, D. B. Itihas Sangrah, 7 Vols.

Pogson, Capt. W. R. A History of the Boondelas. Calcutta 1828.

Potdar and Mujumdar. Hist. Miscellany.

Puntambekar, S. V. A Royal Edict on the Principles of State Policy and Organization.

Raddi. Shivaji.

Ranade, M. G. Rise of the Maratha Power.

Rawlinson, H. G. Shivaji the Maratha.
Source Book of Maratha History. Vol. I.

Rice, B. L. Mysore. 2 Vols. Westminister 1897.
Mysore and Coorg. London 1909.
Epigraphia Karnatika, Part X. 1905.

Russel, R. N. Castes and Tribes of C. P. 4 Vols.

Sainsbury, E. B. Calender of the Court Minutes etc. of the East India Company 1668–70.

Sardesai, G. S. Shivaji Souvenir. 1927.

Sarkar, J.   History of Aurangzeb. 4 Vols.
             Shivaji and His Times. 1929.
             Studies in Moghal India.
Savarkar, V. D.   Hindu-Pad· Padashahi.
Schouten.   Voyage de Gautier Schouten aux Indes
             Orientales, 1658-65. 2 Vols. Amsterdam 1707.
Scott, Jonathan.   Ferishta's History of the Dekkan.
             2 Vols. Shrewsbury 1794.
Sen, Dr. Surendranath.   Administrative System of the
             Marathas.
                          Foreign Biographies of Shivaji.
                          Historical Records at Goa.
                          Military System of the Marathas.
                          Shiva Chhatrapati.
Sewell, R.   A Forgotten Empire. London 1900.
Smith, V. A.   Oxford History of India.
Sullivan, Sir Edward.   Conquerors, Warriors and
             Statesmen of India.   London 1866.
Takakhav, N. S. and Keluskar, K. A.   Life of Shivaji
             Maharaj.
Tavernier, J. B.   See Ball.
Thevenot, J. de. Voyages en Europe, Asie et. Afrique.
             5 Vols. Amsterdam. 1727.
Tod, Col. The Annals and Antiquities of Rajasthan. Ed.
             by W. Crooke. 1920.
Vaidya, C. V.   Shivaji the Founder of Maratha Swaraj.
                          History of Mediæval India.
Valentyn, F.   Oud en Niew Oost-Indien. 5 vols.
             Dordrecht 1724.
Waring, E. Scott.   A History of the Marathas. London
             1810.
Wheeler, J. T.   Madras in the Olden Time.
Wilks, Lt. Col. Mark.   Historical Sketches of the South
             of India.   3 Vols. London 1810-17.
Yule, Sir Henry.   Diary of W. Hedges. 2 Vols.

French

La Compagnie Indes Orientales et F. Martin by P. Kaeppelin.

La Mission du Madure by J. Bertrand; English Translation in the 'Nayaks of Madura.'

Memoires of F. Martin. English Trans. by S. N. Sen.

The Journal of B. Deslandes. English Trans. by J. Sarkar.

Histore de Sevagi et de son successeur by J. D'Orleans. English Trans. by J. Sarkar.

Thevenot, Monsieur de. Works.

Voyage des Indes Orientales by M. Carre.

Dutch

Dagh–Register. Vols. up to 1680.
    Translation in Mss. kindly lent by Rev. H. Heras. Some extracts were translated by my friends, Prof. Brij Narain of Lahore and Prof. Molesbergen of Batavia.

Dutch Records. India Office.

German

Iversen, Volquard. Reise–Beschriebungen. Orientalische Reise–Beschriebung. (Translations through the India Office.)

Marathi

Acworth, H. A, and Shaligram, S. T. Powadas. 1911.

Amatya, R. Ajna–patra. 1923.

Apte, D. V. and Divekar, S. M. Shiva Charitra Pradipa.

Bambardekar, V, A. Konkan–chya Itihasa–chi Sadhane.
    Mathgaon Shila–lekh.

Bendre. V. A. Sadhan Chikitsa. 1928.

Bhat, B. V. Maharastra Dharma. Dhulia
    Ramdas and Shivaji. „

Bhate, G. C. Sajjangad and Samarth Ramdas.

Bhave, V. L. Marathi Daftar–Rumal 3. 1928.

Chitragupta Bakhar.

Dongre, M. G. The Geneological Tree of the Bhonsale Family.
    Shri Sidhanta Vijaya.

S. 2.

Kayastha Prabhunchya Itihasachi Sadhane.

Kelkar, N. C. Aitihasik Powade. 1928.

Keluskar. K. A. Life of Tukaram.

Khare, G. S. Jantri or Almanack.

Khare, V. V. Maloji Wa Shahji. Poona 1920.

Kulkarni, B. S. Account of the Chitnis family and Sanads.

Mawjee, P. V. and Parasnis D. B. Sanads and Letters. 1913.

Modak, B. P. History of the family of Adilshahis of Bijapur.

Modak, G. V. The Campaign of Pratapgad. 1927.

Patrasara–Sangrah. 2 Vols. Poona.

Proceedings of Annual Conferences of the Bharat Itihas Sanshodhaka Mandala of Poona.

Pingulkar, V. P. Savantawadi Sansthancha Itihas. 1911.

Quarterly of the Bharat Itihas Sanshodhaka Mandala.

Qualmi Bakhar, 91 or 96.

Rajwade, v. K. Aitihasik Prastavana,
Marathanchya Itihasachi Sadhane.
Vols. 4, 8, 9, 15, 24.
Tanjavarcha Shilalekh.

Ramdas and Ramdasi Series:— Dasabodha.

Sabhasad, K. A. Shiva-Chhatrapati–Chen Charitra.

Sahvichar–Baroda. October 1931.

Samarthanchen Samarthya.

Sane, Rao Bahadur. Patre Yadi Vagaire.

Sardesai, G. S. Marathi Riyasat.
Shivasansmriti. 1927.

Shedgaonkar Bakhar. Ed. by V. L. Bhave.

Shivacharitra Sahitya. Vols. 1–3.

Shiva Digvijaya. Nandurbarkar P. R. and Dandekar, L. K. Baroda. 1895.

Shivapratap. Baroda.

Shivacharitra Nibandhavali. 2 vols. Shri Shivacharitra Office, Poona.

Shivaji–Nibandhavali. 2 Vols. Shri Shivacharitra Office.
Sirjotishi. Gomantakanchya Itihasachi Sadhane.

Sanskrit

Gagabhatta. Shivarajaprashasti.
Jayarama. Pranal-parvat–grahan–akhyanam. Ed. by
Divekar, S. M.
Radhamadhav–vilas–champu. Ed. by Divekar,
S. M.
Paramanand. Shivabharat by Divekar, S. M.
Shivaraj-Rajyabhishek–Kalpataru.

Hindi

Bhushan's Granthavali. Benares 1907.
Lal Kavi. Chhatraprakash. Allahabad 1916.
Sampurn Bhushan. Bharat I. S. Mandala, Poona.
Rao Bahadur Gaurishankar Ojha, The. History of
Rajputana.

Persian

Khan, Hamid-ud-din. Ahkam-i-Alamgiri.
Khan, Khafi. Muntakhab-ul-lubab.
Lahori, A. H. Padishahnamah.
Nurullah, Sayyid. Tarikh-i-Ali Adil Shah II.
Ruqat-i-Alamgiri.
Sanads with the Rajasaheb of Mudhol.
Sanads with B. 1tihas S. Mandala. Poona.
Tarikh-i-Shivaji. Translated by J. Sarkar in Modern
Review 1907 & 1910.
Zahur, Md. Muhammad-namah.
Zubairi, Md. Ibrahim. Basatin-i-Salatin.

Urdu

Bashir-ud-din Ahmad-Urdu translation of Basatin-i-Salatin

Kanarese

Keladi Nripa Vijayam.

Portuguese

Pissurlenkar, Pandurang. Shivaji.

ABBREVIATIONS

A. Dow. History of Hindustan—*Dow.*

Basatin-i-Salatin— *B. S.*

English Factories —*E. F.*

J. Grant Duff-History of the Marathas-*Duff.*

Jonathan Scott. Ferishta's History of the Deccan-*Scott's Deccan.*

Hague Transcripts Series I at the India Office- - *I. O. D. Records or Dutch Records.*

Kinkaid ahd Parasnis. History of the Maratha People. Vol. I.-*Kinkaid.*

Letter Books or Despatches from the Court of Directors to the Factories in the East—*L. B.*

Manucci. Storia Do Mogor--*Manucci.*

Original Correspondence-*O. C.* (India Office) *C. O.* (Public Records Offlce.)

Patra Sar Sangrah-*P. S. S.*

Papers Unavailable at Bombay--*B. P. Unav.*

R. Orme. Historical Fragments—*Orme.*

Shiva Bharat—*Sh. Bh.*

Shivaji the Great Vol. I. Part II. Shivaji Vol. I.

Shivcharitra Nibandhavali, *Sh. Ch. N.*

Shivacharitra Pradipa—*S. Ch. Pr.*

Sir J. Sarkar. Shivaji & His Times—*Sarkar.*

Surat Factory Outward Letter Book—*O. L. Book.*

Vol. I

SHAHJI

CONTENTS

CHAPTER I

Nature and extent of the records. The Dutch Records, The Records in London, Value of the Records at Bombay. Use of the European Records. General value of the European Records. Light on Afzal Khan's tragedy. Issues of Shaista Khan's surprise, Was Shaista Khan's daughter captured by Shivaji? Shivaji's audience with Aurangzeb. Imperfections of the Persian and European material.

CHAPTER II

The incorrectness of available geneologies. The ancestry of Sajjan Sinha, Rana Sajjansinha of the Solar Dynasty. Rana Dilipsinha, a commander of the Bahmani Kingdom. Heroic deeds of Sidhoji. Bhairoji or Bhimaji, Rana Devaraj and Ugrasen. Dominion of the Bhosles in 1454. The Ghorpades of Mudhol, Guerilla Warfare. Mudhol rulers under Bijapur. The Bhosles of Devagiri. Maloji. Tentative chronology of Shivaji's ancestors.

CHAPTER III

Shahji's personality and education. Marriage of Shahji. Vicissitudes of war in the Deccan. Jadhavrao's desertion to the Moguls (1621-30). Capture of Poona by Shahji, 1621, The seige of Bijapur by Amber. Bijapur described. The battle of Bhatvadi in 1624. Shahji in Bijapur service (1625-28). The recall of Mahabat Khan. Estimate of Malik Amber. Demise of Ibrahim Adil Shah. Desertion and return of Shahji. Shahji in Khandesh. The Imperial army in the Deccan, 1630. Arms of the Mogul army. Mode of Mogul warfare. Method of Maratha warfare. Jadhavarao's murder. Revolt of Shahji. Revolution at Daulatabad. Shahji's monarchy. Shah Jahan's war with Bijapur. The Mogul retreat from Bijapur and Parenda. The end of the Nizam Shahi Kingdom. Shahji, the king-maker. The capture of Junner by Shahji. Siege of Parenda by the Moguls. Internal discord at Bijapur. The brutal murder of Murari Pandit. Shah Jahan against Bijapur. Treaty between Shah Jahan and Adil Shah. Capture of Udgir and Ausa. The submission of Shahji. Shahji's work. Chronology.

CHAPTER IV

A review of Shahji's position. Acquisition of new jagirs. Vijayanagar in the throes of dissolution. Aggressions of the Naik of Ikkeri. The Royal city of Ikkeri described. Muslim alliance against Vijayanagar. Rebellion of Timmaraj. The first expedition into Malnad (1637–1638). Second expedition into the Karnatic (1638). Third expedition in 1639. The result of the campaign. Vigorous policy of Shriranga. Mir Jumla's defeat at Vellore. Treaty between Vijayanagar and Bijapur. Victories of Shriranga. Conquests of Mir Jumla. Campaign against Shivappa of Ikkeri in 1644. Expedition under the Khan-i-Khanan in 1644–5. Mustafa Khan's campaign in 1646–48. Campaign against Ginji in 1648. Cause of Shahji's imprisonment. Release of Shahji. Secret support to Swarajya. Shahji and Baji Ghorpade. The burning of Mudhol. Chronology.

CHAPTER V

Power of Mir Jumla. Shahji's victory over Mir Jumla in 1651-52. Shriranga in the field. Situation in the Deccan. The last ten years of Shahji. Tegenapatam captured by Shahji (1661). Porto Novo taken by Shahji. The capture of Tegenapatam and after. The war between Shahji and Lingama Nayak. Bahlolkhan's raid in Tanjore. War between Tanjore and Madura. Horrible consequences of the war. Second rebellion and imprisonment of Shahji. Shivaji, an independent King. Interview of father and son. Shahji at Bangalore. Shahji's work in the Karnatic. Policy of consolidation. The Maratha revenue system in the Karnatic. A veiw of Shahji's life. Shahji, the inspirer of Shavaji. Chronology.

LIST OF ILLUSTRATIONS

ERRATA

	For	Read
P. 15 & 35	Geneologies	Genealogies
P. 35 & subsequent pages.	Geneological	Genealogical
P. 36 n	Todd	Tod
P. 40	Whose English translation	The Eng. translation of which
P. 52	Extensive tank	An extensive tank
P. 56	1645-1661 Baji Raje	1645-1664 Baji Raje
	1661-1703 Maloji	1664-1700 Maloji
P. 110	Virshapattan	Vrishapattan
P. 133	Salatin-i-Basatin	Basatin-i-Salatin
P. 162	Kempa Gauda	Kemp Gauda.

CHAPTER I

INTRODUCTION

1. Nature and extent of the records

The nature and scope of the historical sources utilized in these volumes demand a close study at the outset. All the indigenous and foreign sources available at persent have been pressed into service for writing the history of Shivaji. Several biographies written on the basis of Marathi chronicles have been discarded, because these are more or less full of fiction, fable, traditional lore, racial bias, romance, chronological inconsistencies, and historical inaccuracies. Since the learned historian Rajwade mercilessly exposed the serious defects [1] of Marathi Bakhars, there has been aroused a keen spirit of quest for original documents. The efforts of the last thirty years have been finally crowned with success. The eminent scholar Sir J. Sarkar has thoroughly examined, criticised and adjudged the value of the sources for the history of Shivaji. Their intensive study led him to make a very cautious and sparing use of the Marathi material and to rely on the contemporary Persian and English Records. He has surely overstated the claim of both the sources by writing that 'the only *contemporary* records of Shivaji's and even Shambhuji's times that now survive are in English and Persian and not at all in Marathi'. The contemporary records are also in Dutch, French and Portuguese. It is to the credit of Sir Jadunath to have first utilized some material available in the last two European languages. Though on account of the sack and destruction of the State archives during the long period of the Maratha war of liberation (1682-1707), no State papers, letters, memoirs or histories have survived, there are diaries, letters, Firmans,

---

1: See appendices for a searching criticism of the Bakhars.

S. 3.

grant-deeds, legal documents and similar papers in Marathi and Persian which are very helpful in the construction of the history of the times of Shivaji. The learned and indefatigable historians like Rajwade, Parasnis and Khare made the collection of the Marathi material their life work. The B. I. S. Mandal of Poona has laudably supplemented their efforts, so that during the last thirty years many scholars and societies have immensely enriched this source. Though this perplexing mass of spurious and genuine literature requires a most careful and impartial analysis and critical examination, its value cannot now be underrated.

2. The Dutch Records

The Dutch material alone has not been tapped by Sir Jadunath Sarkar. The Dutch Factory Records in the India Office, both in English and Dutch, contain little material on Shivaji. The Dagh-Register is a mine of information, but being in the Dutch language, it remained a sealed book to us for a long time. The relevant portions have now been translated and are of great value in giving information, among other things, on the career of Shahji in the Karnatic and in constructing the history of the struggles between Bijapur and Shivaji on the western coast of India. The English and Persian material is not at all sufficient on the two preceding topics. Moreover, but for letters preserved in the Dagh-Register up to 1664, the history of the conquest of Kudal by Shivaji would have remained incomplete. After 1665 references to Shivaji in the Dagh-Register become too meagre, as the Indian letters were from that time copied into a different register, known as " Incoming Letters." Some of these letters concerning the activities of Shivaji are fortunately preserved at Batavia and the Hague. All the relevant documents available at Batavia have been secured by me. Then the Hague Records were examined for several months, and a list of all the documents dealing with Shivaji up to the end of 1669 was made. All these extracts have been translated

into English and included in these volumes. The search for
further documents covering the period of 1670—1680 will
require at least six months more. Hence these could not be
included in this edition.

3. The Records in London

The English Records are the most extensive, most
reliable and the best preserved of all the European records
available to us on Shivaji. These consist of consultations
and diaries of the Councils, copies of the letters sent and
received from Surat, Bombay, Rajapur, Karwar, Fort St.
George, etc. There are many volumes of Letter Books
containing the despatches of the East India Company to
their settlements and agents in the East Indies. The
numerous volumes of original correspondence (O. C.) in the
India Office and C. O. at the Public Records Office in London
have preserved copies of many important letters received by the
Company from all its settlements. Then the Miscellaneous
Records contain abstracts of letters from Surat, Bombay,
Persia, Gombroon,[1] etc.

4. Value of the Records at Bombay

Still the Bombay Record Office contains some material
on the period of 1630 to 1680. There are three manuscript
series in which matter on Shivaji's life is available to some
extent. These are:—

Surat Diaries No. 1 (1659-1696).

Outwards or outward Letter Book of the Surat Factory
(1630—1700)—4 Volumes.

Inwards—Vol. I (1646—1701).

The dearth of material is fortunately supplemented by
volumes known as " Papers Unavailable in Bombay." These
are typescript copies of letters, consultations, etc., which
were available in the India Office but missing in the

---

1. Cf. S. A. Khan, Sources for the History of British India in the 17th
   Century.

Bombay Record Office. The cream was extracted by Mr.
Forrest in his Home and Maratha Series, there yet remains
a good deal in them relevant to our period. The presence
of these volumes partially obviates the necessity of getting
copies from the India Office.

5. Use of the European Records

More than a thousand extracts directly or indirectly on
the career of our hero have been reproduced *verbatim* or
referred to in these volumes. These are not only " very
important for fixing dates, and invaluable in corroborating [1]
facts, admitted by native historians," but for filling up many
gaps in the life of Shivaji. In the absence of these records,
it would not have been possible to have any detailed and
reliable account of the conquest of Kudal,[2] the capture of
Rajapur and dealings of the Raja with the English,[3] the first
sack of Surat,[4] the frequent raids on Surat,[5] the negotiations
regarding compensation between Shivaji and the English,[6]
the Karnatic campaign,[7] Shivaji's expeditions against[8]
Janjira, the war between the Raja and the English for the
occupation of Khanderi,[9] and raids on Hubli, Karwar, and
many towns in Kanara and Khandesh. These have proved
to be of highest value in supplying confirmatory evidence
on many doubtful subjects, like Shivaji's coronation, literacy
and marriages, Netaji's desertion and reclamation, Sambhaji's
revolt and return, Shivaji's flight to Rangana, and so on.
Similarly, much light is shed on many other controversial
subjects.

6. General value of the European Records

Several important and extensive works have been written
on the life of Shivaji. Each scholar has attempted in his

1. Shivaj Chapter III.   2. Shivaji Chapter VI.
3.   „   „   VI.   4.   „   „   VII.
5.   „   „   XI.   6.   „   Chapters XII, XIII, XV, XVI.
7.   „   „   XIX.   8.   „   Chapter XX.
9.   „   Chapters XXI, XXII.

own way to throw light on the main incidents and deeds of the hero, but the details have like blind alleys still to be lighted up. Every scholar must have performed the insuperable task of selecting a certain version or constructing a new story of some incident of the hero's life. The psychological process of selection and construction from a contradictory and confusing mass of details cannot be usually laid bare by a writer. It is to burden the book with details in which the ordinary reader is not interested. But those who, out of curiosity, desire to test the veracity of facts, require the complete material before them, so that they may judge whether the task has been judiciously and impartially performed by the various writers.

This point can be illustrated by selecting four thrilling adventures of the career of Shivaji, such as the murder of Afzal Khan, surprise of Shaista Khan, audience with Aurangzeb, and escape from Agra. There are several disputable points in each story and these need solution. It will be seen that the contemporary English Records furnish a reliable evidence on the various phases of Shivaji's life.

7. Light on Afzal Khan's tragedy

(a) *The strength of Afzal Khan's army* — The English letter of 10th December 1660 states that the Khan was sent with 10,000 horse and foot. This is borne out by Tarikh-i-Ali (II. 7), but Shivaji Pratapa, Rairi Bakhar, 91 Q. Bakhar, Tarikh-i-Shivaji have 12,000 force.

Sabhasad says that there was infantry also besides 12,000 horse.

Chitnis, however, gives the figure of 30,000 men.

(b) *Demolition of temples* — There is no mention of it in the English letters. The Dutch Dagh-Register and the Portuguese records as given by Mr. Pissurlencar do not refer to it.

The Rairi Bakhar is silent on the matter.

The Chitnis B. and the Shiva Digvijaya remark that the Goddess at Tooljapoor and the God at Pandharpur were removed soon after the news that the Khan was going to demolish them.

The Sabhasad B. and the Shivabharat allege that those at Tooljapur and Pandharpoor were desecrated.

(c) *Shivaji's treachery*— The contemporary English letter of 10th December 1659 clears up the *issue of the murder* of Afzal Khan. Its words are:

" Because the queen knew with that strength he was not able to resist Shivaji, she councelled him to pretend friendship with his enemy; *which he did*, and the other (whether through intelligence or suspicion it's not known) dissembled his love toward him, and sent *his mother* as a hostage, assuring him of his reality. "

This letter is explicit on the point that Afzal Khan was advised by the queen to have recourse to dissimulation and treachery and that Shivaji learning of the treacherous design, endeavoured to counteract the plot by various methods in self-defence. It was thus a fight of wits in which Afzal was ultimately outwitted by the shrewd and courageous Shivaji. Ravington did not consider the murder of Afzal Khan as an act of treachery. This contemporary view of the tragedy confirms the statements of the Marathi chronicles.

(d) *Weapons used for murder*— Did Shivaji seriously injure Afzal Khan with his *Waghnukh and dagger* or did he use his dagger only or the sword ? On analysis the evidence filters down to this:—

1. Sabhasad— Waghnukh and dagger, while Khan's head was cut off by Sambhaji Kavji.

2. Shiva Digvijaya (169)—Waghnukh and sword, while the Khan's head was severed by Yesaji Kank.

3. Chitnis (61)—Waghnukh and sword, while the Khan was beheaded by Yesaji Kank and Tanaji Malusare.

4. Jedhe Karina—Waghnukh and sword.

5. 91 Qalmi · Bakhar (34) — Dagger and sword; the Khan's head was cut into twain by Shivaji himself.

6. Tarikh-i-Shivaji — Waghnukh, dagger, sword, *Shamsah* and other weapons. Shivaji used the first two in opening the stomach and then he cut the Khan into two with his sword.

7. Shivabharat (20-16-23)— The Bhawani sword only—there is no mention of a Waghnukh at all.

8. Rairi B.—Dagger concealed in his right arm.

9. English Letter—Dagger from out of his bosom.

10. Fryer—'Slips a stiletto from under his coat sleeves.'

11. Khafi Khan.—Dagger only.

12. Manucci.—A small and very short lancet.

13. Jedhe Sakavali. ⎫
14. Basatin–i–Salatin. ⎭ No mention.

The last eight sources which are mainly contemporary throw a doubt on the use of the well-known Waghnukh.

8 Issues of Shaista Khan's surprise

In the daring exploit of Shivaji in which he surprised Shaista Khan, the following questions still remain doubtful. In case of a fresh enquiry, the European records are of great help.

(1) What was the strength of Shaista Khan's army ?

(2) Did Shaista Khan put up in Shivaji's house at Poona?

(3) With how many men did Shivaji or any one of his captains, proceed to the Khan's camp ?

(4) How was he surprised by Shivaji ?

(5) How did the Khan make his escape ?

(6) Where did the Khan receive injuries ?

(7) How many and which important personages died in the scuffle ?

(8) Was Shaista's daughter captured by Shivaji ?

(9) Was Jaswant Singh won over by Shivaji and thus persuaded to remain neutral during this night attack ?

Let us take up these questions *seriatim.*

(1) *Strength of Shaista's army.*—Shivaji Pratap (p. 90) says that Shaista and Randulla Khan were sent with a force of 60,000, but according to the—

91 Q. Bakhar (43) and

Rairi Bakhar (14)—80,000.

Sabhasad Bakhar (35)— 1,00,000 horse, besides elephants, camels, war–chariots, etc. An ocean-like army with 32 crores of rupees was sent.

Chitnis (96)
Shiva Digvijaya
Manucci (II. 25)
Carre
Thevenot   } Do not mention the number of troops.
Guarda
Grant Duff
Orme
Dow

(2) *Shaista's Residence.*—The evidence on this point is analysed below:

Camp alone is mentioned in—

(*a*) Shivaji's Letter quoted by Mr. Gyffard from Rajapur, dated 12th April 1663, says that Shivaji ' got into his tent to salam. '

(*b*) 4th May 1663—A trusty servant of Rustam Jamah who was specially sent to enquire into the matters, makes the same report.

(*c*) In a letter of 24th May 1663 from Kolhapur by the English merchants: "Shivaji going into Shaista Khan's tent."

(*d*) 25th May 1663.—Surat Letter to Madras—'Shivaji did lately in his own person set upon the tent of Shaista Khan.' [1]

(*e*) Sabhasad (Pp. 33-34)— Nabob's tent and Nabob's pavilion.

Sabhasad (P. 49)—" Shivaji is very expert in treachery; when he entered my camp, he jumped forty cubits from the ground and entered the pavilion ? "

(*f*) Chitnis (p. 18) and Chitragupta— Several times the the word "Tent" has been used.

1. See Shivaji Vol. I, pp. 80-84.

(g) Thevenot—Having been informed that on a certain night he would be on guard near the tent of the General, the Raja went there with his men, and being let in by his Captain, he came to Chast Can.

(h) John L'Escaliot, in a letter dated 26th January 1664—" Hee therefore with 400 as desperate as himself enters the army undiscovered, comes to the generalls tent, falls in upon them, kills the guard. "

(i) Orme (Fragments, p. 11)—"They got into the tent of Chasset Khan after midnight, who escaped with a severe wound in his hand. "

(j) Carre—The Mughal General was far removed from his army, in a camp badly fortified and near a seraglio where he passed his time giving himself up to love and pleasures.... Shivaji conducted his troops up to the middle of the enemy's camp. "

(k) Dow (III. 367)—"Cutting their way through the screens which surrounded the tents of Shaista Khan, they entered that in which he slept."

Palace or House is the place of the incident:

1. Shiva Digvijaya (P. 220).—The house where Shivaji formerly lived.

2. Shivaji Pratap P. 90)—Palace.

3. 91 Q. Bakhar (43', Rairi Bakhar (Pp. 14-15) and Tarikh-i-Shivaji mention Lal Mahal, thus giving the impression that the incident took place in Shivaji's palace.

4. De Guarda (P. 66)— " He entered the lodging of Sextaghan which was in the very houses that Neotagy and Seuagy had built, and posted behind the walls of these houses he began to affect a breach with hand pikes, a strong wind prevented the noise which would otherwise follow, for Sextaghan himself had slept in the house."

5. Scott (P. 10 —" Passing without alarm to the Palace."

6. Grant Duff—House built by Dadaji Kondeva.

7. Manucci (II. 104)—" Outside it, he lived in a mud house that he had caused to be built near a tank. "

S. 4.

8. Sarkar (P. 88)—" Took up his residence in the unpretentious home of Shivaji's childhood. "

We cannot ignore the evidence of the authentic contemporary letters. There could be no mistake in reporting on such a simple point. It appears to me that Shaista Khan and his personal retinue stayed in tents pitched in the compound of the Lal Mahal. The " unpretentious house " of Shivaji would have been too small for a rich grandee and a general of the rank of Shaista Khan. Some persons might be occupying the house itself, but the greater portion would have put up in tents. The sudden attack might have been led by Shivaji by jumping over or mining the compound wall. Escaliot, Carre, Thevenot and Fryer confirm the testimony of the English letters.

(3) *The number of men accompanying Shivaji in his attempt to surprise Shaista Khan*—Shivaji's own letter quoted by Gyffard—12th April 1663—400 choice men.

24th May 1663—400 men.

25th May 1663 Surat Letter—400 of his men.

There is unanimity in the English letters on this point, but the evidence of the Bakhars is contradictory.

Chitnis (98)—2 to 3 hundred men.

Sabhasad (33)—2 hundred men.

Shivaji Pratap (98)—5 to 7 hundred men.

Shiva Digvijaya (220)—4 to 5 hundred men.

Tarikh-i-Shivaji–300 men.

Khafi Khan—2 hundred Marathas.

De Guarda—Netaji and not Shivaji with 80 men.

(4) *Shaista Khan's surprise*—The difference in the statements on this point will be clear from the following evidence.

Shivaji's letter quoted by Gyffard—" Shivaji got into his tent to salam and presently slew all the watch. "

The Nabob was in bed— Chitnis (98), Rairi (15), Khafi Khan (Elliot VII, p. 270), Scott (P. 10), Manucci (II. 105).

The Nabab had not gone to bed, but was sitting in the company of his wives. Sabhasad (P. 33).

The Khan was in bed, but his wife was first awakened by the noise. Shiva Digvijaya (221), Sarkar (P. 90'.

" He came to Chasta Can, who being awakened........."
Thevenot.

(5) *Method of Khan's escape.*—There is no mention of an escape from a window in the five contemporary letters, neither in the Sabhasad, 91 Q. Bakhar (46) and Chitnis, nor in Thevenot, Escaliot, Fryer, Carre, Manucci, Dow, Orme, and Khafi Khan.

All these contemporary accounts are confirmed by De Guarda, Sh. Dig. and Sh. Pratapa.

Rairi (15) says that " Shaista Khan leapt over a wall that was in his way and got safe beyond it. "

Grant Duff seems to have given currency to this story and it has been accepted by the later historians.

In face of the unanimous evidence from contemporary writers, we cannot accept the statement of G. Duff.

(6) The statements regarding the injuries received by the Khan are also contradictory.

Khan's thumb was cut off—Rairi (15), Khafi Khan, De Guarda.

Khan's small finger was cut off-Shiva Digvijaya (222', and G. Duff.

Khan's two fingers were cut off-Chitnis.

Khan's three fingers were removed-Sabhasad, Chitragupta and Dow.

English letter-wounded.

Bernier (187)-severely wounded.

Thevenot-"wounded in the hand."

Escaliot-wounded Shaista.

Carre-wounded with two sword cuts.

This point, I hope, will soon be settled by a close enquiry from the accounts of Shaista Khan left by the English and Dutch Factors who had personal interviews with him and from the paintings available to us. For the present, we should restrict ourselves to the use of the word 'wounded' only.

(7) *Murder of Women*:- A very detailed list of the killed
persons is given in the English Letters.   Herein it is said that
several ladies and maids were murdered by Shivaji.

During the affray which took place in that pitch darkness
of the night, it is quite possible that a few ladies should have
fallen in the scuffle in which blows were being indiscriminately
given.

Sabhasad (83) remarks that it was Chimnaji Bapu who
performed this deed and not Shivaji.

Scott (P. 10) and Sarkar (P. 90)-"Some female servants
were also slain."

Chitnis,
Raire Bakhar
Shiva Digvijaya   make no mention of the slaughter
Manucci   of women.
and Grant Duff

De Guarda's opinion deserves attention:—

" Neotagy offered no insult to the women, for this sex
is much venerated in Hindustan and they observe their
customs better than the Europeans.   These soldiers (nestes)
had special reason for this, as it was the order of Sevagy who
while he lived was both obeyed and loved." (P. 69.)

9.   Was Shaista Khan's daughter captured by Shivaji ?

Out of the five letters available on Shaista Khan's
surprise, the Surat letter of 25th May 1663 alone gives the
news of a daughter of the Khan having been carried away
by Shivaji. The same statement is made by Escaliot and
Thevenot, probably on the reports of the English Factors at
Surat.   Both assert that Shivaji treated her with respect and
sent her back on getting a large sum of money as ransom.

The Bakhars of Chitnis, Sabhasad, Rairi, etc., make no
mention at all. Such a romantic event could not have been
ignored by the Maratha chronicles. Hence the story does not
seem to be true. The incident could not have escaped the
notice of Manucci who had personal acquaintance with Shivaji
as well as Shaista Khan.

(9) *Jaswant Singh*, a great patriot at heart, was never reconciled to Aurangzeb's rule. It is, therefore, natural that he might have yielded to the overtures of one who was carrying on a war of Hindu liberation against all odds.

The English letters, Manucci (II. 104), Dow (III. 367) Orme (Fragments, p. II) and Scott (P. 10) refer to a secret understanding between Shivaji and Jaswant Singh, but there is no mention of it in Chitnis, Sabhasad and Shiva Digvijaya.

Rairi and 91 Q. Bakhars wrongly assert that Jai Singh Mirza Raja was also sent along with Shaista Khan on this service. De Guarda has left a glowing account of Shivaji's diplomacy in this matter.

"Jassomptissinga was a Gentio. Sevagy took advantage of this (fact) for he was a (Hindu) and sent him one night a rich present of precious stones, a large quantity of gold and silver with many rich and precious jewels. With these marvellous cannons Sevagy fought and reduced that fortress." (P. 64)

"Jassomptissinga was less devout and more ambitious and so did not attend to these scruples; he was much obliged for the presents and still more for the promises for which he confederated with Sevagy promising not to obstruct his cause and even to connive at what (Quanto must be a misprint for quando) he might design anything against the Mouros." (P: 66)

10. Shivaji's audience with Aurangzeb

There seem to be as many versions as there are writers regarding Shivaji's audience with Aurangzeb.

The account of *Shivaji's appearance* in the Hall of Audience at Agra is variously given in different histories:

Sabhasad—Shivaji made three salutes and offered a Nazar.

Chitnis—Shivaji did not make any obeisance, but the present was offered by Ram Singh on behalf of Shivaji.

Shiva Digvigaya—Though Shivaji had agreed to salam

the king, yet he lost consciousness in rage and hence did not bow before the throne.

91 Q. Bakhar and Rairi—No salam was made either on approaching near or returning from the throne.

Tarikh-i-Shivaji—A low arch was put up to make Shivaji bow his head before the throne, but Shivaji passed through it with head backwards. He made no salam and was dismissed without any ceremonies.

Dow—Shivaji did not make the usual obeisance and showed contempt and haughty demeanour. So he was dismissed, but through the intercession of Princess Zeb-un-Nisa he was given a second audience. Shivaji again behaved rudely and even asked the Princess' hand. Upon this Aurangzeb ordered him as a mad man from his presence.

Alamgir Namah.—He kissed the ground before the throne and made a large present.

In my opinion, Shivaji was too shrewd to ignore the simple truth that a defeated foe and an uncrowned commander could not claim equality with the Emperor who was also his conqueror. Besides, he would not give offence to the Emperor from whom he had come to solicit the viceroyalty of the Deccan. It is very unlikely that Shivaji could jeopardise the chances of the success of his mission by neglecting the ordinary formalities at the very outset of his interview. Therefore, the version of the Sabhasad Bakhar and Alamgir Namah is acceptable here.

Shivaji's place in the Durbar.—With regard to the place where Shivaji was asked to stand in the Durbar, there is as usual much difference.

91 Q. Bakhar and Shiva Digvijaya—Shivaji sat near Rohilla Khan, the Prime Minister.

Rairi—They stood by the side of Rahim Khan, a Pathan.

Alamgir Namah—He was given a seat near the throne among celebrated nobles.

Manucci—Instead of giving him the promised position,

he assigned him the lowest place in the first circle of nobles within the golden railing.

Sabhasad and Chitnis—He was asked to stand behind Jaswant Singh.

As the statement of Sabhasad and Chitnis is partially borne out by the English letters, it is to be preferred to others.

The story of Shivaji's swoon—The two contemporary English letters do not make any mention of Shivaji's fainting away in the Court. The Bakhars like the Sabhasad and Chitnis have the same version. The account is confirmed by Manucci, Thevenot, Carre, D'Orleans, Orme, Dow, Duff and the authors of the Tarikh-i-Shivaji and Alamgir Namah. The story of Shivaji's fainting is given by Shiva Digvijaya and Khafi Khan and adopted by such historians as J. Scott, Mill, Elphinstone, Beveridge, Montgomery, Martin, Douglas, etc. All contemporary and ancient authorities are unanimous on the point that Shivaji did not fall down in a swoon. Even Khafi Khan has expressly stated that Shivaji *pretended* to faint away.

Attempt to commit suicide—The story of Shivaji's readiness to commit suicide in the Durbar is given by Orme on the authority of Thevenot. It is as unbelievable as the statement of Sabhasad that Shivaji wanted to kill Maharaja Jaswant Singh. The latter had done no wrong, on the contrary had all along done very estimable service to Shivaji. Moreover, it was no fault of the Maharaja to stand in the front rank. Therfore Sabhasad's statement is most improbable.

The guard on Shivaji—The Shiva Digvijaya and the Rairi Bakhar state that Fulad Khan was appointed with 10,000 men to keep watch on Shivaji. This number is reduced to half by Sabhasad, and augmented to 25,000 by Chitnis. Manucci's figure seems to be most moderate when he writes that three corps of guards were posted round Shivaji's tent.

Shivaji's escape—Sabhasad, Chitnis and Shiva Digvijaya tell us the story of the baskets. It is confirmed by Fryer and Manucci (II. 139). But the Rairi Bakhar states that Shivaji went out with the men who were carrying the fruits. The contemporary English letters confirm the old Bakhars and hence their version alone is acceptable.

Grant Duff has given the story that Shivaji and Sambhaji after getting out of the baskets, were carried away by a fleet horse to Muthra. This version might have been taken by him from Manucci (II, 139). But it is unsupported by the Bakhars. According to Shiva Digvijaya, Shivaji soon became a Bairagi and took the road to Kurukshetra.

Sabhasad and Chitnis affirm that at two cosses outside the city, they left the baskets and *set out on foot* to the village where Shivaji's Karkuns were. There they disguised them-selves as Bairagis and went towards *Muthra on foot*. A similar story is told in the Rairi Bakhar.

The escape on horses under the circumstances seems to be very improbable, and I am inclined to believe the version of the Bakhars as true.

Such details can be easily multiplied, but I hope that it has been fully proved that even important points in the career of Shivaji are yet disputable.

On close scrutiny, the structure of each incident, exploit or expedition falls to the ground; only the foundation or basic fact of a particular event having happened, remains in tact. The details present such a kaleidoscopic variety that they even become vague. For the sake of accuracy and definiteness of details, the help of the English and European records of that period, is of supreme necessity. These throw a flood of light on numerous questions, though at times even these have to be accepted with caution. As a detailed comparison of different versions is sure to lead us to the right conclusions, there is an urgent necessity of the publication of all available material on the heroic life of the Maker of the Maharashtra.

11. Imperfections of the Persian and European material

At the same time, we should not exaggerate the importance of the European records. In fixing the dates, the European despatches are surely useful in showing the lower and upper limits of the time of an event, but in many cases they do not give the exact date. This has to be searched from the Marathi material. For instance, the exact dates of the capture of Mahuli, Salher, Jawhar, Ramnagar, Satara, etc., of the murder of Afzal Khan, the raid on Shaista Khan, of Shivaji's departure for Agra, of his release from Agra, and even of his death, are not given. The Marathi Chronologies remedy this defect of the European records by giving many reliable dates.

II. The European extracts chronologically put together are still isolated, or disintegrated facts, nay, even shreds of facts, and are no better than so many unhewn and irregular stones piled up in a chaotic heap. The historian has to weave them together into a fabric, after a critical analysis and a thorough search into their causal relation to each other. In this constructive attempt it is found that many necessary links are absolutely missing. Without the help of the Marathi material, it is impossible to construct an accurate and a thoroughly connected story of Shivaji. Even a cursory study of the fourth, fifth and eighth chapters on Shivaji, will make it evident that the European records furnish a very scrappy information on such important events as the murder of Afzal Khan, the surprise of Shaista Khan, and Jaisingh's campaign into the Deccan. Similarly, Shivaji's wars with the Deccan Kingdoms and the Mogul Empire, are casually and erratically referred to. Though the documents do not supply the whole information on these topics, they shed light on many obscure points.

III. These records are deplorably deficient in furnishing an insight into or even a view of the religious, economic, intellectual, social, or cultural life of the people, nor do they present any picture of the financial organization and administrative system of the time of Shivaji. Again, there is no presentment of the individual life of the hero, his courtiers, family members or the prominent men of his time. The extracts mainly deal with wars, political changes, revolutions and their effect upon the maritime and internal trade that was in the hands of the Europeans.

IV.   It must be remembered that the European records are not naturally expected to speak about the hero, till he sprang into the lime light of fame by the total annihilation of Afzal Khan's forces in 1659.   These give no clue to the hero's early career, nor do they speak of his ancestors. Thus the Sanskrit, Marathi and Persian material alone is useful for writing the history of Shivaji's ancestors.   Prior to 1659 we do not get much confirmation of our data from the European records.

V.   The Persian histories like the Muhammad Namah, Ali Namah, Basatin–i-Salatin, Badshah Namah, Khafi Khan's Muntakhab-ul-lubab are   all written by the proteges of various sovereigns and hence they necessarily suffer from the sins of omission and commission, such as, suppression of impalatable facts, fulsome eulogy of the virtues and exploits of the rulers and their favourites, and unmerited condemnation of their enemies.

Of the same type are the works like the Shiva Bharat, Radha-Madhava Vilas Champu, Pannal Parvat Akhyanam, and Sh. R. Kalpataru.

They are expected to give a grandiloquent account of the exploits of Shahji and Shivaji.   They are also without any chronological data. In fact, they are epics and are thus vitiated by the defects inherent in this literature.   It only means that we must judiciously utilize all these works which are after all interspersed with facts of considerable historical value.

In conclusion, it is superfluous to remark that both the indigenous and foreign sources are indispensable as confirmatory and supplementary to each other. It is now for the reader to judge how far the author has endeavoured to throw aside fables in favour of truth by carefully camparing, critically examining, judiciously investigating and impartially interpreting the vast material at his disposal.

CHAPTER II

THE ANCESTRY OF SHIVAJI

1. The incorrectness of available geneologies

The Marathi chronicles on the life of Shivaji indulge in fable and tradition in writing the history of his near anncestors and they know almost nothing about the origin of the family. The Chhatrapati Raja Pratap Sinha of Satara, a descendant of Shavaji the Great, made a serious attempt for reconstructing a geneological tree of his ancestors in 1828. The original geneology made under his order by Munshi Madhavrao is still available in the Historical Museum at Satara. We learn that the information was collected from many important works.[1]

The geneology made after so much laborious research was accepted as true till recently, but the new documentary evidence shows its incorrectness. Moreover, no details of the careers of the ancestors of Shivaji were known. This gap can now be filled up on the basis of the unpublished grants and the manuscript chronicle of the family of the Mudhol rulers.

2. The ancestry of Sajjan Sinha

The Bhosles trace their lineage from the solar dynasty of Udepur which is itself descended from the great conqueror, Rama of the epic fame. In the 12th century the Solar dynasty had its rule at Chittor and Sisod. One Karan Sinha, Rawal of Chittor, had three sons. After his death, his

1. *Persian books:*— Labbuttavarikh, Firishta, Jame jahannuma, Araya-shamahfel, Khawaif-i-Hindustan, Akber Namah, Tawarikh-i-Babamani.

Hindi books:— Maharaja's Bakhar, Vairat Charitra, Jayapur Bakhar, Udepur Bakhar, Inscriptions on the Pillar of Victory at Chittor, Hindustani Charitra, Kirkol Yadi (Misc. List).

Sanskrit books:—Bhagawat, Vishnu Puran, Manusmriti, Katyayana Smriti, Ramayana, Rajavali, Rajya Mayukha, Jyotish Shastra, Saur Puran.

eldest son, Kshem Sinha ascended the throne of Chittor, while the second son, Maham, became the ruler of Sisod. The latter was succeeded by his younger brother Rahap. These Sisodia rulers were known as Ranas. The eighth descendant of Kshem Sinha was Ratnasinha or Ratnasi of Chittor, while the 10th descendant of Rahap was Lakshman Sinha of Sisod.

It was this Ratnasi and not Bhimsinha or Lakhamsi (Lakshman Sinha) who was the husband of the far-famed Padmini. We need not reiterate the story of the demoniac passion of Alauddin Khilji to take a forcible possession of Padmini, the peerless queen of Chittor and of the brave resolve of 15,000 Rajput ladies to prefer death on the burning pyre to the desecration of their bodies by the Muslims. "The fair Padmini closed the throng, which was augmented by whatever of female beauty or youth could be tainted by Tartar lust. They were conveyed to the cavern, and the opening closed upon them, leaving them to find security from dishonour in the devouring element." [1] This gruesome holocaust was followed by a terrible carnage of the bravest of the Rajputs in the battles with the imperial army. During the life and death struggle with Alauddin for the defence of Chittor, Ratnasi was killed and so was his kinsman Lakshman Sinha (Lakhamsi) with his seven sons. Thereupon Chittor fell into the hands of the Khilji conqueror on 26th August 1303, but Ajaya Sinha (Ajeysi), the only surviving son of Lakshman Sinha continued to rule at Sisod. [2]

To put a stop to the aggressions of the Sisodia Rana, the Delhi Emperor put Chittor under the charge of Maldeva, the Sonigra Chief of Jalor in 1314. Towards the close of Alauddin's reign, the Rajputs of Chittor threw the Muslim officers over the walls, devastated the imperial territory, and asserted their independence. These excursions were probably made under the valourous lead of the famous Hamir, the

1. Todd, Rajisthan, I, p. 311,
2. Ojha-History of Rajputana, I, 446-8; 456-73; 504-514.

son of Ari Sinha who was the eldest brother of Ajaya Sinha.
This boy, as he was brought up by his uncle, gave in
early life proofs of an extraordinary dash and daring. The
two sons of Ajaya Sinha once failed to put down the
rebellion of a robber-chief, but Hamir, though very young,
succeeded in bringing his head as a trophy to his uncle.
Ajaya Sinha was so pleased with this exploit of his nephew
that he accepted him as his successor. In a few years this
noble scion of the solar dynasty, the ruler of Sisod, expelled
Maldeva Chavhan from Chittor and thus brought together
the territories of Sisod and Chittor under his sovereignty.
Since then the rulers of Chittor were known as Sisodia
Ranas; on the other hand, Ajaya Sinha's sons, Sajjan Sinha
and Kshem Sinha, being disinherited by their father, left
for the Deccan as soldiers of fortune. The elder brother
was destined to found a line which gave birth to Shivaji, the
founder of the Maratha Empire.

Ancestry of Sajjan Sinha

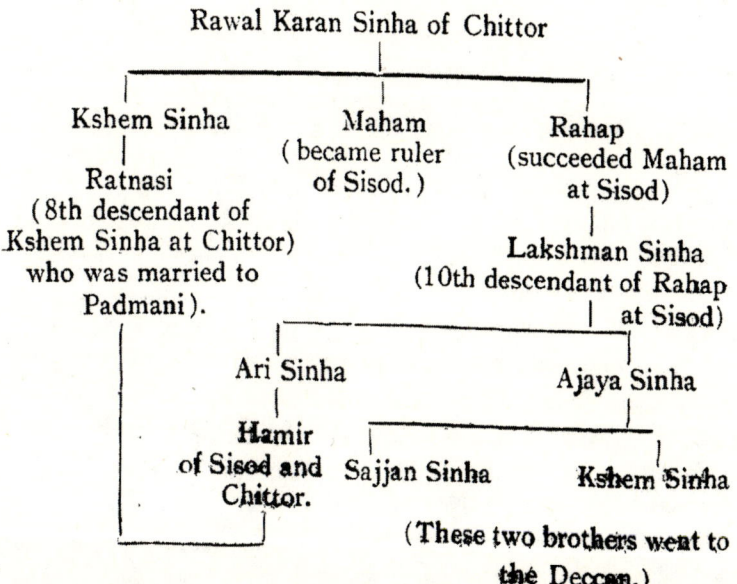

Rawal Karan Sinha of Chittor

Kshem Sinha
Ratnasi
(8th descendant of
Kshem Sinha at Chittor)
who was married to
Padmani).

Maham
(became ruler
of Sisod.)

Rahap
(succeeded Maham
at Sisod)

Lakshman Sinha
(10th descendant of Rahap
at Sisod)

Ari Sinha
Hamir
of Sisod and
Chittor.

Ajaya Sinha

Sajjan Sinha   Kshem Sinha

(These two brothers went to
the Deccan.)

3. Rana Sajjansinha of the Solar Dynasty

It has been seen that about 1320 A. D. Sajjansinha came down to the Deccan with a devoted band of followers to try his luck. A few years after he seems to have entered into the service of Hasan Gangu who afterwards became the founder of the Bahmani Kingdom. Muhammad Shah Tuglaq, Emperor of Delhi, marched towards the south to put down the rebellion of Hasan Gangu and other rebellious captains. In one of the battles fought between the armies of the imperialists and rebellious Sardars, Sajjansinha and his son Dilipsinha distinguished themselves in the service of their master.

Daulatabad was captured by the rebels who chose the valourous Hasan as their king. After the successful establishment of the Bahmani Kingdom in 1347, the first king, Ala-ud-din Hasan Gangu Bahmani, conferred upon the Ranas the jagir of several villages in Mirat, a district in the province of Deogiri, the ancient capital of the Yadavas, which was christened Daulatabad by Muhammad Shah. This jagir is still in the enjoyment of the descendants of Sajjansinha.

4. Rana Dilipsinha, a commander of the Bahmani Kingdom

Dilipsinha had another opportunity of proving his own valour and the chivalry of his Rajput soldiers in the war between the Kings of Gulbarga and Vijayanagar. The Firman granted to him in November 1352 A. D. by the most valiant and victorious Ala-ud-din Hasan Gangu Badshah, is up to this day in the possession of the Rajasaheb of Mudhol who is a direct descendant of Dilipsinha. The latter is addressed as 'Rana' and 'Sardar-i-Khaskhel.' The title of 'Rana' proves that Dilipsinha was descended from the Sisodia Rajputs. In the Firman he is called the grandson of Ajayasinha. This name has been skipped over in the accepted geneologies. Thus we have not to depend upon legends and fables, but on the stern and solid facts of history regarding the ancestry of the Bhosles. The English translation of this first Firman is given below:—

"Being pleased with the valiant deeds displayed on the battle-field by Rana Dilipsinga, Sardar-i-Khaskhel, the son of Sajjansinha and grandson of Ajayasinha, ten villages in Mirat, Taraf Devagadh (Deogiri), are granted to him for the maintenance of his family. So in accordance with his desire they should be given over to him. Dated 25th of the month of Ramzan. 753 A. H."

The Mss. Mudhol Bakhar adds that the jagir was first conferred on Sajjansinha and then confirmed and continued in the name of Dilipsinha. The latter is said to have ruled for 15 years and died in 768 Hijri or 1367 A. D.

5. Heroic deeds of Sidhoji

Rana Sidhoji, the son of Dilipsinha, faithfully served the Bahmani Kings. He was instrumental in putting down the rebellion of Bahauddin, the commandant of the Sagar Fort, and was therefore conferred the command of that territory. After some time, Sidhoji or Sidhaji assisted Firozshah in gaining the Bahmani throne. He was killed in a battle in Hijri 789 (1388 A. D.) and his son *Bhairoji* fought very bravely, though he too was ultimately overpowered by the enemy.

The part played by Sidhoji is thus described by Firishta: "Suddoo, a slave of the royal family commanded in Sagur. He was rich and powerful, and received the Princes with open arms omitting nothing to evince his attachment to them. On the next day, Ahmud Khan and Feroze Khan addressed a letter to Shums-ood-Deen Shah, as also other letters to the principal nobility, stating that their design was only to expel Lallcheen, whose treachery to the late king, and whose other numerous crimes, which had cast dishonour on the royal family, were known to all. They demanded, therefore, that he should be punished, after which, the Princes

promised to pay due submisson to the authority of
Shums-ood-Deen Shah: declaring, till this object were
obtained, they would use every means in their power to
effect his destruction.

Shums-ood-Deen Shah, consulting his mother and
Lallcheen, sent back an answer which served only to inflame
the Princes, who with the assistance of the commander
of Sagur, having collected three thousand horse and foot,
and with the full confidence that other troops would join
them from the capital, marched towards Koolburga.
Disappointed in this expectation, they halted for some time
on the banks of the Bheema, without being aided by any
chief of consequence. It was, however, agreed that the
Princes should advance with the regal canopy carried over
the head of Feroz Khan. On this occasion his brother
Ahmad Khan was raised to the rank of Ameer-ool-Omra,
Suddoo to that of Meer Nobat, and Meer Feiz Oolla Anjoo to
to the office of Vakeel, or Minister." [1]

6. Bhairoji or Bhimaji

In a few years, Firozshah succeeded in gaining the
throne. In recognition of the devoted service of the father
and son, the King bestowed the township of Mudhol with
the adjoining 84 villages upon Rana Bhairoji in Hijri 800
(1398 A. D.). This territory is curiously enough even
now in the possession of the descendants of the Rana.
The details of the events relating to the grant of Mudhol
are mentioned in a Royal Firman whose English translation
is given below.

Firman of Firozshah Bahmani to Rana Bhairoji in 1398

"On account of the ignorance of the Ruler and
mis-government due to the short-sightedness of Amirs, some
servants of the Empire had, disregarding their duty, thrown

1. J. Briggs, Hist. of the Rise of the Mahomedan Power in India Vol. II,
pp. 358-359: Firishta's History of Dekkan by Jonathan Scott, Vol. I, pp. 65-66.

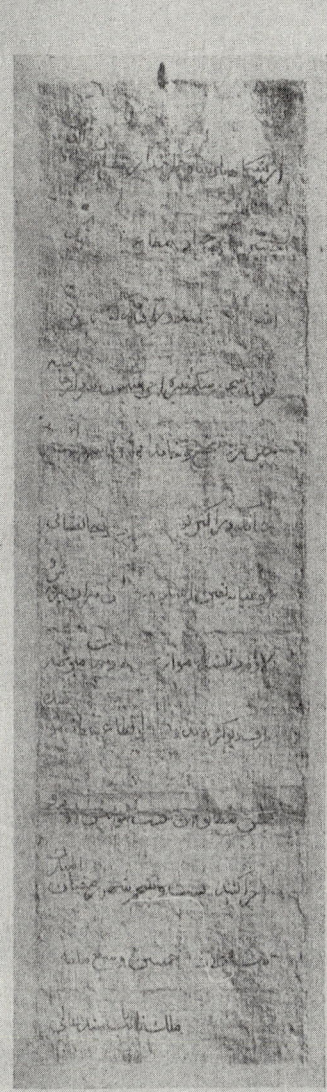

Ala-ud din Hasan Gangu's
grant to Dilipsinha
(A. D. 1352)

Firozshah Bahmini's grant
to Rana Bhairavji
(A. D. 1398)

Ahmadshah's grant to
Rana Ugrasen (A. D. 1424)

off their allegiance and had become so bold as to sow the seeds of treason in the Government of the Kingdom. In this full attention and courage of this disciple of the Almighty was wholly engrossed. To counteract this influence, uproot it and sweep the dirt from the garden of the Empire our action was delayed. So we were obliged to postpone it and afterwards our crystal-clear mind and heart were the recipient of the idea that with the counsel of some loyal and devoted persons attached to us and of those who were gifted with foresight, we should find out those that have full confidence in our policy and are prepared to sacrifice their lives for it, and (with their assistance), we should destroy the ungrateful. Actuated by this resolve, we proceeded towards Fort Sagar with an army and unfured the flag. Rana Siddhaji, Thanedar of Sagar, on receipt of the news of our Imperial presence, came to receive us and loyally joined our cause and girding up his loins eagerly attached himself to us. Acquainting himself of our unswerving resolve, he took great pains and rendered service at the risk of his life. Whatever was told him, was satisfactorily arranged by him. Whenever the enemy tried to surprise us and do us harm, this faithful soul was aware of it and was ready to resist the same and thus he fell and sacrificed himself in the thick of the fight. Shortly afterwards, by the grace of the Almighty our object bore fruit and came within our realisation. At this time I ascended my ancestral throne by great fortune and luck. Siddhaji's son, Bhairava Sing who had fought shoulder to shoulder with his father against our enemies and had showed great courage and ability, attracted our Imperial notice as one deserving of royal favours. So in recognition of these qualities of one deserving recognition, and in view of the sacrifice of his life, Mudhol and the adjoining 84 villages in the Taraf Raibag have been granted as a mark of royal favour to the said Bhairavasingji. So he should take possession of this jagir and enjoy the same from generation

S. 6.

to generation and should be diligent in rendering imperial
service in the cause of the Empire."[1]

Dated 25th Rabiulakhir. Year 800 A. H. (15th January
1398).

It is this Bhairavji, Bhosaji or Bhosla, the first Rana of
Mudhol, from whom the family is said to have got the surname
of Bhosle. The Rana with his two sons quelled the
rebellion of the chiefs of Raibag. His elder son Karansinha
was killed in an engagement with the rebels in Hijri 808
(1405/6 A. D.) and two years later (1407/8 A. D.) the
Rana himself died in the service of his master. Thus he
ruled Mudhol for ten years.[2]

7. Rana Devaraj and Ugrasen

His second son,[3] Devaraj distinguished himself in the
service of the King for 16 years and then his heroic son,
Ugrasen, saved the life of his master Ala–ud–din Ahmadshah
Bahmani when the latter was surprised by a detachment of
the Vijayanagar King in his hunting expedition. In recognition
of this signal service, a Firman was issued in the Hijri
year 827 (1424 A. D.) in the name of Ugrasen which

1. As these Firmans were not available to Mr. C. V. Vaidya, the
distinguished historian of Maharashtra, he has indulged in wrong surmises in
giving a brief career of Sajjan Sinha and his successors in Sh. Ch. N. App.
Pp. 8, 10, 11.

2. In the Mss. Mudhol Bakhar (Pp. 71, 83) he is also called Bhoraji and
Bharavsinha. He died at the age of 47. Hence he must have been born in
1360 A. D. In the Firman he is not called Bhosaji, but the Mudhol Chronicle
gives both the names. Mr. Rajwade's suggestion that the surname Bhosle was
adopted from the village Bhos or Bhose in the Paithan district, cannot be
accepted, unless it is proved that the village was the home of the family.

3. According to Chitnis (13), Devaraj, being the son of Bhosaji, was
known Bhosavant Bhosle. He came to the Deccan in 1200 Shaka and became
a polygar of some tracts on the banks of the Ganga and Bhima. He also
secured the Patilship of Shingnapur. Afterwards the villages of Khanvat,
Hingani, Beradi, Dewalgaon, Verul, Wavi, Mungi were obtained by his
successors and thus they grew into power.

This traditional account is not at all confirmed by the Firmans or the
Mudhol Chronicle. Some of the above-mentioned villages were granted to
Maloji by Nizam Shah as late as the end of the 16th century.

is still in the possession of the Rajasaheb of Mudhol. Its English translation is given here. It is important in mentioning the names of the four generations of the Bhosle rulers and the jagirs enjoyed by them.

From the Court of Sultan Ahmed Shah to Rana Ugrasen in 1424

" The generous mind of this humble servant of the court of God (i. e., the undersigned himself) is always inclined to this that the servants of this Kingdom who have been in service for a long time, are faithful and are doers of good action, may always remain busy in performing their proper and elevating duties and be happy and free from anxiety. The purpose of introducing this expression is that *Sidhji Rana*, Thanedar of Sagar and his son *Bhairava Sing*, who are the great-grand-father and grand-father of *Rana Ugrasen*, son of *Rajsingh Deo Rana*, stood beside us in the period of Firoz Shah Bahmani whose son was the refuge of brotherhood and has now got a resting place in Paradise. At the time of his accession to the throne, Sidhji was of great use (i. e., sacrificed himself). Then in the battle with the Raja of Vijayanagar Ugrasen also displayed great bravery and valour. All that is engraved on our mind.

In the same manner from the beginning of this Kingdom, the ancestors of his family have been faithful and life-sacrificing for this great sovereignty. Therefore the cherishing and sustaining of this family is very necessary and incumbent on our high heart's desire, and for that purpose the Jagir of Mudhol and 84 villages in the dependencies of Raibag which were granted to Bhairva Singh by the refuge of brotherhood (i. e., our brother Firoz Shah) and in the direction of Mirat and the environs of Pathri *some places have been given from old days*, all these we allow with great pleasure, to continue on Ugrasen, so that he may serve us with satisfaction.

Dated the 8th Shawal Year--827 A. H. = 3 Sept. 1424"

It should be marked that the ancient Jagir in the

district of Mirat near Daulatabad was being enjoyed even in 1424 A. D. by the Bhosles of Mudhol.

8. Dominion of the Bhosles in 1454

Rana Ugrasen alias Indrasen with his brave brother Pratapsinha was engaged for several years in carrying on a war in the inaccessible parts of the Konkan. In one of the battles, Ugrasen fell a captive in the hands of the Shirke chief of Khelna, but was ultimately released by his heroic sons [1] (1453-5 A. D.). For this service the brothers got as jagir some part of the Wai Pargana.[2] Thus it will be seen that by 1454, the Sisodia Bhosles enjoyed jagirs in such distant places as Mudhol, Raibag, Wai and Devagiri. After Ugrasen's death, his two sons, Karansinha and Shubha Krishna, faithfully served the Bhamani ruler for several years. But on account of some misunderstanding, the younger brother Shubha Krishna with his uncle Pratapsinha went to the ancient family jagir in Devagiri and settled down there about the year 1460. Thus the families of these two brothers were separated.

9. The Ghorpades of Mudhol

The elder family which was ruling at Mudhol, obtained the name of Ghorpade for scaling the *fort of Khelna* (*Vishalgad*) with the help of ropes tied to an iguana (Ghorpad), and the new title of ' Raja Bahadur ' in place of ' Rana ' was conferred upon the rulers of Mudhol. This important event which proved to be the turning point in the history of the family, has been briefly described by no less a personage than the Bahmani King himself in his Firman granted to Rana Bhimsen. The unrestrained encomiums showered upon this ' Tiger ' and ' Rustum of his age ', exhibit the great esteem in which he was held by his master, Muhammad Shah Bahmani. In the Konkan wars this family came to be

---

1. Firman of Ala-ud-din II to Karna Sinha and Shubh Krishna in 1454 A.D.
2. Mss. Mudhol Bakhar, p. 120.

attached to Usaf Adil Khan who afterwards became the
founder of the Bijapur Kingdom. Thus their fortunes were
for centuries afterwards bound up with the Bijapuri Kings.

Muhammad Shah's Firman to Rana Bhimsen who was
made Raja Ghorpade Bahadur

" In these auspicious times our lasting Empire is
spreading, and all our objects and wishes are fructifying by
the blessing of the Almighty. At such an auspicious juncture,
Sayad Azim Humayun, expert in the art of arms and
writing, faithful, one whose position has been recognized
by the world, the chosem of the Amirs of the Durbar, the
representative of the Empire, Malik-ul Tujar Muhammad
Gawan *alias* Khaja Jahan, brought to our Imperial notice tha
Rana Bhimsing, the son oj Karansing and the grandson of
Ugrasen, the tiger in the forest of courage and bravery, the
soaring bird in the ocean of valour, the pre-eminent among
men, the mighty, the skilful man of actions, the leader
of warriors, the Rustum in conquering forts, the vanquisher
of tigers, the destroyer of military arrays, the greatest
well-wisher of the throne (Dowlat), ever ready to sacrifice his
life, a lover of truth, worthy of royal grace and favours,
the commander of three thousand foot and horse, displayed
wonderful manliness and uncommon bravery in conquering
the forts in the Konkan. Having secured hundreds of 'Samars'
called ' Ghorpads ' with the help of the Deccanees, and
having tied ropes round their waists, he made them ascend
at night the ramparts towering to the sky. By that very
means, the father and the son scaled the fortress with some
brave men when the watchmen were asleep, and they
suddenly presented themselves on the tops of the walls like
the God of Death himself. They unsparingly cut down
the guards and sent to the abode of the God of Death
with their swords all those that offered resistance and opened
the castle gates. Those brave men of the army that
waited outside the gates of the castle rushed in and with

the aid of their weapons sent the enemies to the next world. Thus he conquered the fort and acquired fame and glory. At this critical opportunity *Karansing was killed and fell into the jaws of death on the battle-field.*

Bhimsing's loyalty and his hard exertions from the beginning of his life, his heroism and bravery have been greatly appreciated by us and consequently in return for such service, unequalled heroism and exertions, the possession of Mudhol with its 84 villages has been given to him as heretofore, with the object of perpetuating the House. Besides this, the forts in the two Parganas of Raibag and Ben (Wai) have been handed over to him and in place of the title 'Rana' the high title of 'Raja Ghorpade Bahadur has been conferred upon him and the flag with the sign of 'Ghorpad' (Iguana) has also been given to him. Henceforth he should use it (as his banner).

He should ever remain grateful for these gifts and should be ever ready and diligent in expanding the Empire and be intent on service from generation to generation.[1]

Dated the 7th day of Jamad-ul-Awwal San 876 = 22 Oct. 1471.

10. Guerilla warfare

It should be remembered that the Prime Minister Muhammad Gawan opened a campaign for the conquest of the Konkan to avenge the disgraceful defeat and the total annihilation of the Muslim army under his predecessor Malik-ul-Tujar at the hands of Shirke of Khelna and the Maratha ruler of Sangumeshwar in 1455. The method of guerilla warfare for which the Maratha troops were afterwards so famous under Malik Amber and Shivaji, is seen at its best in the wars between the Bahmani forces and the Konkan irregulars. It is worth noticing that the Muslim army under Gawan was unable to capture Khelna or the

---

1. A detailed account of the capture of Khelna is given on pp. 139-143 of the Mss. Mudhol Bakhar. The Firman is reproduced on pp. 145-46 of the same Bakhar.

Formidable Fort (Vishalgad). It was the Maratha force under Karansinha and his son Bhimsing or Bhimsen that ultimately succeeded in conquering the impregnable castle from its Maratha ruler.

After the murder of Muhammad Gawan, the Bahmani Kingdom fell into confusion, and the provincial governors began to rebel against the imperial authority. During these troublous times the help of the loyal rulers of Mudhol was eagerly sought by the Bahmani Kings. ' At present some evil-doers have started quarrels and are now showing eagerness to fight. At this juncture, the presence of one who has stood the test by trustworthiness and valour, is highly desirable at the capital." [1]

11. Mudhol rulers under Bijapur

Two years after the establishment of a new monarchy at Bijapur, the first Sultan Usaf Adilkhan confirmed the ancient Jagir, Mansab and title on Raja Kheloji Bahadur Ghorpade and made him ' Sarfraz ' in 1491 (Firman 6). He most faithfully served his masters and even laid down his life in defending Bijapur during the invasion of Amir Barid in 1514 at the battle-field of Allapur. Later on, his son Maloji who was then more than 30 years old, very bravely saved the life of Sultan Ismail in a war against Vijayanagar in 1520 and this exploit has been faithfully described in the Sultan's Firman itself (No. 9). In consequence of his valour, he was exempted from performing salutation in the court. The King also permitted the use of the Morchals to the rulers of this family. Even after four hundred years this emblem is still in vogue in this distinguished house. Raja Karansinha, the grandson of Maloji, took such an important part in the famous battle of Talikot in 1565 that he had to sacrifice his life in the cause of his master. For this faithful service his son

---

1. Firmans 7th and 8th of the Hijri year 901 or 1496 A. D. and 896 or 1491 A. D. in the name of Raja Kheloji Ghorpade.
2. Mudhol Bakhar, Pp. 184-212.   3. Ibid. P. 213 et seq.

Cholraj was raised to the dignity of the commander of the seven thousand horse and given *Torgal* and some territory of the Raichur Doab for the expenses of this army. (Firman 10). Later on, Cholraj and his uncle were employed in subduing Bancapur and Sira which were under the Vijayanagar Polygars. 26 villages in the Vijayanagar Kingdom proper and 4 villages to the south of Sira were conferred upon Cholraj. He finally laid down his life in a Karnatic expedition in 1578. It is worth noticing that the Bijapur kings were employing the Maratha Sardars for conquering the Hindu rulers of the Karnatic after the fateful battle of Talikot and they were conferring Jagirs upon them for their faithful services. All the three sons of Cholraj were long employed in subjugating the Polygars of the Karnatic, who now and then gathered such a strength as to inflict a defeat on the Imperial army and to capture some part of the annexed territory. After a faithful service of 20 years, Piraji was succeeded in 1598 by his son Pratapsinha who won many distinctions in the Bijapur Court (Firman 11). The employment of Shahji for the same purpose and the bestowal of a Jagir upon him were merely a continuation of the same old policy of pitting Hindus against Hindus. The Ghorpades and other Maratha Sardars were also employed in the Karnatic expeditions after 1636, as they had been frequently employed before. When Shahji was surrounded in the fort of Mahuli in 1636 by the Bijapur army under Randulla Khan, Pratap Sinha and his son Baji Raje Ghorpade, were serving under the Bijapur commander. The very first opportunity taken by Shahji to wreak vengeance upon his Ghorpade kinsmen was to stir up the cousins of Raja Pratap Sinha for requesting the King of Bijapur to grant them a share in the ancestral Jagir which was being solely enjoyed by the Ghorpades of Mudhol. By his influence Shahji secured a portion of the Jagir for Pratapsinha's cousins Baharji and Maloji, and thus weakened the Mudhol rulers. This and

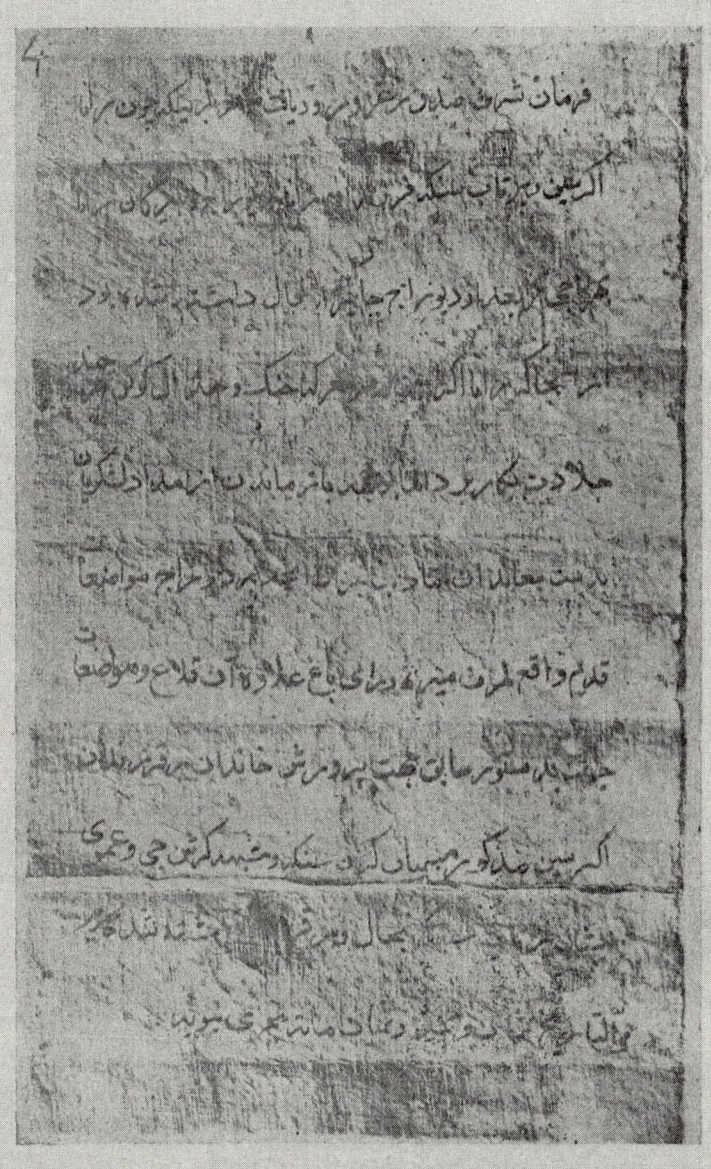

Wai is continued in the names of
Karan Sinha and Shubh Krishna
(A. D. 1454)

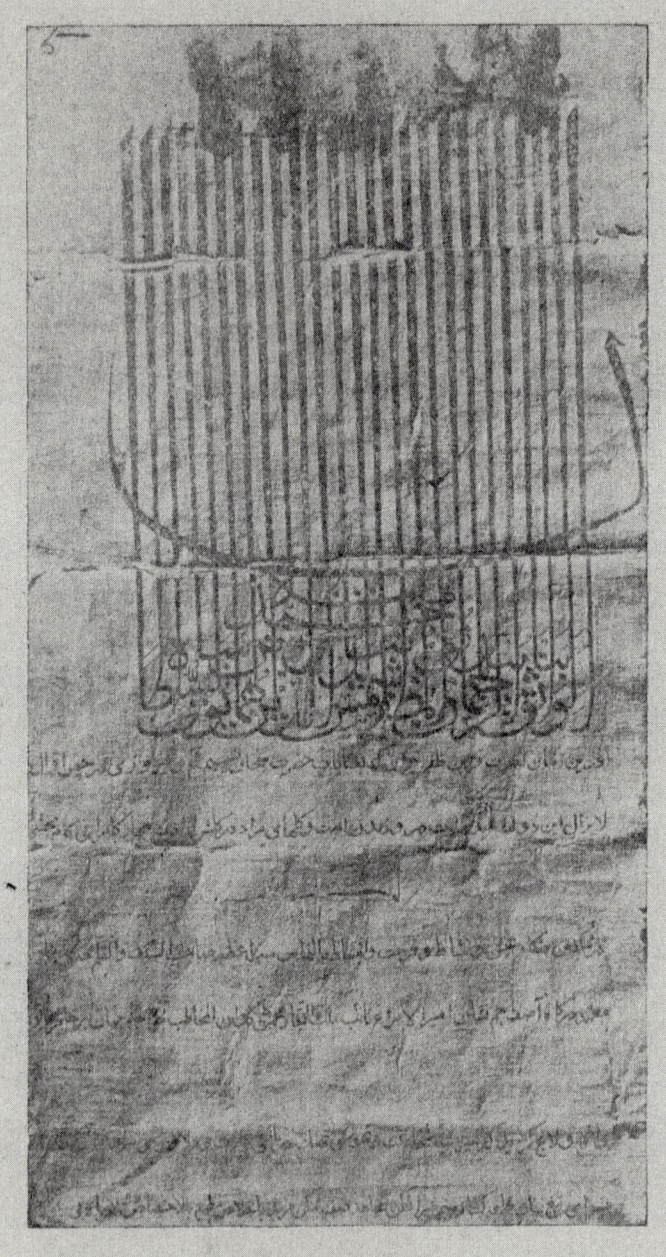

Rana Bhimsinha made Raja and
Ghorpade Bahadur (A. D. 1471)

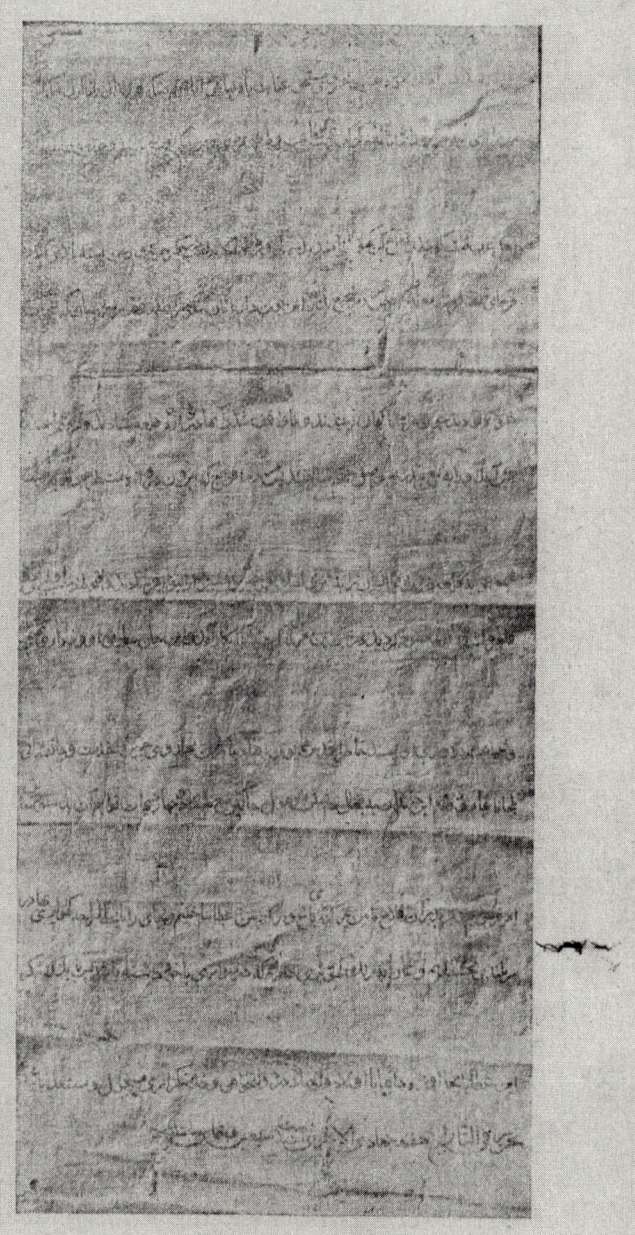

Rana Bhimsinha made Raja and
Ghorpade Bahadur (A. D 1471)

the other family feuds embittered the relations of the two branches of the Bhosle family to such an extent that the Ghorpades thwarted the Bhosles in their attempt to throw off the Muslim yoke. They remained ultra loyal to the Bijapur Kings up to their overthrow by Aurangzeb and then they transferred their allegiance to the Mogul monarch against the national interests. The Ghorpade family founded principalities at Kapsi, Gajendragarh, Sondur, Dattwad, etc. which have lasted up till now. The greatest contribution of the Ghorpades during the war of independence against Aurangzeb was in the form of the matchless general Santaji Ghorpade whose very name struck terror into the hearts of the Moguls.

12. The Bhosles of Devagiri

Having reviewed the history of the Ghorpades up to the time of Shivaji, we take up the study of the younger branch of the Bhosles. The famous Shivaji is a lineal descendant of Shubha Krishna whose successors continued to live in Devagiri for several centuries. In time they adopted service as captains in the Nizam Shahi army and rose to important positions by dint of their daring and valour. No firmans are yet available with the scions of this family. From the dynastic trees which have come down from various sources, it appears that Rupasinha, Bhumendrasinha, Dhopaji, Barhattji, Kheloji, Jankoji, Sambhaji, Babaji, Maloji, and Shahji were the names of the direct ancestors of Shivaji. This geneology is critically examined in the appendix.

The preceding account makes it clear that Sajjansinha migrated with his younger brother to the Deccan about 1320 A. D. Nothing is known about him till he got an opportunity to serve Hasan Gangu in the fifties of the fourteenth century.[1] There is no mention of the grant of the Patilship of Shingnapur in the firmans. Chitnis

---

1. The famous Bahmani Kingdom was founded by Hasan Gangu in 1347 and it was ably ruled by him till his death in 1358.

S. 7.

knows nothing about the exploits of the Ranas described here on the basis of the firmans. Keluskar and Takakhav, as well as Kincaid and Parasnis who have followed Chitnis in this account are *ipso facto* incorrect.

Sarkar too has relied upon the traditional account and made certain observations on Shivaji's ancestors, which, we hope, will be revised by him in the light of these documents.

" Agriculture was their original occupation, as with most Marathas. But the break up of the large monarchies of Western India, (namely, the Bahmani at the end of the 15th century and the Nizam Shahi at the beginning of the 17th) opened to the ablest men among them the chance of rising to military power and lordship over land. The history of Shivaji's family illustrated this transformation of the tiller of the soil by successive stages into the bandit, the captain of mercenaries, the feudal baron, and the sovereign ruler, which was so frequent during the troubled times that followed the downfall of central powers like the Bahmani or the Delhi empire and ended only with the establishment of British paramountcy and British peace." [1]

The Firmans clearly prove that the Bhosles were neither agriculturists nor bandits. They did not rise to power at the close of the Bahmani Kingdom, but their fortunes shone from its very beginning. Even in 1454 they possessed Jagirs in Mudhol, Raibag, Wai and Devagiri, while later on Torgal and some territories in the Karnatic were granted to them.

Nothing is known of the several descendants of Shubha Krishna either from the Maratha chronicles or the documents which have been discovered up till now. This gap is closed up with the material available on the career of Maloji, the grand-father of Shivaji.

13. Maloji

By referring to the geneological trees of Shivaji's ancestors in the appendix, it will be seen that Sambhaji is

1. Shivaji P. 16.

common in three lists and is shown as the father of Babaji in
two of them. Shedgaonkar Bakhar (P. 2), however, gives Maloji
as the name of Babaji's father. It is difficult to choose between
the two till same confirmatory evidence is available. Still a
recent Bakhar can not be much trusted. Babaji is said to have
been born in 1530, and to have lived up to 67th year of his
age (Raj. V. 367). He had two sons Maloji and Vithoji who
were born in 1550 and 1553 (Sh. Dig. and Chitnis), but
in Shedgaonkar B. (P. 2) Maloji's birth year is said to be
1552. It is said that Maloji entered into Jadhavrao's
service in 1577 A. D., i. e., at the age of 27 or 25 years
(Duff), but, according to Shiva Digvijaya, in the year 1599
A. D., that is, when Maloji was 49 years old. Further on,
it is alleged that Maloji's wife did not have any issue for
a number of years, hence she sought the benediction of a
Muslim saint Shah Sharif. When afterwards two sons were
born to her in 1594 and 1596/7, they were named Shahji and
Sharifji after the name of the saint (Sh. Dig. 37-38). It
is evident now that, according to this account, Maloji
passed the first 49 years of his life at Verul as an agriculturist.
He and his brother migrated to Sinkhed for service and
became sentries or guards in Jadhavrao's mansion at
Sinkhed on a monthly pay of 5 pagodas. The contradictory
statements in the preceding account cannot be verified from
any other source. But we cannot believe that Vangoji
Naik Nimbalkar, the chief of Phaltan, would have given
away his sister Dipabai or Uma in marriage to Maloji, if
he were an ordinary cultivator or a sentry in the service
of Jadhavrao.

The Shivabharat introduces Maloji as a Maratha
ruler of the Solar dynasty in the Maharashtra. This
heroic son of Babaji was staying in the district of Poona
and tried to extend his power over the territory adjoining
the banks of the Bhima and the mountainous region

of the Sahyadris. He married Vangoji Nimbalkar's sister
Uma [1] by name, built extensive tank on the Shambhu
Hill, constructed many mansions, gardens, wells, rest-houses,
etc.. He had grown so powerful that several feudatory
Rajas were at his command. This famous Sardar was
invited by the Nizam Shahi King to fight on his side
against the Bijapur Sultan and therefore he and, sometime
after, even his brother Vithoji went over to Devagiri
with their large armies. The brothers distinguished
themselves in the Nizam Shahi service and obtained a new
jagir from their master. The military services of Maloji
are recorded in the Tanjore Inscription. The fortress of
Ausa was besieged by the Bijapur general Dilawar Khan,
but it was most heroically defended by Maloji. Four
years later, the said Dilawar Khan joined Nizam Shah and
he carried fire and sword into the Bijapur territory. In
this destructive expedition the general was assisted by the
Nizam Shahi troops under Maloji. Then Ibrahim Shah's
brother Ismail became a rebel and raided the territories of
Kolhapur and Belgaum. He was helped by Nizam Shah with
troops under Maloji. For services like these the latter secured
the command of 5,000 horse, and thus became a great noble
of the Nizam Shahi State. We learn from a document of 1596
A.D. that Patgaon on the bank of the Bhima was in their jagir.
This town must have been really given to Babaji Bhosle
(Nos. 10-11 of P. S. S.), and it rose to very great prominence
in the days of Shivaji when the Mogul armies used to encamp
there. The Poona Jagir was entrusted by the brothers for
management [2] to their ministers. While Maloji was staying

---

1. Radha-Madhava Vilas Champu (267), the Tanjore Inscription and a
document (Rajwade VIII. 71) confirm this name, but the Bakhars name her
Dipabai. That this latter name is incorrect is also clear from a letter of Shahji
in which he gives 'Umai' as the name of his mother who seems to have been
living up to the end of 1644 (No. 498 P. S. S,). It is likely that Dipabai
might be her name before the marriage.

2. The names of the two brothers occur together as managers of the jagirs.
P. S. S. Nos. 26-29; 36, 92,

at Davagiri, a son was born to him and he was named Shahji.
Two years after another son was born and he was named
Sharifji. These names are said to have been given in honour
of a saint whose name was Shah Sharif. In the 5th year
of Shahji's age, Maloji was sent with a large army to put
down a rebellion. However, in the battle of Indapur [1] he
was killed [2] in 1606 A. D. His wife was dissuaded from going
Satti with her husband for the sake of her sons. Vithoji
became the guardian of his nephews, and kept peace and
order in the estates which had been confirmed upon them
by King Murtiza Nizam Shah. It appears that Maloji and
Vithoji obtained the title of Sargiroh (Leaders of Armies).
They were granted the three Parganas of Ellora, Dheradi,
Kannrad and some more villages in the districts of
Jafrabad, Daulatabad and Ahmadabad in 1606. [3] Thus it is
now evident that Maloji Raje held two large estates, one
at Poona and its surrounding regions, and the other in the
several places of the Nizam Shahi Kingdom. He was an
eminent Sardar even before migrating to Daulatabad, but
his status must have been much improved by the acquisition
of the new Jagirs. He is said to have constructed the temple
of Ghrisneshwara at Ellora which exists up till now. This
Maloji Raje Bhosle also constructed a tank at Shingnapur,
and granted some land and money to a religious
society there. [4] This town continued in the possession of
the family, as is borne out by a document of December
1611. [5] There are some grants by Vithoji Raje Bhosle
of the year 1613. [6] He must have died before 1621,

---

1. A taluka in the Poona District,
2. Shedgaonkar Bakhar wrongly gives 1542 Sh. or 1620 A. D. as the year
of Maloji's death.
3. P. S. S. Nos. 26–29.
4. P. S. S. No. 35.
5. P. S. S. Nos. 53, 54, 55.
6. P. S. S. Nos. 62, 95.

though there are grants of his sons from 1616 to 1636. [1]

14. Tentative chronology of Shivaji's ancestors

A. D. 1303   Ratansi and Lakshman Sinha died in the siege of Chittor.

1320?   Sajjan Sinha migrated to the Deccan.

1340?   Sajjan Sinha entered into the service of Hasan Gangu.

?   Sajjan Sinha fought against the Imperial army.

1347   Sajjan Sinha got a grant of a few villages in the Meerat district in the province of Devagiri.

1352   The grant of this jagir was confirmed upon Dilipsinha.

1367?   Sidhoji was made Mir Naubat.

1388   Sidhoji was killed in a battlle.

1398   Bhairoji or Bhosaji was granted Mudhol with eighty four villages.

1405   Karansinha, the eldest son of Bhosaji, was killed in a battle.

---

1. P, S. S. Nos. 72, 127, 130. The names of Vithoji's sons were:—

Sh. D.g. 36—		Sh. Bh. III 3-4—	
Sambl aji,	Kheloji,	Sambhaji,	Kheloji,
Parsoji,	Nagoji,	Parsoji,	Nagoji,
Mayaji,	Trimbakji,	Mambaji,	Trimbakji,
Makaji,	Maloji,	Vakkaji,	Mallaji,

Rajwade XV. 395 has Kakaji for Vakkaji out of the seven names. 91 Q. Bakhar (2) mentions ten sons and names Kheloji and Mambaji only.

P, S. S. has several rames mentioned in many grants:—

Sambhaji Nos. 56 127, 176, 169,	Ekoji No. 130 ?
Dasoji No. 72 ?	Kheloji Nos. 317, 380, 382, 418.
Maloji Nos. 127, 178	Parsoji No. 412.
	Trimbakji Nos. 484, 485.

There is, however, one grant of Vithoji Raje (No. 204 of P. S. S.) in 1624 March to the Karkun of Shirwal. If it is a genuine document, it will mean that Vithoji was alive in 1624, though he is said to have died before 1621 (No. 127), Though a large part of the administration of his jaghirs was handed over to his sons and there was a division of gold among the brothers in February 1623, P. S. S, Nos. 177–78. The grant No. 204 is of the same type as No. 291 from Malik Ambar in April 1629, though he had died in May 1626. Such are also the grants Nos. 169 and 176, as Sambhaji died in 1621.

A. D. 1407 Bhosaji died in the service of the King.

1423 Devaraj died.

1424 Ugrasen succeeded.

1454 Some villages in Wai Pargana were granted to Ugrasen.

1455? Ugrasen died in taking a Konkan fort.

1460? Shubha Krishna went over to his jagir in Meerat and left his elder brother Karansinha in the enjoyment of the Mudhol Jagir.

1471 Karansinha was killed in conquering the fort of Vishalgad.

1471 Bhimasinha became the first Raja Ghorpade Bahadur. His family was to use a flag with the emblem of Ghorpad (iguana) on it.

1491 Kheloji was made Surfraz.

1514 Kheloji was killed in an attack on Bijapur by Kasim Barid.

1520 Maloji saved the life of Sultan Ismail.

1522 He was exempted from prostration in the court.

1530? Babaji Bhosle was born.

1550 or 1552? Babaji had a son whom he named Maloji.

1553/4? Maloji's younger brother Vithoji was born.

1565 Raja Karansinha died in the battle of Talikot. His son Cholraj was given Torgal and a command of seven thousand horse.

1578 Cholraj died and was succeeded by Pilaji.

1596 Patgaon on the Bhima was under Babaji Bhosle.

1598 Pratapsinha succeeded Pilaji.

1602 Shahji was born to Maloji's wife Uma.

1604 Sharifji was born.

1606 Maloji and Vithoji got new jagirs from Nizam Shah.

1606 Maloji was killed in the battle of Indapur.

A. D. 1616–36 Various grants made by Vithoji's sons are
.   available.
1621   Vithoji died.
1636   Pratapsinha and his son Baji aided Randulla
        Khan against Shahji.

The Bhosle and Ghorpade rulers of Mudhol

Years of rule.

1352—Sajjan Sinha died.
1352-67—Dilipsinha.
1367-86—Sidhoji.
1386-1407—Bhosaji.
1407-23—Devaraj.

1548-1565—Karansinha.
1565-1578—Cholraj.
1578-1598—Pilaji.
1598-1645—Pratapsinha.
1645-1661—Baji Raje.
1661-1700—Maloji.

1424-1455?—Ugrasen. (Mudhol Bakhar P. 120 makes it
        1457, for he is said to have governed for
        34 years).
1455-1471—Karansinha.
1471-1491—Bhimasinha.
1491-1511—Kheloji (Mudhol Bakhar P. 212 puts 25
        years' rule).
1511-1531—Maloji.
1531-1548—Akhaiji.

CHAPTER III

SHAHJI—THE KINGMAKER

1. Shahji's personality and education

Shahji, the son of Maloji, is said to have oval eyes, a fine, parrot-like nose, a beautiful face, long arms and a handsome body. He was generous, [1] mild, wise, brave, valorous, and deeply learned in Hindu law-books and literature. His court-poet Jayarama has compared him to Arjuna in bravery, to Vikramaditya in generosity and King Bhoja in learning. [2] The poet has explicitly stated that a part of a stanza was composed in Sanskrit by Shahji himself for being completed by him as a test of ready wit and power of versification. His sons, Sambhaji and Ekoji, were also fairly fond of poetry and literature. They too composed lines to test the poetic powers of Jayarama. The names of about 75 poets and Pandits who were at one time or another in the service of Shahji, are mentioned by the poet. This assembly of Indian intelligentsia recruited from various parts of the country, represented a Babel of tongues, such as Sanskrit, Prakrit, Persian, Kanada, Hindi, Urdu, etc. Shahji living in the company of such learned men who spoke thirty-five languages, must have become a poly-linguist.

The poet has finally expressed Shahji's contribution to the revival of the sacred Sanskrit literature in a couplet. "The Vedic word which had been lying insensate for a long period, was brought to senses by the valour of Shahji. She prayed Brahma to divide India into two parts between Shahji and Shah Jahan. The former protected the Vedas and other sacred literature against the inroads of the

1. Sh. Bh. II, 13-20.
2. Radha Madhava Vilasa Champu, 217-18.

Mlechhas and revived the same by his generous donations."
It is now evident that Shahji was fairly educated in classics,
was intensely fond of the company of scholars and anxious
to revive the almost dead Hindu literature at a time when,
on account of the neglect or persecution of Muslim kings, it
had reached its lowest ebb.

2. Marriage of Shahji

At the time of the death of his father, Shahji was
four years old. Hence he must have been born in 1602.
Sharifji was two years younger. Both these sons were
brought up by their mother under the general supervision
of their uncle, Vithoji. ' When Shahji grew to handsome
and lusty manhood, when he had shown himself to be a
generous and valiant youth endowed with excellent qualities,
he was married to Jijabai, the beautiful daughter of
Jadhavrao who is said to be as rich as Kubera, the God
of wealth. This Lakhoji Jadhavrao was descended from
the Yadava Kings of Devagiri or Daulatabad. He was
the *Deshmukh* of Sinkhed and had the right to
command 10,000 horse in the Nizamshahi Kingdom. Shahji's
brother Sharifjji was soon married to Durga, a daughter
of Vishwasraja, the chief, of Junner. (Sh. Bh. VIII.
10-15; II. 65). Shahji's marriage must have taken place
in 1619-20, for then only he would be a youth of 17 to
18 years of age. ² The Shiva Bharat states that this
valorous warrior Shahji who was comparable to Bhishma
and Prithwiraj of old, soon afterwards rose to the first
rank among the Nizamshahi nobility.

1. Sh. Bh. II, 44, Kincaid (I, 114) and G Duff (P. 40) wrongly place the
birth years of the two brothers in 1594 and 1597 A. D.

2. Chitnis, G. Duff and Khare place the marriage of Shahji in 1604 A. D.,
while the dissension created in the Rangapanchami festival is said to have
occurred in 1599 (G. Duff 40-41). Sh. Dig (43) gives 1603 and Shedg. mentions
1605 as the year of Shahji's marriage. All the Bakhars wrongly state that this
marriage took place in Daulatabad. G. Duff (P. 41) places the scene of marriage
at Ahmadnagar. He too is wrong, as it was then in the possession of the Moguls.

It will be seen that the Shivabharata makes no reference to the anecdotes of the Bakhars. For instance, it is not said that on the day of the Rangapanchmi in the Holi festival Lakhoji was very much impressed with the graceful and charming figure of Shahji who was merely a boy of five years; that he publickly expressed the desire that Shahji and his daughter Jijabai would make a fine couple, and that taking advantage of this public offer, Maloji pressed his claims to the recognition of the betrothal. But the ladies of Jadhavrao's household resented their connection with an ordinary soldier in their own service. Thereupon Maloji is said to have left Ahmadnagar on a pilgrimage to Tuljapur. There he received the benedictions of the Goddess Bhavani, and on his return invited Lakhoji to a duel. On the other hand, the 91 Q. Bakhar and the Shedgaonkar Bakhar relate the story that Maloji, to obtain the hand of the daughter of Jadhavrao, proceeded with Nimbalkar of Phaltan to Daulatabad where they threw two dead pigs into a mosque. The aggrieved Muhammedans approached the King for redress. But it was found out that Maloji had committed that atrocity to revenge himself on Jadhavrao. The latter was called to the Court and reprimanded for not giving his daughter in marriage to Shahji. In the meantime, Maloji, instead of being punished, was conferred the dignity and title of the lord of 5,000 horse [1] and given Poona and Supa [2] in fief, and made commandant of the forts of Shivneri and Chakan with the title of Raja. Thereupon his marriage was celebrated with great eclat in 1604.

This unreliable account has been followed by Waring, Grant Duff, Kincaid, Takakhav and even by Sir J. Sarkar,

1. Sh. Dig. (P. 42). Other Bakhars mention a mansab of 12,000 horse being conferred on each one of the two brothers, Maloji and Vithoji. See Waring.
2. Sh. Dig. (P. 44) adds Paramati, Sangamner, Chandwad, Shevgaon, Patode, Ambade and others; Nasik with its 27 forts; and ten Parganas and Mahals in the province of Malwa, but there is no confirmatory evidence. It is said that even the city of Burhanpur was given to Maloji This assertion is wholly unreliable.

but the Sabhasad Bakhar or the contemporary letters and
authors like Jayarama and Parmanand do not refer to this
romance and hence we have discarded it.

3. Vicissitudes of war in the Deccan.

It is well-known that in 1600 Ahmadnagar was ceded to
Akbar after its most heroic defence by the illustrious Chand
Bibi and the ignoble murder of this amazonian queen by her
perfidious nobles. Malik Amber and others removed the new
king Murtaza Nizam Shah II first to Ausa and then to
Parenda forts. In 1607 Amber captured Junner and made
it the seat of Nizam Shahi Kingdom.[1] Then in 1610 he
founded the new city of Khirki[2] near Daulatabad and brought
the king to that city.

These successes of the Abyssinian minister exasperated
Jahangir who in 1610 appointed Khan Jahan Lodi, a general
of the relief forces, to help the Khan Khanan for crushing
the versatile Malik Amber. This Lodi was the second son
of Daulat Khan Lodi, a distinguished warrior of Akbar's
time, and rose to the high rank of 5,000 horse on account
of his martial talents. In spite of this additional force,
even Ahmadnagar had to be surrendered to the Deccanis.
Though Khan Jahan displaced the Khan Khanan as Viceroy,
yet he was no match for Amber who succeeded in cutting
off a large part of the Mogul army in the Konkan by
means of his guerilla bands. Jahangir, being enraged at the
incapacity of his generals, once more sent the Khan Khanan
in 1612 to the Deccan. During this campaign success
smiled upon the Imperialists on account of Muslem and
Maratha desertions from the army under Malik Amber.
The victorious Moguls captured and plundered the new
capital of Khirki, then demolished its magnificent buildings
and even burnt the city to ashes. The war was temporarily

1, Brigg's Firishta III. 315-20.

2. Khirki or Kharki signifies the Rock City from 'Khark' which means
a rock. Its name was changed into Aurangabad by Aurangzeb. (Basat–
in-i-Salatin. P. 221).

brought to an end by Prince Khurram in 1617, when the Malik bowed before the storm, ceded the Balaghat which had been seized from the Moguls, surrendered Ahmadnagar and other forts, and gave valuable presents to pacify the Prince.

Three years after in 1620, the Malik broke the treaty and once more vigorously began his offensive against the Imperialists. After a severe struggle in which the Mogul and Nizam Shahi territory was mercilessly devastated, the Moguls were besieged in Balapur and Burhanpur. The Maratha light horse even advanced as far as the environs of Mandu itself. At such a critical time of national disaster, all eyes turned towards Prince Khurrum, but he refused to march until he was permitted to take his eldest brother Khusrau a hostage with him. The extreme necessity of saving his honour at that time of an impending crisis, compelled Jahangir to comply with Khurrum's demand. Success soon smiled upon this prince. His advance guard easily drove the Marathas from Mandu and pursued them with great slaughter across the Narbada. The Prince rapidly marched to the relief of Burhanpur. The Deccanis raised its siege at the very approach of the Imperial army, and were then pursued to the very gates of Khirki, the capital of the Nizam Shahi Kingdom. Malik Amber was defeated within sight of Kharki in 1621. The capital was again captured and demolished. Another Mogul division advanced to relieve Ahmadnagar. Hard pressed from all sides, Malik Amber offered submission to Shah Jahan. A peace was concluded by which all the three Deccan monarchies accepted to pay a tribute of 50 lakhs of rupees. It appears that Jadhavrao, Shahji and Nimbalkar of Phaltan bravely fought on the side of Amber in this war. Shahji by his constant raids upon the Moguls, proved his valour, dash and generalship for the first time.

The prince retired to Burhanpur, and busied himself

in the organization of the Deccan provinces. In that very year (1621) he put to death his elder brother Khusrau. This unnatural crime was condoned by Jahangir for various reasons. Soon after the Persians laid siege to Qandhar. As its fall was imminent, Shah Jahan was commanded to hasten back from the Deccan. Being afraid that Nur Jahan's junto would jeopardise his claim to the throne during his absence in Afganistan, he refused to obey the orders. His revolt, defeat and flight [1] need not be described here. It will suffice to see the result of this internecine war on the Deccan. Malik Amber, freed from the danger of a vigorous offensive of the Moguls, turned his energies to the consolidation of the state. However the ill-fated Kingdom was dogged by a series of misfortunes, the first of which was the desertion of the most prominent noble Jadhavrao.

4. Jadhavrao's desertion to the Moguls (1621-30)

Bitter enmity was accidentally created between the Bhosles and Jadhavrao. One day at the end of a court levee in 1621 there was a very great rush in the retinues of the various war-lords. The elephant of one Sardar Khandagale getting out of control, trampled several men. Jadhavrao's son, Dattaji, ran to control the animal. In the scuffle, Vithoji's sons Sambhaji and Kheloji and then Shahji too advanced to save their friend Khandagale against Dattaji. The latter was killed in this fight, and hence Jadhavrao returned with his retine and killed Sambhaji and wounded his son-in-law Shahji. The king himself came upon the scene and separated the two parties. He was disgusted

1. " Concerning the Affairs of the Mogal with his Son, they said that Sultan Chorrom, having been twice routed, had at last retreated with some few followers into the Dominions of Cutab-Sciah; and that his Father had given over pursuing him and, being retired to his own Court, left him there in quiet; that Cutab-Sciah did not assist him out of his Territories out of respect to himself, but let him enjoy the possession of a certain small circuit in his Country to which he had retired". Travels of Petro Della Valle in India. Vol. II, P. 419.

with the pride, power, and prestige of Jadhavrao and began to mature schemes against this powerful lord. Thereupon this premier Maratha chief with all his adherents left Daulatabad in October 1621 and allied himself with the Moguls against his master Nizam Shah[1]. The defection of this Maratha baron was also the fruit of the policy of Prince Shah Jahan who, as Viceroy of the Deccan, had been sowing intrigues amongst the Nizam Shahi nobles. Up to 1630 Jadhavrao was with the Moguls as is stated in a Surat letter and in the Maasir-ul-Umrav.[2] He was treated with special honours. Even the princes of the royal blood did not enjoy such an eminent position.

" The manner in which the Moghuls received and rewarded him, is, in itself, a proof of the great power and consequence which the Mahrattas had by that time attained. A munsub of 24,000, with 15,000 horse, was conferred upon him, and such of his relations as accompanied him were all raised to high rank." [3]

5. Capture of Poona by Shahji, 1621

In 1620 Poona seems to have been governed by one Rayrao on behalf of Bijapur. This place was governed from the fort of Bhuleshwar or Daulatamangal. At the news of the termination of the friendly relations between Adil Shah and Nizam Shah, Rayrao began to collect money by oppressing the subjects. Shahji was despatched against him by Malik Amber to turn him out of the

1. Sh. Bh. Chapter III; E. F. 1618-21, pp. 317 n. 318, 332 Cf. Jahangir's Memoirs (II. 218) :—

" In the sixteenth new year (of Jahangir's reign i. e. 1621 A. D) it was reported to me (Jahangir) that Jadao Rao Kaitha (or Kathia) who is one of the leading Sardars of the Deccan, by the guidance of good fortune and reliance on God had elected for loyalty and had been enrolled amongst the loyal servants, Bestowing on him a dress of honour and a jewelled dagger, I sent a gracious Firman to him by the hand of Narayan Das Rathor."

2. E. F. 1624-9, p. 176, 6 February 1627.

3. G. Duff, p. 43 and confirmed by the Maasir-ul-Umrav.

district. On the faithful performance of this service Shahji obtained the Mokasa or superintending powers of the Parganas of Poona and Shirwal from Nizam Shah. This incident still more embittered the relations of the two monarchies. [1]

6. The siege of Bijapur by Amber

The desertion of Jadhavrao and the conquest of Poona were taken advantage of by the Moguls and the Bijapur ruler in cementing their alliance and jointly invading the Nizamshahi territory. Thereupon Malik Amber concluded an alliance with Golconda, and by forced marches surprised and defeated the Bijapur troops at Bidar. After plundering that magnificent city, he hastened towards the capital of Bijapur itself and laid siege to it. At the same time he devastated the surrounding country, and raised the siege only on the arrival of a large reinforcement from the Imperial army. The allied Bijapuri and Imperial forces then advanced into the Nizamshahi territory to wreak vengeance upon the Malik, and encamped near the village of Bhatwadi. [2]

7. Bijapur described

The great traveller Mandelslo who visited Bijapur in 1639 has left this impression of the city:—

" The City of Visiapour is of such a largeness, that it is above five Leagues in compass. The walls which are very high, are of Free-Stone, encompass'd with a great Ditch, and several Fortifications, mounted with above a thousand great Pieces, of all sorts, Iron and Brass. The Kings Palace is in the midst of the City, from which it is divided by a double wall, and two Ditches, being above 3500 paces in compass. He who commanded there in the time of Sultan Mamedh Ideshacn (Muhammad Adil Shah) the Son of

1. Sh. Ch. Sahitya I, 16–17; 19–30.
2. Elliot VI, pp. 412, 415.

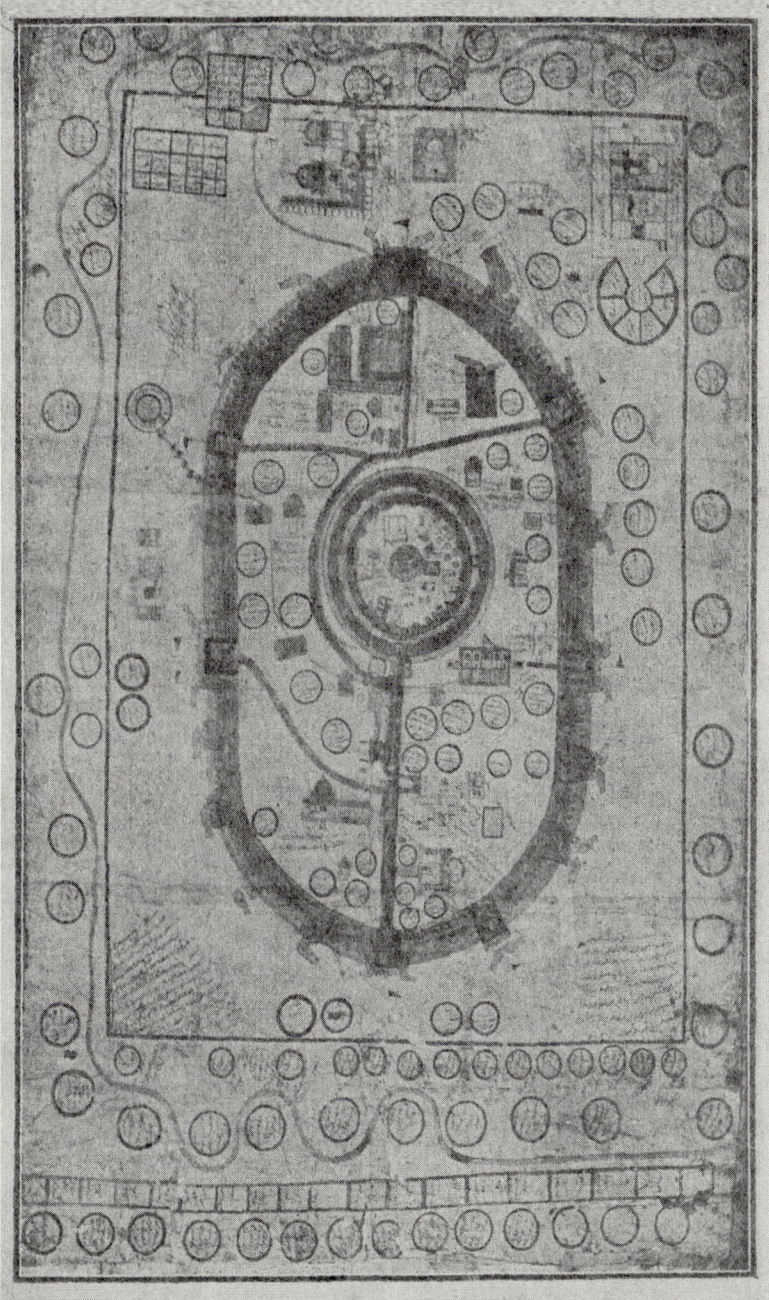

Plan of Old Bijapur City. (Bijapur Mus.)

View of Bijapur.

of Ibrahim, was called Mammouth–Chan (Mahmud Khan)
by Countrey an Italian, born at Rome. His command
extended also over the City, and the 5000 men who kept
Garrison therein, besides the 2000 who were the constant
Garrison of the Castle. The City hath five distinct Suburbs,
where the principal Merchants have their habitations and
particularly in that of Schanpour, where live most of the
Jewellers. The other Suburbs are called Gurapour,
Ibrahimpour, Alapour and Bomnenaly. The Inhabitants
are Decanins, that is, of the Kingdom of Decam, or Benjans,
Moguls, and Jentives, of whom an account hath been
given before." [1]

All these various suburbs and places of interest can be
seen in the accompanying plan of the city which has been
photographed from the original, now kept in the Bijapur
Museum.

8. The battle of Bhatvadi in 1624

The Shiva Bharata contains a detailed description of
this battle. It is said that the Bijapur army was under Mulla
Muhammad who was assisted by the feudal armies of Mustafa,
Masaud, Farhad, Sarja Yakoot, Khairat, the Brahmin
Dhundiraj, [2] Ghathe and many other Maratha chieftains.
The Mogul army was officered by such veterans as Lashkar
Khan, Jalal Khan, Khanjir Khan, Sikandar Khan, Bahadur
Khan, Brahman Udairam, Vishwanath, and Jadhavarao with
his three sons.

The Nizamshahi army was commanded by Malik Amber,
Fateh Khan, Mansur, Atashkhan, Joharkhan Shahji, Sharifji,
sons of Vithoji, Hambirrao Chavan, Mudhoji Nimbalkar,
Bramhan Nrisinha Pingle, Sundar Raja and others.

In October 1624 the invading armies of the two allies
were boldly faced at Bhatvadi or Bhaturi, 10 miles distant

---

1. Mandelslo's Travels into the East Indies. Pp 72–73.
2. J. Ch.: Sh. Bh. Chapter IV; Sh. Ch. Pr. Pp. 53-4, and Tanjore Inscription.

S. 9.

from Ahmadnagar, by the Nizamshahi war-lords. Many Maratha Sardars distinguished themselves on the battlefield of Bhatvadi. Sharifji, the younger brother of Shahji, was killed in an action with a Mogul commander Manchehr by name. Shahji particularly distinguished himself for his generalship by ultimately routing the army of this commander. Jadhavrao and Udairam are said to have fled away from the field without striking a blow. Mulla Mahammad [1] fell at an early stage of the fight, and many officers of the allied army including Ikhlas Khan and Farhad Khan of the Bijapur forces, were made captives. Farhad Khan was disgracefully executed, and his army broke up in utter disorder. So were other chiefs of the imperial army imprisoned, but Khanjar Khan with several other commanders made an escape to Ahmadnagar which they prepared for a siege. The rest of the fugitives sought refuge in Barhanpur. The victorious Malik Amber lost no time in laying siege to Ahmadnagar as well as Barhanpur, and in capturing the whole Mogul territory of the Balaghat. This crushing defeat was also followed by two great disasters to Bijapur. The rich town of Sholapur which had long been a bone of contention between Nizam Shah and Adil Shah, was stormed and captured by the former. Moreover, the triumphant king sent a large army, numbering 60,000 strong to once more invest Bijapur itself. The metropolis escaped from the fury of the besiegers, but they burnt down, destroyed and razed to the ground the new and fine suburban city of Nauraspur which had been lately built with a great taste by Ibrahim Shah. [2]

The remarkable victories of Malik Amber over the combined armies of the Delhi Empire and the Bijapur State spread his fame far and wide. The world did little know that the brilliant successes were not all due to the energy

1. This account from the Persian sources is not so reliable as that of P. D. Valle who learnt the news at Goa only a few days after the battle.
2. J. Ch.; Sh. Bh. Chapter IV; P. S. S. No. 224. 18 September 1625.

of the octagenerian Amber, but were to be largely attributed to the valour and tactics of Shahji and other Bhosle commanders.

Malik Amber's chances of success in inflicting another serious blow to the Imperialists grew more brilliant by the union of Prince Shah Jahan who had retreated from the north to take refuge in the Nizamshahi Sate. Shah Jahan vigorously pressed the siege of Barhanpur for several months, but the city was most heroically defended by the Rajput levies. At last, a relieving force was brought by prince Parvez and Mahabat Khan. Thereupon Shah Jahan and Malik Amber raised the siege of Barhanpur and retired towards the Balaghat.[1]

Pietro Della Valle, the famous Italian traveller has referred to this battle of Bhatvadi in these lines:—

" On October the one and thirtieth (1624) news came to Goa that Melik Amber, who for a good while successfully warr'd against Adil-Sciah, at length in a victory had taken one Mulla Muhamed, General of Adil-Sciah's Army and much favor'd by him; who by his ill demeanor towards the said Melik (even so far as to endeavour to get him poyson'd) was the occasion of the present warr, wherein Melik's chief intent was to revenge himself on the said Mulla Muhamed: whom being thus taken, they say, he beheaded and caus'd him in that manner to be carry'd about his Camp with this Proclamation: that this Traytor Mulla Muhamed, the cause of the warr and present discords between Adil-Sciah and Nizam Sciah, (to whom this Melik is Governour, otherwise Friends and allies, was thus in the Name of his Lord Adil-Sciah, as a Traytor and disturber of the publick Peace, put to death. By which act Melik meant to signifie that he had no evil intention against Adil-Sciah, but onely took up Arms for the mischiefs done him by Mulla Muhamed, whom he

---

1. Beni Prasad, History of Jahangir, Pp. 390—95; E.F.1624—9, Pp. 151—153, 161, 316. Gladwin, P. 76,

desired to remove from the Government of Adil-Sciah and from the world. Yet it was not known how Adil-Sciah received this action, and what end the business would have.

In this warr, they say, the Mogol favoured Adil-Sciah against Melik and supplied him with 20,000 Horse, but, be that how it will, Adil-Sciah hath hitherto always gone by the worst and sometimes been in great danger; Melik who is a brave Captain, having over-run all the State almost to the Gates of Vidhiapor, which is the Royal City of Adil-Sciah where he hath sometimes been forced to shut himself up as if it were besieged. A few moneths before Adil-Sciah put one of his principal Wives to death, for conspiracy which she was said to hold with Melik, and for having been a party in promoting this warr, out of design to remove Adil-Sciah from the Government as one become odious to his own people, either through his covetousness, or inability (being infirm), and to place his son in his room, who therefore was in danger too of being put to death by his Father when the conspiracy was discovered. "[1]

9. Shahji in Bijapur service (1625-28)

In the campaigns against Sholapur and Nauraspur the Bhosles performed signal service, but instead of giving Shahji due honour and dignity, the Nizam Shahi government rewarded his cousins for the victory. This act naturally created a suspicion in his mind against Malik Amber, Nizam Shah as well as his cousins. Mutual jealousy soon grew into enmity among the cousins. In a short time, Shahji was satisfied that his stay at the court was no longer safe. Like his father-in-law Jadhavrao, he decided to retire from that service. Ibrahim Adil Shah of Bijapur was raging for revenge on Malik Amber for the brutal indignities piled upon him and his general during the late war. He offered the honourable post of Sarlashkar of the Bijapur army to Shahji and thus

---

1.   The Travels of Pietro Della Valle in India. Vol. II. Pp. 442-443.

a new alliance was made against Malik Amber.[1] This was the first desertion of Shahji which has not been noticed by many historians, but has been fully described by the Shiva Bharat and confirmed from the Tanjore Inscription and other sources. For instance, in the famous letter[2] written by Shivaji to Maloji Ghorpade of Mudhol, it is said that Shahji went to Bijapur in the reign of Ibrahim Shah before the death of Malik Amber which happened on 14th May 1626. Hence the desertion of Shahji must have ocurred in 1625.

In the beginning, Shahji Bhosle Adil Shahi began to act as an independent chief in his Jajir of Shirwal, Poona and Karyat Patas, but he suffered a terrible defeat at the hands of Sabaji Anant, the commander of Nizam Shahi troops which were sent to oust him from his possessions. The Bijapur army which came to assist Shahji was cooped up by the Nizamsahi forces in the Salpa pass in December[3] 1625. This reverse was soon after retrieved, as he successfully resisted the armies of Malik Amber which were again sent to capture his Jagir.[4]

Thereafter Shahji showed a wonderful activity during the brief period of his service in Bijapur. By his intervention he secured from Adil Shah an order for the restoration of the Jagir of Karyat Talib under the Governor of Fort Panhala, to Sambhaji and Dhoraji Mohite in January 1626.

Impressed with the power, valour and determination of Shahji, Ibrahim Adil Shah granted him the title of Sarlashkar, showered favours upon him and employed him against Mudhoji Nimbalker of Phaltan who was completely defeated. Then his troops were employed in subduing the Karnatic, the Kerala district and other tracts.[2] By his victories there, he brought an immense booty to Bijapur and thus improved the prosperity of the kingdom.

1. P. S. S. Nos. 227, 226,. 28 July 1625, 16 January 1626; 4 February 1626. Sh. Bh. V. 1-13.
2. Shivaji Vol. II, p. 281.
3. P. S. S. Nos. 222, 225. 19 December 1625.
4. Sh. Bh. V. 14-15; Raj. XV. 345.

It is evident that Sarlashkar Shahji had won his laurels as a general and statesman under Bijapur. Even under Malik Amber he first held the Mokasa of Poona and Shirwal, and later on distinguished himself in the battle of Bhatwadi and after. Hence his name could not first occur in recorded history in 1628, nor was he a petty captain during the regency of Malik Amber.[3] In a grant of 8th March 1628 Shahji called himself Sarlashkar, 'Maharaja,' 'the shelter of ministry,' 'and the refuge of valour.'[4] These titles must have been bestowed upon him by the Adil Shahi state.

The political situation rapidly took a different turn by the recall of Mahabat Khan in the beginning of 1626, the death of the octagenerian Malik Amber in May 1626 and that of King Ibrahim on 22nd September,[5] 1627.

10.   The recall of Mahabat Khan

The recall of an experienced general and a subtle diplomat like Mahabat Khan to the north, had an adverse effect on the situation in the Deccan. His successor Khan Jahan Lodi did not possess the energy, diplomacy, generalship and prestige of his predecessor to successfully withstand the guerilla tactics of which Malik Amber was a consummate master. The factions at the court, the succession disputes, the *coup de main* of Mahabat Khan in capturing Jahangir as well as Nur Jahan, and removing the Premier Asaf Jah from the administration, the rebellion of Shah Jahan and lastly, the death of the drunken Prince Parvez, very much weakened the Imperial cause in the Deccan. A graphic account of these events is given by President Kerridge in his Surat Letter of 29th November 1626 to the Company.

1. P. S. S. Nos. 226 290.
2. Sh. Bh, V. 20.
3. Sarkar, Shivaji, P. 18; M. R. 1917 September. P. 284.
4. P. S. S. No. 262.
5. O. C. 1264, 4 January 1628. P. S. S, No. 431; Beni Prasad, History of Jahangir, 415, 422.

" Asaph Chaun being father–in–lawe by marriage of his
daughter unto the Prince Charome, the Kings third sonne,
who (as you have doubtlesse bin advertized),
Murder of Khusrau. murthering his elder brother, (Khusrau), rebelled
against his father and by force of armes
aspired unto the crowne; in which attempt having susteyned
sundry overthrowes, hee lastlie fledd from the King his army
unto Bengall, and thence by way of Musulopotan (Masulipatam)
unto Decan, where hovering under the protection of Malik
Amber hee submissively sought reconciliacion, which his
said father in--lawe (being still in favour) mediating by
intercession of his sister, the predominant
Mahabat Khan recalled. Queene, obtained that Mahobett Chaun,
gennerall of the King his army, Charoomes
feirce enimy, should bee dismissed from that charge; who
after long deniall resigneing and comeing unto the court,
the King being then some 40 course from Lahore in his
progresse towards Cabull, his pavillion with his family and
attendants being pitched on the side of a
Mahabat's camp. river and his nobles on the other, the said
Mahobett Chaun with 8 or 10,000 horse came
suddainly unto him, slewe all such as seemed to question
or dislike the manner of his coming, and, having accesse
unto the King his presence, tooke him imediatelie with
him unto his owne tents; whereupon the Queene amasedlie
(amazedly) fledd unto hir brother and friends on the other
side the river, by a bridge purposelie made for passage
to and from, which imediately after was cutt downe to
prevent others from going over. The King, after private
conference with the said Mahobett Chaun, was with great
reverence returned againe unto his pavillion, and the Queene
by his command sent for; who rendering all dutie, refused to
come untill a feild weare tryed twixt hir friends and enimyes;
which the next morning she with them put
Surrender of Nur Jahan. in execution, and passing the river (hardlie
foordable) were encountred by Mahobutt
Chauns armie on the Kings side, who, though by farre the
lesse nomber, with the slaughter of about 5,000 menn put the
Queene and hir friends to flight. She hirselfe, after assurance

given by Mahobet Chaun for hir safety, came into the King.
Hir brother recovered a castle of his owne with many of

Asaf Khan's
flight. his friends; some were slaine, but most,
pretending the Kings service, weare pardoned
and continewed in office. Assaph Chaun, being
beseidged in his castle (of Attock), surrendered on assurance
of life, and hath ever since untill verry latelie remained
closse prisoner in the custodie and charge of Mahobett Chaun,
not withstanding the Queenes uttmost dilligence and the

Disaffection
against
Mahabat. Kings perswadeing an accord twixt them; all
which tyme Mahobett Chaun hath governed,
nothing having been granted without him,
and in such extremitie that the insolence of
his followers hath grieved not only the campe but the
inhabitants of Cabull also, who, instigated by some great
men, att a signe given slewe in an instant almost 2,000 of
his souldiers, that expected noe such massacre, and their
fellowes in revenge have since done divers outrages err both
sides could bee pacified, which the King lastly effected, and

Release of
Jahangir. being againe returned neere the river
aforemencioned where the Queenes friends
weare overthrowne, she hath with sundry of
them reinforced hirselfe for the delivery of hir brother, in
such manner as the armies of both have been at point of
joyning battle, but still prevented by the Kings endeavours
to accord them, which (as report newlie gives out) is
seemingly effected, both the mencioned favorites having
exchanged hostages and Asaph Chaun delivered; yet newe
and greater stirrs suspected, Carome having passed with

Shah Jahan's
wanderings. 3,000 horses onely from Decan through this
country unto Sindey, determining (as was
supposed) to have fledd into Persia; but
Sultan Parveis, the Kings second sonne and eldest then
living, who lately obteyned this cittie and the country
about it, being deceased within this 30 dayes att Brampore
(as is supposed by poyson) and the army there under
command of Chan Irhan, an especiall friend of the Prince
Caromes, his hopes are againe revived, and except the King doe
pardon his offences (thereby endaungering his owne state

Shahji.

Shivneri.

Shivneri.

and life) newe and great stirrs are like to bee raised, his
sonnes army daylie encreasing and hee on his
Shah Jahan's bid for the throne. returne from Sindee to Gusurat. Wee have
thought requisite to give you this particular
relacion of these troubles, as well for that
some circumstances in your business depend thereon as
that the inhabitants doe generally feare they are not yet
quieted, for the Prince Carome his farther hopes will cause
great stirrs both in court and country, who although hee
bee nowe the eldest living of the Kings children, yett hath
hee a younger brother (Shahriyar), marryed
Rival claimants to the throne. to the daughter of the beloved Queene
aforesaid, the sonne (Dawar Bakhsh) also
of his elder brother being a hopefull gentleman and
indubitate heire in favour of the King, and all of them
competitours for the kingdome." [1]

11. Estimate of Malik Amber

The famous Dutch traveller, Petro Della Valle has given
an interesting account of Malik |Amber and of the then
situation of the Deccan. It is not fully reliable, because
it is based upon hearsay. However, a popular view of
the personality of the great warrior, shrewd statesman and
the most enlightened financier of the Deccan was recorded by
him in 1620.

" The Nizam Sciah now reigning, is a boy of twelve
years old, who therefore doth not govern it, but an
Abyssine Slave of the Moors Religion,
Power of Malik Amber. called Malik Amber, administers the state
in his stead, and that with such authority,
that at this day this Territory is more generally known and
call'd by the name of Malik's Country, than the Kingdom
of Nizam Sciah. Nevertheless this Malik Amber governs not
fraudulently, and with design to usurp, by keeping the King
shut up, as I have sometimes heard; but according as I
have better understood since from persons inform'd nearer
hand, he administers with great fidelity and submission

1. O. C. 1241. Surat to the Company. 29 November 1626. Cf. Elliot **VI.**
Pp. 425-30.

S. 10.

towards the young King, to whom nevertheless they say, he hath provided, or already given to wife a Daughter of his own, upon security that himself shall be Governour of the whole state as long as he lives. This Malik Amber is a man of great parts, and fit for government, but, as they say, very impious, addicted to Sorcery; whereby 'tis thought that he keeps himself in favour with his king, and that for works of Inchantments, (as to make prodigious buildings, and with good luck, that the same may last perpetually and succeed well) he hath with certain superstitious us's in these countries committed most horrid impieties and cruelties, killing hundreds of his slaves' Children, and others; and offering them as in Sacrifice to the invok'd Devils, with other abominable stories which I have heard related; but because not seen by myself, I affirm not for true. The Ambassador of this Nizam Sciah in Persia, is that *Habese Chun*, an Abyssine also, whom I saw at my being there.

Of strange things, they relate that Nizam Sciah hath, I know not where in his Country a piece of Ordnance so vast,

The Malik-i-Maidan cannon at Parenda

that they say it requires 15,000 pound of Powder to charge it; that the ball it carries, almost equals the height of a Man,[1] that the metal of the piece is about two spans thick, and that it requires I know not how many thousand Oxen, besides Elephants to move it; which therefore is useless for war, and serves onely for vain pomp. Nevertheless this king so esteems it, that he keeps it continually cover'd with

---

1. Another account of this cannon when it was in the possession of Adil Shah, comes from the pen of Mendelslo.

"There is not any Prince in all those parts so well stored with Artillery as the king of Cuncam (Konkan in Bijapur). Among others, he had one Brass piece, which required a Bullet weighing eight hundred weight, with five hundred and forty pound of fine powder; which did such execution, as was reported, that at the siege of the Castle of Salapour (Sholapur), at the first firing, it made a breach in the wall of forty-five foot in length. The Caster of it was a Roman born, and the most wicked of mankind; since he had the inhumanity in cold blood, to kill his own son, to consecrate that monstrous Piece, with his blood, and to cast into the fire, wherein he had melted his Metal, one ef the Kings Treasurers, who would call him to account for the charge he had been at therein. But it is time we prosecute our Voyage." Mendelslo's Travels into the Indies. Lib. II. Pp 77-78. Cf. Cousens, Guide to Bijapur, p. 45.

rich cloth of Gold, and once a year comes in person to do it reverence, almost adoring it; and indeed, although these kings are Moors, yet they still retain much of the ancient idolatry of the Countries, wherein Mahometism is little, or not yet universally setled."

Even the Mogul historian, Motamad Khan who frequently revels in abusing the 'dark, ill-fortuned, Abyssinian slave,' has eloquently testified to his eminence. "In warfare, in command, in sound judgment and in administration, he had no rival or equal. He well understood that predatory warfare, which in the language of the Deccan is called *bargiqiri*. He kept down the turbulent spirits of that country, and maintained his exalted position to the end of his life and closed his career in honour." [1]

12. Demise of Ibrahim Adil Shah

Ibrahim Adil Shah is said to have been a great patron of scholars, poets, historians and musicians. He ardently loved music and used to worship Saraswati, the Hindu goddess of music. As he was often surrounded by Hindu musicians and Brahmins and was given the title of 'Jagat Guru'—world-teacher by his Hindu admirers, he was disliked by his Muslim co-religionists. This tolerant and learned monarch was succeeded by his minor son Muhammad Shah on 12th September 1627. At this time, the Bijapuri army consisted of one lakh foot, 52,000 horse and 955 elephants.

13. Desertion and return of Shahji

The regency began to follow a reactionary policy. All the Brahmin and Hindu Sardars were kept in custody. Shahji too was afterwards insulted by the new Padshah,[2] and consequently he thought it unsafe to continue there under

1. Beni Prasad, History of Jahangir. P. 423. Cf. J. Sarkar, Mod. Rev. September 1909.
2. Sh. Bh. IX. 26-27; VIII. 5-8.

the altered conditions. Secondly, though on the one hand, the death of Malik Amber and the desertion of the two noble Maratha lords had weakened the Nizam Shahi Kingdom, it was, on the other hand, resuscitated by the cession of the territories formerly lost in the wars with the Mogul. Khan Jahan Lodi, the Mogul Viceroy in the Deccan, treacherously gave back to Murtaza Nizam Shah all the territory that Akbar and Jahangir had wrested from the dynasty with so much loss of men and money. But the commandant of the Ahmadnagar fort refused to obey the order of this Viceroy, and thus that fortress alone did not pass into the possession of Nizam Shah.[1]

The political situation changed with the inauguration of Shah Jahan's rule. He proceeded in person to the Deccan to put down the rebellion of his Viceroy, Khan Jahan Lodi, and demanded the restoration of the imperial territory from Nizam Shah. In case of refusal his Kingdom was threatened with fresh invasions under the Emperor himself. The Daulatabad court invited Shahji to return, and he gladly accepted the offer to usefully serve[2] the state which had been the patron of himself and his ancestors. On his way, he took legal possession of his Poona Jagir for which a grant was formally made by Nizam Shah in May[3] 1628.

14. Shahji in Khandesh

In 1628 when the Moguls advanced against the fort of Bir, the Sultan sent Shahji and a party of siledars with 6,000 horse to make a raid in East Khandesh and check the Moguls there. But Darya Khan Ruhela slew many of the raiders and expelled them from the tract lying between the Tapti and the Purna. About one year after the return of Shahji to Daulatabad, his father-in-law Jadhavrao also renounced the cause of the Moguls for the

---

1. Khafi Khan in Elliot. 2. Sh. Bh. VI. 8. 3. P. S. S. Nos. 262, 274, 275. It appears that Shirwal or Subhanmangal remained with Jayanapant Lingras under Bijapur for some time to come. Sh. Ch. Sahitya I, pp. 22,24.

benefit of the old Nizam Shahi state, but unfortunately
he could not long live in peace there.[1]

15, The Imperial army in the Deccan, 1630

Mendelslo has given a detailed composition of the
imperial army that marched to the south. The names of
the chief officers and the strength of the battalions under each
of them will be interesting (Appendix). In 1630 Shah Jahan
marched with an army of 144,500 horse, besides elephants,
camels, mules, and horses for transport. This force was
divided into four brigades and was respectively commanded
by Shaista Khan, Iradat Khan, Jai Singh and one by the
King himself.

However, Manrique puts the figure at 400,000 horse.[2]
According to him, the total strength of Shah Jahan's army
in 1640 was 10,61,330 horse under 7,250 Umras, Mansabdars
and Ahadies. There were besides 128,000 horse belonging to
the four highest lords and the royal princes themselves. Thus
the nominal strength of the cavalry alone was twelve lakhs.
Shah Jahan was at Burhanpur in April, 1630.[3]

16. Arms of the Mogul army

The arms and weapons of the Moguls are thus described
by Manrique:

"The offensive Arms of the Horse are, the Bow, the
Quiver, having in it forty or fifty Arrows, the Javeline, or
a kind of long-headed Pike, which they dart with great
exactness, the Cymitar on one side, and the Ponyard on the
other; the defensive is the Buckler, which they have always
hanging about their necks."

17. Mode of Mogul warfare

The method of Mogul warfare as seen by this impartial
European, deserves our special attention.

1. Sh. Bh. VIII. 20; Orme Mss. Vol. 331. Rajvade is wrong in saying
that Jadhavrao returned to Daulatabad in 1625. R. M. V. Ch. P. 56.
  2. Vol. II, 273, Pp. 275-278.   3. E. F. 1630-1636, Pp. 22, 33.

"They know nothing of the distinction of Van–guard, main Battle, and Rear–guard, and understand neither Front nor File, nor make any Battalion, but fight confusedly without any Order.

Their greatest strength consists in the Elephants, which carry on their backs certain Towers of Wood, wherein there are three or four Harquenbuses hanging by hooks, and as many Men to order that Artillery. The Elephants serve them for a Trench, to oppose the first attempt of the Enemy, but it often comes to pass that the Artificial Fires, which are made use of to frighten these Creatures, put them into such a disorder, that they do much more mischief among those who brought them to the Field, than they do among the Enemies. They have abundance of Artillery, and some considerable great Pieces, and such as whereof it may be said, the invention of them is as ancient as that of ours. They also make Gun-powder, but it is not fully so good as what is made in Europe. Their Timbrels and Trumpets are of Copper, and the noise they make, in order to come to some Military Action, is not undelightful. Their Armies do not march above......Cos, or Leagues, according to the measure of the Country, in a day; and when they encamp, they take up so great a quantity of ground, that they exceed the compass of our greatest Cities.

In this they observe an admirable Order, in as much as there is no Officer nor Souldier, but knows where he is to take up his Quarters; nor can there be any City more regularly divided into Streets, Markets and other publick places for the greater communication and convenience of the Quarters, and for the distribution of Provisions." [1]

18. Method of Maratha warfare

The Nizam Shahi and Adil Shahi states had Muslim as well as Maratha feudal lords. For a long time Maratha

---

1. Travels of F. S. Manrique. P. 40,

levies seem to have followed the guerilla tactics of warfare
and their system had been adopted even by the Muslim forces,
so that Malik Amber was considered to be a consummate
master of predatory warfare. The Moguls of the time of Akbar
had no faith in the efficacy of this method and even slighted
it, till later on they learnt its value by terrible reverses in the
Deccan. Jahangir and Shah Jahan won over many Maratha
chiefs like Jadhavrao and his sons, Shahji and his relatives,
Kheloji and his brothers, and several Muslim war-lords
like Mukurrab Khan. The presence of their levies in the
Mogul armies taught the latter the supreme value of the
lightning and furious attacks on masses of the enemy forces
of carrying victories to their logical ends by way of hot
pursuit of the demoralised forces, of pillage and
destruction of the camps and transportation of the most
valuable booty, of an immediate and eccentric retreat, of
dispersing in all directions for avoiding war and afterwards
uniting in their place of bivouac. Rapidity, enterprise, energy,
courage, simplicity, perseverence in each individual soldier,
and bravery, discipline, versatility on the part of the whole
army are the virtues necessary for such a system of warfare. A
rapid succession of paralysing blows grows like an avalanche
in its destructive effects, so that the morale of the army is
reduced to its lowest level. Shivaji was a past master in the
art of predatory warfare. His successors faithfully followed
it in the long war with Aurangzeb who, though at the climax
of his power, could not maintain the morale of his troops
against the secret, furious and sudden attacks of the Marathas.
So that this system finally made the Hindus triumphant and
brought about the destruction of the Mogul Empire.

19. Jadhavrao's murder

Soon after the accession of the minor King
Muhammad Shah at Bijapur, Murtaza Nizam Shah saw
an opportunity of regaining his lost territory, and so he
commenced a war against Bijapur. But his army was
defeated first at Kayji Dharur and then at Kundri

Kannur in 1628. The Nizam Shahi premier Fateh Khan
had brought the misfortune of defeat upon his kingdom,
and yet he wielded an abundant influence upon the king.
The latter was persuaded by one minister Hamid Khan
to imprison Fateh Khan and then to arrest Jadhavrao who
was unjustly suspected of being at heart with the Moguls.
It was thought that in case the old experienced Jadhavrao
who knew all the secrets of the state, joined the Moguls,
he would cause irrepairable loss to the kingdom. The
plot was thus put into action. One day the king suddenly
withdrew from the Audience Hall and thereafter a few
Muslim courtiers under instructions from the king fell upon
Jadhavrao and his sons in the Court Hall. The latter bravely
fought to the last, so that Jadhavrao, his sons Raghuji and
Achaloji, and even his grandson Yeshwant Rao were killed
in June 1630. Thereupon Jadhavrao's brother Bhauji,[1] his
wife Girjabai and other members of the family, fled first
to Sindhkhed near Jalna and thence to the Moguls for
protection.[2] Hereafter they served the Moguls for the
destruction of the Nizam Shahi State.

20. Revolt of Shahji

The barbarous and cruel murder of the most
prominent Hindu noble of the Nizam Shahi Kingdom,
was full of important consequences. Other Hindu and
Muslim nobles found out that their lives and properties
were quite unsafe in the hands of the King. Shahji, the
son-in-law of Jadhavrao, was mortally afraid of the
coming conspiracies. He and his wife had every reason
to avenge the death of their nearest kinsman. So he
put up the banner of revolt and started from the
impregnable fort of Parenda on a plundering expedition.[3]

1. In Bad. Namah the names of the two brothers of Jadhavrao are given as
Jagdev and Bahadurji.
2. Urdu Basatin-i-Salatin, P. 229; Sh. Bh. VIII. 20-32. The names of
Jadhavrao's sons are given in Sh. Bh. IV. 26 as Raghuji, Achalaji, Jaswantrao
and Bahadurji, but Jaswant Rao should be replaced by Dattaji, the former was
his grandson.   3. Sh. Bh. VIII. 33.

He created a mighty disturbance in the Adil Shahi and
Nizam Shahi territories and strengthened Poona. From
seven other grants it appears that Poona was in his
possession[1] up to 1630.

Murar Jagdeva Pandit was sent with a large force
from Bijapur to subdue and punish Shahji. The Pandit
captured Poona and Indapur, set fire to the towns,
destroyed and burnt down all in that district.[2] Then he
built a fort on the Bhuleshwar hill which is some thirty-
two miles distant from Poona. Abarao was appointed as a
commandant of this new fort called Daulatamangal to look
after the administration of the newly conquered district. In
two grants Murari Pandit is styled ' Maharaj, Rajadhiraj'—
the Emperor and the King of Kings.[3] Meanwhile Shahji had
retreated to Shivneri and taken refuge with Shrinvas Roa
alias Vijayaraj. There his son Sambhaji was married to
the chief's daughter Jayanti.[4] Then he left his family there
and thought out a plan to save himself from the persecution of
the Nizam Shahi and Adil Shahi Kingdoms. As Shahji had
taken an active part in supporting Khan Jahan Lodi, he
thought it proper for saving his Jagir of Poona and the new
conquests, to throw himself on the Emperor's mercy and
procure a promise of pardon for his past offences by accepting
the Mogul service. He entered into correspondence with Azam
Khan, the Mogul Viceroy who forthwith sent information to
the Emperor. Shah Jahan was fully aware of the bravery,
strategy and versatility of Shahji, and consequently he
welcomed this Maratha noble for the conquest of the Nizam
Shahi Kingdom. The alliance of the Deccan monarchies was to
be weakened by the separation of Shahji.[5] The Raja with two
thousand cavalry went to have a personal interview with the
Viceroy, and there he was granted the dignity of 5,000 horse,

1. P. S. S. Nos. 274–279, 282, 285, etc..
2. P. S. S. No. 332; Rajvade. 18. Pp. 29, 44.
3. P. S. S. Nos. 337-8, November 1631, No. 363. September 1633.
4. P. S. S. Nos. 264—267; Sh. Bh. VIII. 10–18,
5. E. F. 1630–36. Pp. 159–60. 10 June 1631.

S. 11.

a robe, various other emblems of honour, and two lakhs of rupees. His son Sambhaji, relatives and dependents were also similarly honoured. Many of his cousins as Kheloji, Parsoji, Maloji, and Mambaji, as well as the sons of his uncle Vithoji, were taken into service at this time. Then he was deputed to conquer Junner, Sangamner and the Konkan districts for the Moguls.[1] Thus the Bhosles became the vassals of the Moguls for some time and began to capture territories for being annexed to the Delhi Empire.

Raja Chandar Rao More and Baji Valvale were sent by the Bijapur court with their own contingents to conquer the Konkan up to the port of Dabhol. They siezed Mahad, Chodegaon, Nizampur and a few other places from Nizam Shah. Siddi Marjan, the Subedar of Talkonkan, marched out of Chaul to oppose them. He was defeated and slain, and thus Chaul fell into the hands of the Adil Shahis. This victory was soon followed by a rout of the troops of Baji Valvale who was slain at Kolar near Chaul by Siddi Saba Amber Khani who had been reinforced with the troops of Ikhlas Khan from Daulatabad. He re-took Chaul and other parts previously captured by the Adil Shahis, and returned to the Konkan.[2] We have no light on Shahji's activities in that part. On the other hand, he seems to have been in the party of the pursuers of Daria Khan who had revolted against his master Shah Jahan. The rebel had made an escape into Bundhelkhand, but even there he was brought to bay by Shahji. In a fight the Maratha hero pierced him with many arrows and despatched him to the other world. Then Shahji returned to Shivneri[3] where for the first time his heart was gladdened to see his newly borne babe who was named Shivaji from the goddess Shivai after whose name the fort was styled Shivneri. The Orme Mss. Vol. 331 records that Shahji was invested by the Moguls with the Jagirs of Junner

Sangamner, Beejzapore (?) and Bugole (?) on the borders of Rajapur.

21. Revolution at Daulatabad

The murder of Jadhavrao, the rebellion of Shahji, the invasion of the Moguls, and the alliance of Bijapur and Shah Jahan forced Murtiza Nizam Shah to remove his prime minister, Mukurrub Khan who, on being degraded, went over to Shah Jahan. Malik Amber's son, Fatch Khan, was restored to liberty and the dignities of the prime minister were conferred upon him on 18th January[1] 1631. He desired to make an alliance with the Moguls, but many nobles were against this policy. He was apprehensive of the king turning against him on that point. Hence, that revengeful, impulsive and passionate Abyssinian, instead of being grateful to his generous master the king, is said to have put him to death[2] in February 1632. Basatin—i—Salatin, however, does not charge him with the crime and states that the King was suddenly struck with insanity and soon succumbed to that disorder. Fateh Khan set up Hussain Shah, the seven years old son of Murtiza Nizam Shah, upon the throne. The premeir was universally suspected of poisoning the King and was therefore detested by the people and the nobility.[3]

Sabaji Anant, Sewaji Pandit, Sakhoram and other officers went over to the Moguls. Similarly, the Muslim nobles deserted the cause of the prime minister, so that he was reduced to extremities. To add to his miseries, a severe famine desolated the country and created such a scarcity of provisions and fodder that thousands began to die of starvation. Under such circumstances he was unable to oppose the Moguls. He petitioned Shah Jahan to extend his protection to him. It was promised to him only when he

---

1. Sh. Ch. Pr. P. 54.   2. Sh. Ch. Pr. P. 54.

3. 'The whole of the nobility attached to the unfortunate prince, were put to death by the ruffian. Grant Duff (P. 47) gives the name of Takurrib Khan who disgusted by the change, and dreading the consequences to himself, went over to the Moguls and got the rank of 6,000 horse.

delivered the jewels, elephants, etc. belonging to the King. Then the Emperor restored his jagir which had been before confiscated from him and conferred upon Shahji.

22. Shahji's monarchy

The latter deserted the Moguls, repaired and strengthened the old fort of Payamgad (Pemgiri), named it Shahgad and laid the foundation of an independent monarchy. Thereafter he raised an army and began to lay waste the adjacent country. Within a short period he was able to conquer a large territory. So that his new acquisition extended from Poona–Chakan to the Konkan on one side and from Junner and Sangamner[1] to the precincts of Ahmadnagar and Daulatabad. His rule extended over Nasik and Trimbak. There is Shahji Raje's grant of 31st December 1629 to the officer of Pandiapedgaon (P. S. S. No. 302). There are other grants of July 1631 (P. S. S. Nos. 333-4) for the same town. Then two grants relate to the continuance of the donation to a mosque at Nasik in 1632 and 1634(Nos. 349, 375). Thus during 1632-36 he had seized Nasik and Trimbak. It is evident that a large part of the Nizam Shahi Kingdom was in the hands of Shahji even up to the loss of Daulatabad.

He also succeeded in persuading the commandant of Jalna to cede the fort to him, but the Moguls outbid him, and hence it was delivered to them on 7th October 1632, so that Shahji's troops had to retreat in disappointment.[2] He appealed to the generosity of Muhammad Adil Shah. It was impossible for the King to send any assistance as he had entered into alliance with Shah Jahan through his ambassador Shekh Muayyan-ud-din.[3] The aim of the mission was to separate Bijapur from an alliance with the Lodi. No sooner was the object fulfilled by the rout and death of the Lodi than Shah Jahan changed his policy. He.

1. P. S. S. No. 376–Shahji's grant of 1634. Orme Mss. Vol. 331.
2. Crme Mss. Vol. 331.
3. Muhammad Namah gives Shekh Mughanniya as his name.

treacherously hurled his force into the Bijapur territory. As soon as the ambassador left the precincts of Bijapur, news was brought of the Mogul raids on Dharur which had been before captured by Bijapur from the Nizam Shahi State. A detatchment was despatched under Malik Amber Jan of Bidar after the Mogul ambassador who was arrested and brought back to Bijapur. Shahji who had been pushed aside since his assistance was no longer necessary to the imperial arms, set up a new Hindu monarchy. He now joined Adil Shah and thus saved the Deccan monarchies from being swallowed up by the Mogul Emperor.

23. Shah Jahan's war with Bijapur

Though Shah Jahan took Fatch Khan under his wing, he did not slacken his efforts of conquering the Nizam Shahi Kingdom from the nobles who had rebelled against Fateh Khan. Several armies were despatched one after another to desolate the country and capture strong forts. For instance Nasrat Khan was sent against Qandhar which was soon delivered up to him. Iradat Khan laid siege to the impregnable fort of Parenda, but being foiled in his attempt, he proceeded to the fort of Dharur on the Krishna to capture it for the Moguls, because it formely belonged to the Nisam Shahi Kingdom. Bijapur was not ready for this treacherous attack, hence the fort capitulated to the Mogul commander without any serious fight. It has been seen that this attack on the Bijapur territory was rightly looked upon as a violation of the treaty. Therefore an alliance was concluded by Muhammad Adil Shah with Qutub Shah and the Nizam Shahi barons who were against Fateh Khan. Even the Portuguese secretly assisted Bijapur with ammunition.[1]

24. The Mogul retreat from Bijapur and Parenda

The news of the arrest of his ambassador by the Sultan of Bijapur led the Emperor to appoint his father-in-law Asaf

1. E, F. 1630—36, Pp. 59—60. 10 June 1631; P, S. S. Nos. 343, 345.

Jah as commander-in-chief of the war against the two monarchies. The latter raided the country up to Gulbarga with the troops of the principal nobles of the Empire and then proceeded to lay siege to the Bijapur city itself. [1] Many skirmishes took place on a small scale every day, but at last on 13th February 1632 a bloody battle took place wherein the Moguls were defeated, and five generals of theirs were killed. On the other hand, the Bijapur army lost one general Sikandar Ali Khan. Yet the siege continued. The Mogul army wantonly destroyed every thing in the environs of the metropolis. These oppressions set the Bijapuri nobles' blood boiling. On the 20th of February they made a furious charge and fought with the courage of despair, so that they inflicted a serious defeat on the besiegers. The negotiations between the two parties broke down, and hence the Moguls began to retire from the field. The retreating army was pursued by 15,000 soldiers under Murari Pandit till it was out of the borders of the Kingdom. He then marched to the relief of Parenda in the Nizam Shahi Kingdom. The troops engaged in its siege had already beaten a hasty retreat, so that the Pandit stationed himself near the fort. He was fortunate to soon get its possession from the commandant Aga Ruzwan or Haibat Khan on 18th July 1632 by giving 10,000 huns as a reward. The chief cause of the Mogul failure was the dearth of water, fodder and provisions due to a terrible famine prevailing throughout the Deccan in 1631 and 1632. [2]

25. The end of the Nizam Shahi Kingdom

The crest-fallen Asaf Jah was replaced by Mahabat Khan, the Governor of Lahor, as the Viceroy of the Deccan. Circumstances in the south augured success in the campaigns. Knowing that Fateh Khan had niether men nor provisions to defend his capital, Shahji persuaded the Bijapur Government

1. G. Duff (P. 47) gives a different version.
2. Elliot. VII. 243 28-31. Urdu Basatin-i-Salatin. 235-6; Sh. Bh. VII. 53-57.

for entering into alliance with him for despatching an army under Randulla Khan and himself for capturing Daulatabad and thus keeping the Moguls at arms length.   On hearing of the march of this army, Fateh Khan lost heart and proposed to give up the fort to the Moguls, provided he could save the rest of the Nizam Shahi monarchy with their help.   Thereupon a Mogul army marched under Khan Zaman towards Daulatabad, but it found the fort already invested by the Adil Shahis.   The two armies began to fight against each other, and each bombarded the castle to get its possession first.

In the meantime, the Bijapuris opened negotiations with Fateh Khan for not delivering the fort to the Moguls and for accepting their support.   On this condition Fateh Khan readily accepted the offer, and without any declaration of war suddenly opened fire on the Mogul army from the heights of the fortress, while the Bijapur artillery also began to work havoc in the Mogul lines.   Mahabat Khan was naturally enraged on this breach of faith on the part of the Abyssinian premier.   However, he bravely extricated himself from this difficulty situation.

Money and provisions were first successfully given to Fateh Khan by the Bijapurians after the negotiations. A bloody war continued for months under the hill-fortress of Daulatabad and in its environs.   Shahji distinguished himself by his valour on many occasions, but at last he was driven away from Nizampur by Khan Zaman, the son of Mahabat Khan.[1] The Mogul army then occupied the town of Daulatabad. In the meantime Murari Pandit was sent with large quantities of provisions and ammunition for the use of the besieged.   But his haughty and rash temper had alienated the Bijapuri nobles who refused to fight with or

---

1, It is said in Orme Mss. Vol. 131 that during this siege, the wife and daughter of Shahji, with part of his treasure, were by the treachery of Mukuludar Khan, betrayed into the hands of Khan Khanan. They were however sent back through the intervention of the brothers of Jjiabai.

under him. Mutual discord obliged them to retire to a distance of some sixteen miles and leave the field open for the Mogul armies to capture the fortress. In spite of the repeated requests of Fateh Khan, the Pandit refused to send relief to the besieged, unless the fort was first delivered to him. Fateh Khan, being disappointed of assistance from the Adil Shahis, made up his mind to surrender the capital to the Moguls and once more opened negotiations with Mahabat Khan. The latter promptly sent large quantities of gold and provisions with a message to Fateh Khan that on the delivery of the fort, royal favours would be showered on him, and he and his sovereign would be restored to their previous positions. Fatch Khan delivered the fort in June 1633. But the treaty was soon violated by the Viceroy, because the last King Hussain Nizam Shah was sent as a prisoner to Gwalior, and Fateh Khan too ended his life in a prison under the effects of insanity.[1]

The remnants of the territory of the Ahmadnagar State were annexed to the Mogul Empire and thus the Nizam Shahi dynasty came to an end. The most cherished ambition of Shah Jahan was fulfilled, but little did the exultant Emperor think that this extinct dynasty would sphinx-like once more rise from its very ashes through the efforts of Shahji.[2]

26. Shahji, the king-maker

After the conquest of Daulatabad, Mahabat Khan appointed Khan Duran Nasir Khan as the Governor of the uew province and himself went over to Burhanpur. But there were still several Nizam Shahi barons in possession of small territories. Each one became independent for the time being, on account of the disappearance of the Nizam Shahi Government.[3] Siddi Raihan of Sholapur, Siddi Amber of Danda Rajpuri, Siddi Saba Saifkhan of Kalyan,

---

1. G. Duff. P. 49. Pad. N. I, 531.   2. Sh. Bh. VIII. 34-73.
3. Urdu Basatin-i-Salatin. P. 245.

Shrinivasrao of Junner and Shahji of Shahgad began to rule over the territories like independent chiefs. The first three barons thought it safe to acknowledge the supremacy of Muhammad Adil Shah and be confirmed in their jagirs by him. Shrinivasrao remained in suspense, while Shahji chalked out the plan of reviving the Ahmadnagar monarchy by his genius and heroism. He first set up a puppet-king by the name of Murtiza Nizam Shah in the hill fort of Shahgad or Payamgad (Pemgiri) in September[1] 1632. Secondly, this new capital of the Nizam Shahi government was consequently made the centre of rallying all the ancient and loyal soldiers, Sardars and subjects of that monarchy. Thirdly, he was successful in winning over the Bijapur Government for assisting him in this work of resuscitating the dead carcass of the Nizam Shahi Kingdom. Muhammad Adil Shah and his nobles were conscious of the dangers of the Mogul advance. They realized that their own safety lay in creating a buffer state to bear the brunt of the direct aggressions of Mogul imperialism. Shahji rightly wrote to the Bijapur Durbar that out of 84 forts, one fort alone had been possessed by the Moguls, and therefore the Nizam Shahi Kingdom could easily be revived by bringing together the dismembered parts. Murari Pandit who through his conceit and folly had extinguished the Nizam Shahi State and lost Daulatabad, was now sent by the premier Khavas Khan to back up Shahji in this enterprise. The latter, depending upon his own resources alone, had already raised seven or eight thousand horse. Now he obtained the help of Bijapur in the form of 5 to 6 thousand horse under Captain Umbar Khan who was placed by Murari Pandit under the orders of Shahji. The Muslem Sardars of the Nizam Shahi State were not willing to submit to the King-maker, even though Murari Pandit, the reprensentative of Adil Shah, persuaded some of them to show their allegiance to the new sovereign.

1. J. Shak. and Padshahnamah confirm this date, but Muhammad Namah places the event of coronation at Junner.

S. 12.

For instance, Siddi Saba Saif Khan of Kalyan ceded all
the country except the forts to Shahji and proceeded with two
thousand horse to Bijapur for service.   The latter, though
master of the Konkan now, still wanted to punish Saif Khan
for his insurgence, in order that the other Sardars might
learn a lesson from his fate.   Murari Pandit, on his way to the
capital, encamped at Pabal, situated on the confluence of the
Bhima and Indrayani.   Here he made very generous donations
of land and precious articles to the Brahmins in the
performance of the various rites on the day of the solar eclipse.[1]
He performed his weighing ceremony by being balanced against
seven metals, as if he were a king.   During his stay here
the news was brought to him of the surprise and defeat of Saif
Khan's detatchment·by Shahji's troops at Kher, the capture
of Siddi Amber Atash Khan, the commander of Saif Khan's
army, and of the siege of the village wherein the Khan had
taken up his temporary residence.   Murari Pandit promptly
despatched a force to the assistance of the Khan. Thereupon
the Maratha troops retired and the Khan being relieved
from the danger, proceeded to the bank of the Bhima and
then to Bijapur. It is really strange that neither Murari Pandit
nor the Bijapur Government protested against Shahji's
aggression on a nobleman who had sought their refuge.
Thay did not probably desire to break off their friendly
relations with him at that juncture.[2]

It is related in the Basatin-i-Salatin[3] that Saif Khan
on being presented to the King, was given two lakhs of
pagodas and employed in putting down the rebellion of the
Naik of Harpan Halli. The latter was killed by a shot in the
battle, and thus the Khan was crowned with victory.

The most important means to put an end to the existence
of the new state was to remove Shahji from the scenes
of his activities.   Hence the first attempt of the Moguls

---

1. P. S- S. Nos. 363, 372. The Bakhars are wrong in several details of
the part played by Murari Pandit in aiding Shahji.

2, & 3. Urdu Basatin-i-Salatin. P. 247.

was to win him over to their side by friendly means. It is said that Iradat Khan, the new Commander of Daulatabad, tried his best to conciliate Shahji to the Moguls through his cousin Maloji Bhosle. He was promised very high dignities for himself and his relations, because the commandant knew that he would highly improve his own prospects, if he could succeed in extinguishing the Nizam Shahi Kingdom without a war. But Shahji, being the most ambitious, far-sighted and clever man, did not fall into his trap.[1]

Siddi Raihan of Sholapur distinguished himself for his rare determination and bravery by so successfully resisting the siege-operations conducted by the Mogul General Mahabat Khan that the latter was obliged to beat a retreat from Sholapur. Khawas Khan, the prime minister of Bijapur, made a successful attempt to win over the Siddi to the service of Bijapur. Raihan gave up the formidable fort of Sholapur to Adil Shah and in return accepted the jagir of Kolhapur, Khanapur, etc., yielding a revenue of a lakh of pagodas. He was entrusted with the defence of the south-west frontier of the kingdom.[2]

Shahji could not prevent the loss of Sholapur, but he captured all the territory in the Konkan and Talkonkan, as well as some districts in Khandesh. Similarly, the rebellious barons were brought into submission, and the Hindu nobles, actuated by patriotic and religious motives, joined hands with him. For these reasons, the Mogul hostility to him grew to be fierce and malignant.

27. The capture of Junner by Shahji

The new Pemgiri or Shahgad fort was not so strong and impregnable as that of Shivneri, the ancient Nizam Shahi capital. No traditional love and sentiment were aroused by the upstart capital begun by Shahji and named after himself.

1. Some chronicles state that he was offered the rank of 22,000 horse.
2. Urdu Basatin-i-Salatin. P. 245.

Even Shrinivas Rao, the chief of Junner–Shivneri, showed slackness in supporting the cause of the new Sultan and would not consent to hand over the fort to him.   Shahji could not naturally brook recalcitrance among the nobles and on the failure of his conciliatory methods, he was compelled to have resort to a stratagem to oust the chief.   He was successful by some Machiavellian method in capturing the fort.   The fall of this invincible place, was followed by the acquisition of Jivadhan, Sunda, Bhorgad, Parasgad, Harshgad, Mahuli, Khoj and other forts. Murtaza Nizam Shah, the eleven years old king, was brought to Shivneri, and this strong castle subsequently served as a centre for further acquisitions.   Shahji secured a large booty in these conquests and thereby he was able to re-employ twelve thousand cavaliers who had been discharged after the capture of Daulatabad.[1]   He made bold to plunder the environs of even Ahmadnagar, Daulatabad and Bidar.   In 1633 one Khawas Khan was detatched with 3,000 horse towards Ahmadnagar to drive him away.   The Moguls also retaliated by ravaging Chamargunda,[2] the home of the Bhosles, but for some time they could not put any effective check to Shahji's raids.   These grew even worse after the death of Mahabat Khan, the Viceroy of the Deccan, in October 1634. However, the new governor, Khan Dauran, chased Shahji's troops from Daulatabad,[3] Revdanda, Shivgaon, Amarpur, and the pass of Muhri.   On the way to Junner a very large part of the baggage, provisons, arms, ammunition and cattle were captured and some 3,000 men fell prisoners into the hands of the victorious Moguls.   Khan Dauran, having inflicted heavy losses on Shahji, returned to Ahmadnagar in February 1635.

1. Urdu Basatin-i-Salatin. Pp. 247–48.
2. It was situated near the frontier of Mogul Ahmadnagar.
3. Orme Mss. Vol. 331,

28. Siege of Parenda by the Moguls

These victories proved .to be pin-pricks to Shahji,
hence his destruction was considered to be a difficult task.
Mahabat Khan first planned to punish his allies for
recognizing the new monarchy and for inflicting serious
losses during the last Mogul retreat from Daulatabad. He
thought of winning over the Sultan of Bijapur to his side
through the fear of war. For instance, he sent Prince Shuja[1]
to lay siege to the strong castle of Parenda in February 1634.
Shahji, Randulla Khan, Farhad Khan, Ankush Khan, Murari
Pandit and other war-lords had come over there to face the
Moguls. The Adil Shahi armies bravely defended the place
and counteracted all the plans of the Moguls. Murari
Pandit gave an effective relief to the fort. After four months
of an unsuccessful siege, the Mogul armies were withdrawn.
The Bijapuries under Randulla Khan pursued the Moguls up
to Burhanpur and killed many of their soldiers.[2] This
proved the strength of Bijapur and showed that as long as
its nobles were united at heart in its defence and service,
there would be little danger of its dissolution.

29. Internal discord at Bijapur

But the internal concord and mutual good will at
Bijapur soon gave way to discord and distrust. Nawab
Khan Baba Mustafa Khan was arrested with several friends
and relatives by order of Khawas Khan, and confined in
the fort of Belgaum. The new prime minister with unchecked
authority began to oppress the subjects. The King finally
made a plan to throw off his intolerable yoke. Khawas
Khan, on getting scent of the royal disaffection sought for
help from Shah Jahan. The discovery of this conspiracy
still further enraged the king against him.

1. Muhammad Namah has Dara Shikoh. G. Duff (49) and Pad, N. (536)
have Shah Shuja.
2. Muhammad Namah and Basatin–i–Salatin.

Taking advantage of his growing unpopularity, he got his minister murdered by Siddi Raihan in 1635.[1] The murderer was publickly honoured by the titles of Ikhlas Khan and Khan [2] Muhammad Muhammad Shahi, and with the post of a minister. Then Mustafa Khan was released from his confinement and restored to his former dignities and premiership.[3] He enjoyed an annual income of ten million pagodas, ordinarily employed a thousand domestics in his mansion, had three thousand horse at his own charge, and besides kept a large number of soldiers to guard his palace. [4]

The contemporary evidence of Mandelslo on the administration of Khawas Khan is against his condemnatiou by the author of the Muhammad Namah. Being the protege of Mustafa Khan, he is expected to denounce Khawas Khan. But Mandelslo who visited the city only three years after the murder of the premier, has praised his government. His regency had the approbation of the people. Being over-confident of the affection of his people "which he had made it his main business to acquire by a liberality truly royal" and "imagining that the people had so great an affection for him as to proclaim him King, in case there were no other, he resolved to make away with the Prince." Mandelslo first describes his attempt to kill the King, and then states that on his failure he was in return ordered by :the Prince to be murdered.[5]

30. The brutal murder of Murari Pandit

The Pandit was a very great friend and favourite of Khawas Khan. He heard the news of his patron's death

1. In the Muhammad Namah the year of this murder is wrongly given as 1629. Basatin–i–Salatin gives a chronogram of the death and it confirms the year 1635-6. The same year is given in the Haft Kursi. We are informed in the B. S. (252) that Khawas Khan was minister for eight years. Hence it means that his murder took place early in 1636.
2. He was also known as Muzaffar–ud–din Khan Muhammad.
3. Urdu Basatin–i–Salatin. Pp. 250-1.
4. Mandelslo's Travels into the East Indies, p. 77.
5. Mandelslo's Travels into the East Indies. Pp. 75-76.

at Dharwar, and realized that he was unsafe in the service of
Bijapur. On that very night he made for the fort of Halemal
(or Halihal ?), but he was arrested by the local officer and
sent to the capital in chains. On being ill-treated, he used
abusive language against the King. Thereupon untold
barbarities were practised upon that Brahman lord. His
tongue was drawn out; he was dragged through the town,
and his body was hacked into pieces. Such was the pitiful
end of one of the greatest nobles of the land for his life-long
and faithful service under an irresponsible autocrat.
However, these murders did put an end to the civil war
for a time and the confusion and disturbances resulting from
the same.[1]

Mandelslo's account of the murder of Murari differs from
the preceding one.

" One of Chauas-chans Creatures, whose name was
Morary, was advanc'd with ten thousand horse, within five
Leagues of the City of Visiapour; in so much that the
King fearing that General might assemble all the Friends
of the deceased, caused him to be proclaim'd a Traitor against
his Prince, and set his head at a certain price. His own
Army siez'd his person, and recieving intelligence, that
another Lord, named Rundelo, was coming up to the relief
of Chauas-chan, and intended to joyn with Morary, they
sent him by a by-way to the City, whither he came about
eight at night. He sent a Message to the King, proposing,
that if his Majesty would pardon him, and bestow on him
the Government of the Brammenes, he would pay him yearly
twenty thousand Pagodas; but those Propositions were
rejected, and the King ordered him to have his hands cut
off, and his tounge cut out, and that in that posture he
should be led all about the City; but he died by the way."[2]

31. Shah Jahan against Bijapur

The defeat of the two premier nobles of the Empire,
Asaf Jah and Mahabat Khan, opened the eyes of the

1. Urdu Basatin-i-Salatin P. 252.
2. Mandelslo's Travels into the East Indies. Pp. 76-77.

Emperor to the gravity of the situation in the Deccan. Moveover, Shahji's power was fast growing to the detriment of the Empire. The shattered Nizam Shahi State was now so re-organized by the Bhosle statesman as to present a solid front. For the security of the Imperial prestige, it was extremely necessary to put an end to the rising Hindu power.

Having been encouraged by the late internal discords prevailing at Bijapur and being invited by its premier, the Emperor marched to the south with an army of 50,000 men, and himself opened a vigorous campaign against Nizam Shah and Adil Shah in February 1636.

Three Mogul armies proceeded against the Bijapur Kingdom from three directions. One was sent under Sayad Khan Jahan against Parenda which was defended by Randulla Khan. The second marched under Khan Dauran against Bahlol Khan at Bidar in the north-east, and a third advanced under Khan Zaman against Bijapur itself. He entered into the Adil Shahi territory, desolated the country with fire and sword, captured Kolhapur, plundered Miraj and Raibag, and then for sometime encamped on the bank of the Krishna. The Sultan employed the most effective method to baffle his barbarous [1] foe who was working havoc in the country in a remorseless manner. He ordered the whole country round Bijapur up to the distance of twenty miles to be desolated to such an extent that not a blade of grass or a drop of water could be obtained by the enemy. The Mogul army died by thousands for want of provisions and its General jumped at the opportunity of entering into a treaty with the Sultan.

32. Treaty between Shah Jahan and Adil Shah

According to it, Adil Shah was to pay an annual tribute of twenty lakhs of rupees, and to acknowledge the suzerainty

---

1. Sarkar's Aurangzeb Vol. I, Pp. 37-38. We are told that Khan Zaman sold 2,000 prisoners into slavery in the Kolhapur district alone.

of the Emperor. The Nizam Shahi Kingdom was to be put an end to, and its territory was to be divided between the Emperor and the Bijapur King. The latter was given the part comprising the Sholapur and Wangi[1] Mahals, the parganas of Bhalki and Chitagopa, and the Konkan including the Poona and Chakan districts. Shahji Bhosle was not to be taken up in the Bijapur service or even allowed to enter its territory, unless he ceded the country in his possession. This important treaty was ratified by the Emperor on 6th May[2] 1636. It marks the beginning of the end of the Adil Shahi Kingdom, but augurs the fast-approaching extinction of the Nizam Shahi State. The power of Shahji can be judged from the three articles which were included in the treaty itself :—

(1) "The pretence of a Nizam Shahi Kingdom should be ended and all its territories be divided between the Emperor and the Bijapur king. Adil Shah should not violate the new Imperial frontier, nor let his servants hinder the Mogul officers in occupying and settling the newly annexed districts.

(2) "Each side undertook not to seduce the officers of the other from their master's service, nor to entertain deserters, and Shah Jahan promised for himself and his sons that the Bijapur King would never be called upon to transfer any of his officers to the Imperial service."[3]

(3) "Shahji Bhonsla, who had set up a princeling of the house of Nizam Shah, should not be admitted to office under Bijapur, unless he ceded Junner, Trimbak, and some other forts still in his hands to Shah Jahan. If he declined,

1. Wangi, 1 mile East of Bhima and 21 miles S. W. of Parenda; Bhalki, 19 miles N. E. of Kaliani; Chitagopa, 21 miles S. E. Kaliani.

2. Sarkar, Aurangzeb I, pp. 38–40. Basatin-i-Salatin 253. The signing of the treaty was done in May 1636 according to the Basatin-i-Salatin, but the Muhammad Namah places it in May 1635. However, Jedhe Shakavali gives Shak 1557 or 1635–6 and Haft Kursi has 1046 A. H. or 1636 A. D. Cf. E. F. 1630–36. Pp. 216–17; 260.

3. Sarkar, Aurangzeb Vol. I, pp. 38–39.

S. 13.

he was not to be harboured in Bijapur territory or even allowed to enter it." [1]

33. Capture of Udgir and Ausa

There was an article in the treaty for the cession of the forts of Ausa and Udgir. If their commanders were not willing to surrender the same to the Emperor, though they were given the concession of removing their families and private property to wherever they liked, the imperial army was to forcibly capture the forts from them.

It appears that the Nizam Shahi officers did not give up the forts, and hence Khan Dauran was sent to capture *Udgir* [2] which was defended by one Siddi Miftah. After a continuous siege of three months the fort captitulated on 28th September 1636. The Habshi commandant was taken into the imperial service under the title of Habsh Khan.

Another army was despatched under Rashid Khan to lay siege to *Ausa*, but it was long defended by the heroic commander Bhojpal. The victorious army set free from Udgir arrived to strengthen the besiegers. Soon after, on 19th October 1636 the fort capitulated, and its commander also was taken into the imperial service. [3]

34. The submission of Shahji

The treaty with Muhammad Adil Shah not only released the Mogul forces, but brought the help of the Bijapur armies also in the task of crushing the new monarchy set up by the king—maker Shahji. Even before the treaty, he was dislodged from Pedgaon, Chambhargunda, and Lohgaon [4] on the Indrayani river, and forced to take shelter in the hill forts of Kondana and

1, Sarkar, Aurangzeb Vol. I. P. 40.

2. *Udgir*, 35 miles south of Qandhar; *Ausa*, five miles south of the Towraj river which flows into the Manjira.

3, Sarkar, Aurangzeb Vol. I. Pp 44-46.

4. Lohgaon, 10 miles North East of Poona and 3 miles south of the Indrayani

Torna. Shahji's forces evacuated Sangamner, Nasik, Trimbak. and several other hill-castles, when they were hard pressed by Shaista Khan. Junner was for several months the seat of a bloody warfare. The Marathas cut off the supplies of the enemy by their guerilla tacticts. The Mogul army was then recalled from that quarter to give assistance to the main army fighting against Bijapur. The various divisions of the Imperial army had not done much against the powerful Maratha lord whom the late treaty did not unnerve, but instead enthused him to stake his all on the fortunes of war. After the treaty Randulla Khan, Malik Rehan, and Siddi Marjan were despatched by Adil Shah against him. Kanhoji Jedhe, Pratapsinha and his son Baji Ghorpade were serving under Randulla Khan. Shivneri was invested by one division, and the rest of the army was employed in hunting out the King-maker.

Shahji retired to Danda Rajpuri for some time and then he came down to Muranjana. Here he suffered a defeat from Khan Zaman, and leaving behind all his heavy baggage, he proceeded to Mahuli where he made the plan to resist the Moguls for a long time.

According to the Shiva Bharata (IX. 13-19), Shahji saw God Shankar in his dream who told him that Shah Jahan was invincible and therefore he should give up his fight against him, but he should not be disappointed, because his son Shiva who was the incarnation of Krishna, would surely destroy the Mlechhas. According to the Jedhe Chronology, Shahji went to Mahuli on 26th March 1636, but it is wrong, because the treaty was concluded in May. Shahji could not have been pursued before the treaty. The Basatin-i-Salatin expressly states that Shahji was pursued during the rainy season and that Mahuli too was besieged by the allied armies during the heavy rains. While on the one side, Khan Zaman and Randulla Khan vigorously pressed the siege, on the other, the Sultan and his mother were against Shahji's policy of continuing the war and were for surrendering themselves to the Moguls. Finding that under those circumstances opposition was fruitless, he consented in December 1636 to give up the shadowy Sultan to the Moguls, ceded to them Junner and seven other forts still held by him, and was himself permitted to enter the service of Bijapur.

Muhammad Adil Shah confirmed the grant of the ancient jagirs of Chambhargunda, Supa and Poona on Shahji, so that he was to bear the brunt of future Mogul invasions on the Bijapur territory. The Shiva Bharata(IX. 20-31)states that Shahji was allowed to keep his jagir according to the terms of the treaty, and was after some time invited by Muhammad Shah to join his service, so that he might have such a brave, resourceful, and redoubtable general to fight against the Moguls. He was appointed to a very high office[1] in the Bijapuri army. Thus the extinction of the Nizam Shahi State apparently strengthened the Bijapur kingdom by the addition of territory and the transfer of the services of the soldiers and officers of the extinct State.[2]

35. Shahji's work

The causes of Shahji's failure are not difficult to divine:—

(1)   When the powerful kingdom of Golconda agreed to pay a tribute and acknowledge the Mogul sovereignty without a show of a fight, when a long and barbarous war forced Bijapur to come to terms with the Mogul, Shahji alone could not be expected to fight the allied armies of Bijapur and Delhi. Yet the threat of an allied invasion did not intimidate him as it did the Golkonda ruler. Shahji bade defiance to the Emperor and did not submit without a long war.

(2)   The Muslim lords of the old Nizam Shahi State had renounced their allegiance to the new monarchy. The Hindu Sardars like the Ghatges, Thomares, Kharates, Pandhares, Ghorpades, Mohites, Mahadiks, Waghs, Kanks, Chavhans, etc. had rallied round his banner. Shahji's effort to re-establish

1—2   Urdu Basatin-i-Salatin, P. 254; Orme Mss. Vol. 331.

the Nizam Shahi Kingdom appeared to be an attempt of establishing Hindu swaraj. Hence the alliance of Shah Jahan and Adil Shah can be said to be for the purpose of rooting out the budding Hindu monarchy. This incomplete and insuperable task of creating a Hindu State was afterwards taken up by his son Shivaji who succeeded in carving out a new kingdom comprising portions which were wrested from the Mogul, Adil Shahi and Vijayanagar Empires.

36. Chronology

1607	Amber captured Junner and made it the capital.
1610	Khirki was founded. Khan Jahan Lodi was sent to the Deccan.
1612	Khan Khanan was given command of the Deccan.
1617	Treaty between Malik Amber and Shah Jahan.
1619-20 ?	Shahji married.
1920	War with the Moguls begun.
1621	Khirki demolished. Prince Khusrau murdered by order of Shah Jahan. Desertion of Jadhavrao. Capture of Poona by Shahji from Rayrao Adil Shahi. Shahji's uncle Vithoji died.
1624	Battle of Bhatvadi.
1625	Desertion of Shahji to Adil Shah.
1626	Malik Amber died.
1626-27	Sarlashkar Shahji engaged in conquering the Karnatic.
1627	(Sept.) Ibrahim Adil Shah died.
1627	(Oct.) Death of Jahangir.
1628	Shahji returned to the Nizam Shahi State.
1628	Poona re-granted to Shahji by Nizam Shah. Shahji raids Khandesh.
1629	Khan Jahan Lodi's revolt.
1630	Shah Jahan marched to the Deccan.
1630	Jadhavrao's murder. Shahji rebels and accepts service under the Moguls. Poona burnt by Murari.

1630   Shivaji born at Shivneri. A terrible famine raged in the Deccan.

1631   Fateh Khan was released and re-appointed prime minister.

1632   Murtiza Nizam Shah murdered by order of Fateh Khan. Shahji's jagirs restored to Fateh Khan. Hence Shahji revolts against the Moguls, sets up a new monarchy and makes alliance with the Bijapur Sultan.

1632   Jalna secured by the Moguls.
Daulatabad captured by the Moguls.
Shahji sets up Murtiza as king of the Nizam Shahi State. This succession is recognized by Adil Shah and Shahji is assisted by Murari.

1633   Weighing ceremony of Murari Maharaj.
Shahji defeats Saif Khan's forces at Kher.
Shahji captures Junner and makes it his capital, ravages the Mogul country up to Ahmadnagar, Daulatabad and Bidar.

1634   Shahji sustains several defeats from Khan Dauran Parenda invested by the Moguls, but they receive a disgraceful repulse.

1635   Prime Minister Khawas Khan was murdered at Bijapur, and so was Murari Pandit done to death by order of Adil Shah.

1636   Shah Jahan opened a campaign against Adil Shah and Shahji. Udgir, Ausa, Bidar and many other places captured by the Moguls. Bijapur besieged. Treaty concluded between Adil Shah and Shah Jahan. Shahji was besieged in Mahuli. He delivers Murtiza Nizam Shah to the Moguls, while he himself accepts service under Adil Shah.

CHAPTER IV

SHAHJI IN THE KARNATIC

1. A review of Shahji's position

At the end of the war, Shahji with all his family, followers and wealth was taken to Bijapur by Randulla Khan and presented to the Sultan. The latter conferred upon the Raja his jagir of Poona and Supa, and within a short time deputed him for the conquest of the Karnatic as second-in-command to Randulla Khan. Shahji had been a virtual king of a part of the Nizam Shahi State for six years. During this period he had assisted Bijapur in the reduction of the fortresses of Daulatabad and Parenda, and was in turn aided with men and money by the Bijapur government against the Moguls.

The Raja staked his all for maintaining his position against the greatest Muslim Empire of the world. The murders of Khawas Khan and Murari Pandit in Bijapur had removed the stalwart champions of maintaining the Nizam Shahi Kingdom as a buffer state. The new premier Mustafa Khan was for alliance with the Moguls. Hence the bait of receiving a part of the Nizam Shahi territory was made a sufficient excuse for not only renouncing the cause of Shahji, but for openly allying with the Moguls for the destruction of their former ally. This volte face brought about the ruin of the Nizam Shahi State as well as of its heroic defender. Shahji was naturally exasperated at the treacherous defection of Bijapur in his hour of trial and hence he did not wish to serve under it. The Sultan of Bijapur had, however, made it a specific term of the treaty that Shahji could not be taken up in the Mogul service. So that even against his will he had to accept service in the Bijapur Government. The latter was also rightly apprehensive of the danger of allowing such a daring and experienced statesman to remain in Poona. He had made himself very popular by ruling the whole country from Poona to Nasik. His presence in these parts which were recently brought under the jurisdiction of Bijapur, might have led to a revolt. So the Raja was ostensibly sent for the conquest of the Karnatic, but in a way it was an exile to him. One can easily imagine the attitude of Shahji to the government of Bijapur. He could never be reconciled to his new position of gilded slavery. He was still in the prime of youth, and hence his righteous indignation and passion for revenge might have taken a subtle and subterranean turn in making his son Shivaji an instrument for the re-conquest of the parts which were under him as a virtual ruler of the Nizam Shahi State.

2. Acquisition of new jagirs

But before starting for the Karnatic, Shahji took a subtle step of reducing the power of the Ghorpades and of enlarging his own possessions. There is a firman of 1637 A. D. referring to a partition deed. Shahji and Maloji who was the grandson of Vallabhsing, complained to the Sultan of Bijapur against Raja Pratapsinha of Mudhol for having withheld their share from the family estates which then consisted of Mudhol with 84 villages, the Parganas of Torgal and Wai, and many villages in Karad and the Karnatic. Shahji was granted the rank and command of 5, 000 horse, 26 villages in Karad, half the Pargana of Wai and half of the family possessions in the Karnatic. Similarly, Maloji got a command of 2, 000 horse and 30 villages in the neighbourhood of Vijayanagar for the maintenance of his rank. Thus Shahji was able to revenge himself on the Ghorpades who had helped Randulla Khan in reducing the fort of Mahuli. To his original estate of Poona and Supa the new jagirs in the Wai and Karad Parganas were[1] added. The adjacent jagirs of the Ghorpades and Bhosles became a source of frequent disputes between

1. See Persian Grant and its translation No. 1.

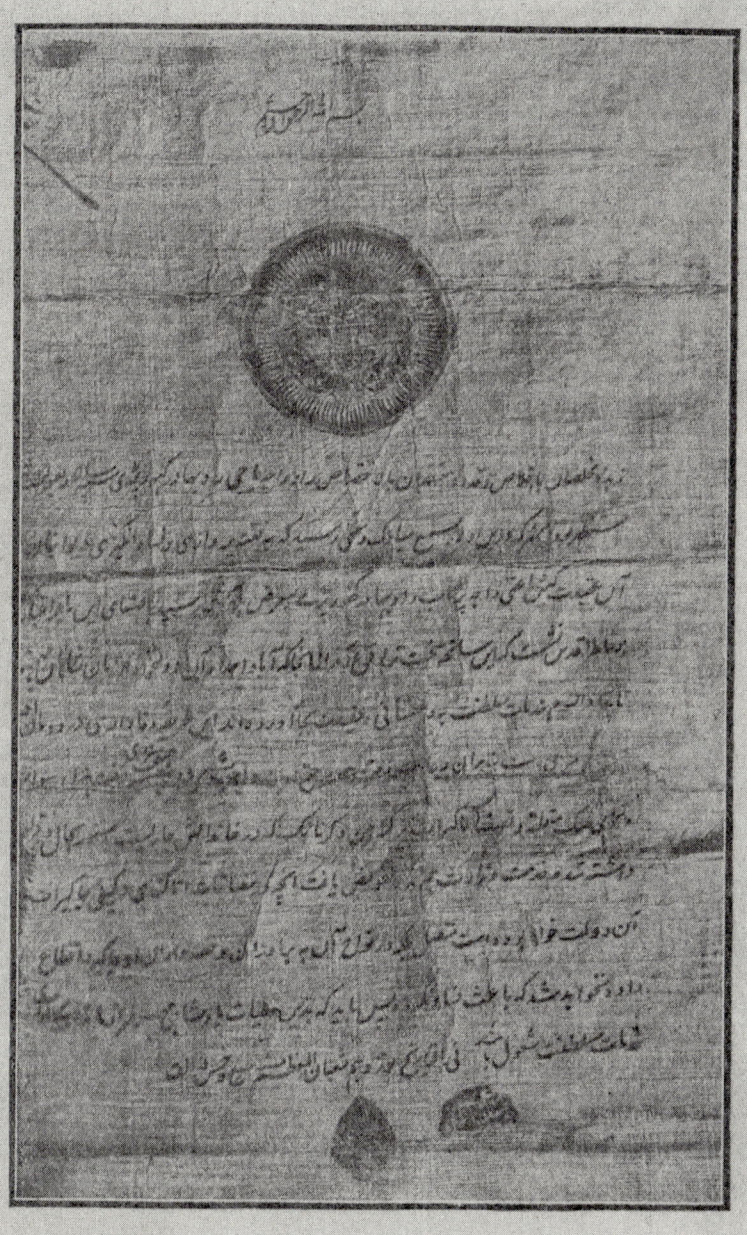

(2) Baji Ghorpade made Vazir and
Commander of 7000. No more Partition.

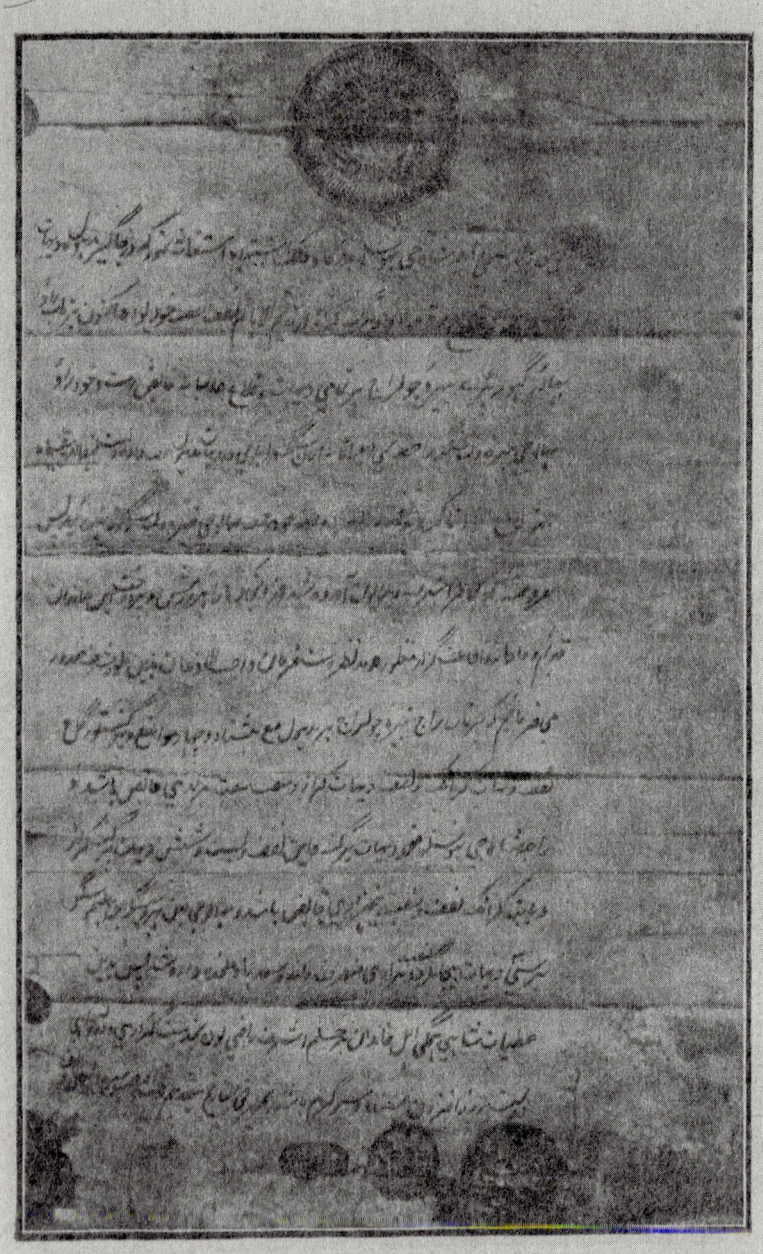

(1) The Deed of Partition.

the two branches. It appears that Raja Pratapsinha, while he was living in his jagir of Wai, was shot dead by some secret junta in 1646. His ashes were interned at Shilewadi. This tragic death has been mentioned in another Firman which was issued in 1647 to give assurance to his son Baji Ghorpade that in future no jagirs would be conferred upon his kinsmen in the neighbourhood of Anagundi and Kampli. Baji was made a minister, and command of 7, 000 horse was confirmed upon him.[1] The rest of Shahji's life is spent in the Karnatic. The Bakhars have recorded almost nothing about it, but the Shivabharat, Radha Madhav Vilas Champu and the Tanjore Inscription usefully supplement the data obtained from the Persian, English, Dutch and Portuguese sources. The part played by Shahji in the history of the Karnatic for one generation can be understood only when the complicated events of the dying Empire of Vijayanagar are studied in detail.

3. Vijayanagar in the throes of dissolution

Vijayanagar, the greatest Hindu Empire of Southern India, passed through the throes of dissolution from 1614 onwards. Revolutions at court, civil wars, factions of the nobility, murder of princes, frequent revolts of satraps, a series of crimes and catastrophies, depopulation and desolation, these undermined the Emperor's power and exhausted his financial resources. During the short period of 28 years, eight Emperors rapidly succeeded each other on the tottering throne of the Empire.[2]

4. Aggressions of the Naik of Ikkeri

The Ikkeri kings had ruled in the Shimoga district and along the coast from the beginning of the 16th century.

1. See Persian Grant and its translation No. 2.
2. Sewell, Forgotten Empire. pp. 222-234. Sewell gives this list: Ranga (1619), Rama (1620-22), Ranga (1623), Venkata (1623), Rama (1629), Venkata (1636). It was this Venkatpati Raja who made a grant of Madraspatam to the English in 1639. O. C. Nos 1690, 1695, 1718, 1751.

S. 14.

Their territory included Aranga and Gutti below the Ghats in South Kanara. Keladi was their capital up to 1560, and Ikkeri up to 1639. Then they made Bednur or Nagar their chief place. Its walls were of great extent, forming three concentric enclosures. In the citadel was the palace, of mud and timber, adorned with carving and false gilding. A bird's-eye view of the weakening of the central government and of the mutual dissensions of the provincial governors is given by the famous Dutch traveller, P. D. Valle who visited Ikkeri in company with the Portuguese ambassador in 1623.

" The Prince Venk-tapa Naieka, was sometimes Vassal and one of the Ministers of the great king of Vidia–Nagar which the Portugals corruptly call Bisnaga; but after the downfall of the king of Vidia-Nagar, who a few years age by the Warrs rais'd against him by his neighbours, lost together with his life a great part of his Dominion, and became in a manner extinct; Venk–tapa–Naieka, and also many other Naieki, who were formerly his Vassals and ministers, remain'd absolute Prince over that part of the state, whereof he was governor; which also being a good souldier, he hath much enlarg'd, having seiz'd by force many territories of divers other Naieki, and Petty princes his neighbours; and in brief, is grown to that reputation, that having had Warr with the Portugals too, and given them a notable defeat,[1] he is now held for their Friend, and for the establishment of this friendship they send this Embassage to him in the name of the king of Portugal, the Ambassador being styl'd, Ambassador of the State of India."

---

1. He extended his dominions on the north and east to Masur, Shimoga, Kadur, and Bhuvanagiri (Kavaledurga), and on the west and south to the sea at Honore (North Kanara), by victory over the queen of Gersoppa, the pepper queen of the Portuguese, who was a feudatory of Bijapur. By espousing the cause of the queen of Olaya against the Bangar raja, he came into collision with the Portuguese who call him Venkapor, king of Canara. " Mysore and Coorg, p. 157.

5. The royal city of Ikkeri described

As the royal city of Ikkeri or Hikeri remained a storm
centre of war in subsequent history, its realistic description
by P. D. Valle who stayed there for a few days in 1623 or so,
will be very interesting.

"After a small journey further we arrived at Ikkeri,
which is the Royal City of Venka-tapa Naiek where he holds
his court; having travell'd since morning from Ahinala to
Ikkeri but two Leagues; This city is seated in a goodly plain,
and as we entered we pass'd through three gates with forts
and ditches, but small, and consequently, three inclosures;
the two first of which were not walls, but made of very high
Indian canes, very thick and close planted in stead of a wall,
and are strong against foot and horse in any........., hard to
cut, and not in danger of fire; besides, that the herbs which
creep upon them, together with themselves, make a fair and
great verdure and much shadow. The other inclosure is a
wall, but weak and inconsiderable; But having pass'd these
three, we pass'd all. Some say, there are other within,
belonging to the Citadel or Fort where the Palace is; for
Ikkeri is of good largeness, but the Houses stand thin and
are ill built, especially without the third Inclosure; and most
of the situation is taken up in great and long Streets, some of
them shadow'd with high and very goodly Trees growing near
lakes of water, of which there are many large ones, besides
Fields, set full of Trees, like Groves, so that it seems to
consist of a city, Lakes, fields, and Woods mingled together,
and makes a very delightful sight. We were lodg'd in
the House, as they said, wherein the king of Belight lodg'd,
I know not whether Kinsman, Friend, or Vassal to Venk-ta-pa
Naieka, but probably one of the above mentioned Royolets;
and to go to this House we went out of the third Inclosure,
passing through the inmost part of the City by another
gate opposite to that by which we enter'd. The House
indeed was such as in our Countries an ordinary Artisan

would scarce have dwelt in, having very few, and those small and dark Rooms, which scare afforded light enough to read a Letter; they build them so dark as a remedy for the greater heat of Summer; However, this must needs have been one of the best, since it was assign'd to the said King first, and now to our Ambassador; although as we pass'd through the midst of the City I observed some that made a much better show."

6. Muslim alliance against Vijayanagar

Bijapur and Golconda, taking advantage of this internal discord and exhaustion, opened a vigorous offensive for its dismemberment in 1637. The treaty of peace with Shah Jahan, the cession of a part of the Nizam Shahi territory and the transfer of the valuable services of an experienced general and a ripe administrator like Shahji, had immensely strengthened the position of Bijapur. Its ruler exhibited a great sagacity in using the new forces and opportunities for the conquest of a crumbling empire and making a pact with the King of Golconda by which the latter was to conquer the Imperial territory on the Coromandel Coast, while the central and western portions were to be captured by Bijapur. Moreover, Muhammad Adil Shah, King of Bijapur, desired to strengthen and glorify the Islamic religion in the Hindu Kingdom, and to win for himself the titles of *Mujahid* and *Ghazi*.[1] The opportunity for a campaign was offered by the mutual jealousies of the petty satraps of the Hindu Empire.

7. Rebellion of Timmaraj

The wars between the Emperor Kodand Rama and his commander Timma Raja are thus described in the Dagh Register of 1631-34.

---

1. Urdu Basatin-i-Salatin, p. 254,

The Emperor imprisoned by Timma Raja

" That the Commander Tijmerage still kept the King of Carnatica in arrest and that there were no signs that he would be released.

That the Tijmerage, Commander of the King of Carnatica, who had revolted against the king and arrested him, and except a few fortresses, had conquered the whole country, had also conquered the fortress Talamver. He hoped that the country would now become quiet, and that the trade would regain a better aspect."[1]

The Emperor was released from captivity

" The Tijmoragie would most likely have to open the roads that he had kept closed so far round Paliacatte and in the kingdom of Carnatica, because the King of Carnatica, who now by the influence and interference of several raides of nobles had been released from captivity, was lying in camp with a big army and pursued the Tijmoragie, and according to everybody'd opinion he would chase him out of his incorporated and usurped countries, if he did not leave them on his own accord."[2]

Peace between the Emperor and Timma Raaj

" Peace was made between the King and the Tijmerage. The latter thereby surrendered to the king all fortresses which he had possessed (except two), and people said that the capture of the two said fortresses had been the only cause that had forced the Tijmerage to come to an understanding and make peace. Let us hope that the countries may live up again and become prosperous again as before, for which the Almighty may give His blessings."[3]

1-3. Dagh–Register 1631–34. Pp. 145, 241, 364. Mr. Sewell merely remarks that the king was devoid of energy. and that one Timma Raya had revolted against him. (Forgotten Empire, p. 233.) On the contrary. the chronicle Ramarajiymu describes him to be quite energetic and heroic. Sources of Vijayanagar History, p. 312.

8. The first expedition into Malnad (1637–1638)

Vira Bhadra Nayak of Ikkeri was enlarging his territory by conquering the neighbouring districts of various rulers. One of them was Kenge Nayak of Basvapattan[1] (Virshapattan of the Sanskrit writers) who, to take revenge for his previous routs and losses of territory, invited the Bijapur King to pounce unawares on the Nayak of Ikkeri. Randulla Khan, under the title of Rustum Zaman was sent with Shahji, Malik Raihan, and others to carry on this war in the spirit of Jihad or religious crusade. With the help of the traitor, Kenge Nayak,[2] the Bijapur army suddenly arrived at Ikkeri. The ruler succumbed to this unexpected attack and fled away to his fort of Kasnauldrug. Rustam Zaman captured Ikkeri, remained there for a month, gave one lakh of huns to the traitor, and then proceeded to attack Kasnauldrug. Vira Bhadra, unable to resist such a vast army, made peace by ceding half of his kingdom and giving 18 lakhs of huns.[3]

Rustam Zaman returned in triumph to Bijapur, but two years after when Vira Bhadra threw off the yoke of submission by refusing to pay up the balance of the stipulated indemnity, the Bijapur forces proceeded against him and in a short time completely subjugated him. However, he was

1. The founder of the Basvapatan family is said to be Dhuma Raja whose son built the fort of Basvapatan and subdued a territory extending from Harihar and Kumasi to Taridere aad Bagur. His successor Hanumappa Nayak was confirmed in these possessions by the Vijayanagar Sovereign and he founded Sante Bennur. Mysore Gaz. II. 437, 447.

2. Muhammad Namah and Sh. Bh. IX, 35 name the ruler as Keng Nayak, but Dr. Aiyangar says that he was Kenge Hanumma, the son of Kenge Nayak, Rustam was assisted by the Rajas of Sunda, Bilige, Tarikere and Banawar. Mysore and Coorg by Rice, p. 158.

3. Urdu Basatin - i -Salatin (p. 254) mentions 30 lakh huns, out of which 16 lakhs were paid in cash and the rest was to be given in instalments.

restored to his principality through the intervention of Shahji.[1]
Since then he became a vassal of the Bijapur Kingdom and
removed his capital to Bednur.[2]

9. Second expedition into the Karnatic (1638)

In this expedition Rustam Zaman (Randulla Khan)
with Shahji Raje marched for the conquest of Bangalore,
while he deputed Afzal Khan to capture the fort of Sira.
Its Nayak came out to negotiate with the commander,
Afzal Khan, but was treacherously killed by him during
the interview. The people heroically defended the fort for
some time, but finally had to surrender it to the superior
forces of Bijapur. Sira was first remorselessly plundered
and then handed over to the traitor, Kenge Nayak, This
treacherous Nayak was afterwards instrumental in
intimidating Kemp Gouda, the chief of Bangalore, into
submission. He gave up the fort with all its property to
Rustam Zaman who appointed Shahji Raje as the governor
of this part of the country, while the Gouda retired to his
stronghold on Savandurga. Then the Bijapur army proceeded
to conquer Shrirangpatam. Its ruler, Kantirava Narasa Raja
Wodeyar, was subdued by Shahji whose valour was much
appreciated by the commander-in chief, Rustam Zaman.
Five lakhs of huns were taken as an indemnity and the
fort was left in the possession of its ruler. Then the Nayaks
of Madura and Kaveripattan were won over to the side
of Bijapur. (Sh. Bh. 11. 4–5.).

10. Third expedition in 1639

On the retirement of the Muslim forces to Bijapur
Kenge Nayak began to collect troops and seek alliance of
other Nayaks. He soon revolted against the Bijapur
authority. Thereupon Rustam Zaman advanced from Bijapur

1. Sh.Bh. XI.6.
2. S. K, Aiyangar, Ancient India, 293–94,

with forced marches to put down his rebellion. At the same time he invited Vira Bhadra, the enemy of Kenge Nayak, to assist him in conquering Basvapatan. This town is said to have been defended by 70,000 warriors of Kenge Nayak. The Bijapurian army consisting of the levies of all the principal war–lords besieged the town. Afzal Khan, Shahji, Badaji (Madaji) and other officers were sent against the main gate of the fort; Siddi Raihan Sholapuri, Peshjang Khan, and Hussaini Ambar Khan, against the second gate; and Ankush Khan,[1] Yaqut Khan and some other generals against the third gate. The garrison is said to have fired 80,000 rounds at the besiegers, but Afzal Khan heroically captured a part of the Peth. Thent he simultaneous advance of other generals broke down the opposition, some 3,700 soldiers of the Nayak were killed in the action and thus after a very severe struggle the entire town was captured. Thereupon Kenge Nayak surrendered the fort and gave 40 lakhs of huns to Rustam Zaman. According to the Shivabharat (IX. 37) the laurels of this victory were won by Shahji.

11. The result of the campaign

The fall of Basvapattan was followed by the conquest of Chiknayakan Halli,[2] Belur[3] (Velapuri), Tumkur, Kandal (Kuningal?) and Balapur, A vast booty was captured in these places and hence Bijapur rapidly advanced in pomp and prosperity. The beautiful suburban towu of Badshahpur and one memorable Palace of Justice[4] (Dad Mahal) were built in the metropolis at that time. It is evident that the Muslim arms succeeded everywhere against the petty Nayaks, each of whom had to fight single–handed against the overwhelming hosts of Bijapur. Now and then some

1. These very names are found in the Shivabharat. IX, 34–35.
2. 30 miles South West of Sira,
3. 20 miles distant from Halbid or Dwarasmudra, Belur might have been plundered, but it remained in the possession of the Bednur ruler for a long time.
4. It is now known as Asar Mahal.

defeated chief like Kenge Nayak raised his head against the Muslims. Similarly, Shivappa Nayak, the successor of Vira Bhadra, made bold to surprise the Bijapuri commander stationed at Ikkeri, took the fort from him and strongly fortified it in 1643. Still within seven years the Bijapur. generals had succeeded in capturing a large part of the Karnatic, depriving the country of vast amounts of wealth, spreading Islam in the Hindu Kingdom,   doing away with several Nayaks, and in reducing the power of the Hindu Emperors. The Muhammad Namah has thus depicted the result of the campaigns:

"As the King thought of spreading and strengthening the true faith, he brought Ram Raja and all other Rajahs of the South under subjection, and the strong temples, which the infidels (Kafirs) had erected in every fort, were completely depopulated. The whole country was conquered in three years and the citadel of dualism and idol worship was given such a rude shock that the knots of the sacred thread-wearers of Setu Band Rameshwar were severed."[2]

12. Vigorous policy of Shriranga

The Emperor Shriranga ascended the throne of Vijayanagar in 1642.   He was young, energetic and jealous of his honour. He realized that it was impossible for him to stem the tide of Muslim advance from Golconda and Bijapur, unless all his satraps co-operated with him by being brought under his hegemony.   But Tirumal Nayak of Madura was totally against the resuscitation of the defunct Empire.   He brought about a triple alliance of the states of Tanjore, Ginji and Madura, but his secret plots were disclosed to the Emperor by the loyal ruler of Tanjore.

13.   Mir Jumla's defeat at Vellore

Tirumal Nayak, to avoid the Imperial wrath, treacherously, called in the aid of Golconda. Its commander, Mir Jumla

1. It is now known as Asar Mahal.
2. Muhammad Namah.

made Vellore the objective of his attack and succeeded in surprising it. But the Emperor with the assistance of Shivappa Nayak of Ikkeri–Bednur was able to expel Mir Jumla's forces from this impregnable fort and make prisoners of a part of the garrison. The Emperor very gratefully conferred many titles and abundant wealth upon Shivappa who, to further assist his lord, defeated several recalcitrant feudatories.[1] Hardly was the Muslim invader repelled, when the two ministers of Shriranga's predecessor who had been dismissed by him, intrigued with Golconda. The East India Company's records mention that one of these, Damerala Venkata who was imprisoned by the Emperor for his treachery, was likely to be released[2] on account of the pressure being put on him by Mir Jumla. It was at this time that Shriranga sought the assistance of Bijapur by promising to pay 150,000 pagodas and 24 elephants.[3]

14. Treaty between Vijayanagar and Bijapur

The Mahammad Namah mentions a treaty made between the Rayal of Vellore and Rustam Zaman which appears to be incredible. But it is possible that, having been exasperated against his insurgent governors whom he alone could not bring into subjection and who were yet falling a prey to the Muslims, the Rayal might have devised the plan of issuing a threat to them by announcing that he would be seeking the help of Bijapur in their reduction. The forces of the Emperor of Vijayanagar and the King of Bijapur were to make conquests conjointly and whenever a fort was to be captured, its moveable property was to be taken by the Bijapurians and the immoveable was to go into the Rayal's possession. Thus the latter could save his country from passing into the hands of the enemy. But the threat had the desired effect, because the treaty was

1. Sources of Vijayanagar History, p. 347.
2-3. E. F. 1642-45, pp. 80, 111.

not observed by the Rayal who rather made common cause
with the local Rajas, refused to be coerced by the Bijapurians,
and prepared to oppose them.

15. Victories of Shriranga

Having got some respite from the invasions of the two
Muslim states by his vigorous policy and having won a few
governors to his cause, Shriranga turned his attention to the
subjection of the rebellious Nayaks of Madura, Ginji and
Mysore. We learn from a letter of October 1645 that the
Emperor had brought his enemies under control and had
restored himself to his original position.[1]

16. Conquests of Mir Jumla

But he had no time to restore peace and order to the
harassed land. The enemies were always knocking at his
doors. Bijapur and Golconda made a common cause against
him and the war began more vigorously than before. Mir
Jumla succeeded in capturing Udayagiri, the capital of the
eastern parts from the Governor Mallaya. Its account is
recorded in the two extracts of the East India Company:

"Having now answered the Surat letters they will conclude
with an account of 'How the warres stand betwixt the king
of Vinagar (Vijayanagar) and the Hollanders. Ever since
the seige of Pullacatt, which was begune the 12th August last,
*he hath bine in warres with the king of Vizapore (Bijapur)
and in the civil warres with three of his great Nagues*;
soe that he to this time never had opportunitie to send a
considerable foorse against Pulicatt, more then 4,000 souldiers
that lay before it to stopp the wayes that no goods should
goe in or out. And now the King of Gulcondah hath sent
his generall, Mier Gumlack (Mir Jumla) with a great armie
to oppose this king; who is advanced to the Jentues cuntry
where the King hath sent Mallay, who hath got togeather
50,000 souldiers (as report saith), whereof 3,000 he sent

1. E. F. 1642–45, p. 290.

for from Pullacatt, to keep the Moors from intrenching upon
this Kings country. Soe there is now remaining before
Pullacatt but one thousand.[1]

"This countre is at present full of warrs and troubles
for the King and three of his Nagues are at varience, and
the King of Vijapoores armie is come into this country on
the one side and the King of Gulkondah uppon the other,
both against this King. The Meir Jumlah is Generall for the
King of Gulcondah, whoe hath allreadie taken three of the
Kings castles whereof one of them is reported to bee the
strongest hould in his kingdome; where Molay (Malaya) was
sent to keepe it, but in short tyme surrendered it unto the
Meir Jumlah, uppon composition for himselfe and all his
people to goe away free; but how hee will be received by the
king we shall advice you by the next, for this newes came
unto us but yesturday."[2]

The allied troops laid siege to Vellore itself and
completely defeated the Rayal. Subsequent to its fall, all
the eastern portions of the Empire fell like ripe fruits into the
hands of Mir Jumla. Thereupon the English East India
Company obtained the renewal of their grant from Mir Jumla,
the Suzerain of Madras. Similarly, the Dutch who were
given freedom to reside and trade in Tegenapatam, were
granted the farm of the town of Palicat by the Vijayanagar
King. This town seems to have passed into the possession of
Mir Jumla in 1645 and of Bijapur in 1651. The details of
these events are told in various Dutch documents.[3]

17. Campaign against Shivappa of Ikkeri in 1644

Let us now turn our attention to the activities of the rulers
of Bednur. Virabhadra was defeated but not crushed by
the Muslim army. His younger brother and general Shivappa

1. E. F. 1646–1650. P. 25. Fort St. George to Surat. 21 January 1646.
O. C. 1974.

2. E. F. 1646-1650. P. 26. Fort St. George to Surat. 10th February 1646.
O. C. 1975. Cf. O. C. Nos. 1652, 1696, 1718, 1859, 1952, 2046.

3. Dutch Records, Series I, Vol. 15, No. 484; Vol. 17, Nos. 518, 532;
Vol. 18, No. 539. Mack. Mss. 201, pp. 10, 24, 25, 27, 31, 32 38, 46, 62.

subsequently subdued Bhairasa of Karkala, invaded Malayalam and entered Coorg. Swelled by his victories, he murdered[1] Virabhadra, and himself ascended the throne. He was one of the most distinguished kings of the line. He raided Manjrabad, Vastara, Sakkarepattan and Hassan. He greatly enlarged Bednur (Bidnur or Bidanur) and made it a central emporium of trade. " Being in the direct course of trade by the Hosangadi ghat, it rapidly increased in size and importance, until there was a prospect of the houses reaching the number of a lakh, which would entitle it to be called a Nagara. The walls were 8 miles in circumference, and had 10 gates, named the Killi, Kodial, Kavaledurga, &c. The palace was on a hill in the centre, surrounded with a citadel, and the whole city was encircled by woods, hills and fortified defiles, extending a great way in circumference. " [2]

Father Leopardo Paes, then travelling in Kanara, says that Shivappa had amassed enormous treasure, that his possessions extended from the Turdy river to Kasargod or Nilesvar, and that he had a standing army of from forty to fifty thousand men. There were more than thirty thousand Christians among his subjects, originally natives of Goa and Salsett. [3]

On learning the news of the fall of Ikkeri into the hands of Shivappa Nayak, Muhammad Adil Shah resolved to proceed to Malnad in person. So he left Bijapur at the head of a large army on 3rd January 1644. But he encamped at Bankapur, the famous outpost of his kingdom, called Dar-ul-Fath, ' the capital of victory' since 11th January onwards. He despatched Nawab Khan Baba Mustafa Khan, and Muzaffar-ud-din Khan-i-Khanan for the conquest of Ikkeri. Shivappa is said to have mightily strengthened the

---

1. But Shivatattvaratnakara, a history of the Keladi Kings, states that Virabhadra became an ascetic and gave his kingdom to his uncles, Shivappa and Ventappa, Sources of Vijayanagar History, p. 346.

2. Mysore Gazetteer Vol. II. P. 464.

3. Mysore and Coorg from the Inscriptions. Pp. 158-59.

fortifications of the place, but to have left its defence to
his generals. The garrison heroically defended the fort for
five days, but when a tower was raised by the enemy to
mount their cannon for the bombardment of the hill-castle,
the defenders were disheartened and they surrendered the
fort. Sagar, another important town at the distance of four
miles from Ikkeri, was also captured. Khan Baba was left
to consolidate this conquest and the main part of the army
returned to Bankapur and then marched on with the King
to Bijapur. Thus in less than three months the campaign
against Ikkeri was over.[1]

18. Expedition under the Khan-i-Khanan in 1644-5

At the end of the rainy season of 1644 another expedition
was sent into the Karnatic under the Khan-i-Khanan with all
the principal officers who had distinguished themselves there
in previous campaigns. Yet the vast force could hardly make
any headway for full one year, on account of either the treaty
of peace with Shriranga or his vigorous opposition. As the
campaign was centred in the Karnul district which was
included in the Golkonda Kingdom, it is evident that Khan-i-
Khanan was assisting Shriranga against Mir Jumla. All
the force was first concentrated to capture the strong fort
of Nandiyal[2] which fell after a severe fight lasting for
four days.

The fall of this important place was followed by the capture
of eight places whose names are thus given in the Muhammad
Namah:— " Sriwal, Kopgonda, Obhali, Porlor, Parkanpulast,
Kanigiri, Kardelmast, Chabakalmarbast.[3] Khaljalm and
Kanikgiri." The king was much gratified with these conquests
and honoured the Khan-i-Khanan with the high-sounding
title of Khan-i-Muhammad Muhammad Shahi. It appears
that some treaty was concluded between the two Muslim

---

1. Muh. Namah and Basatin-i-Salatin.
2. It is written Nandibhal in the Muhammad Namah.
3. Muhammad Namah.

monarchs and hence Abdullah Qutub Shah sent a rich present
to Mahammad Shah to close the war and seal his friendship.

19. Mustafa Khan's campaign in 1646-48

This was the most brilliant of all the campaigns in
the Karnatic.   Nawab Mustafa Khan was sent as
commander-in-chief along with other premier nobles on
5th June 1646. On the way he captured the Gumti Fort
on the Palri river.   It was a stronghold of the robbers
who were laying waste the neighbouring country.   Passing
through Gadag and Lakmeshwar, the Muslim army reached
Honhalli, 12 miles to the west of Basvapatan.   Here
Rustam Zaman was deprived of his command and property
for his disloyalty to the King, but was afterwards restored to
his former honours through the intercession of the Nawab.
Here the latter was met on 3rd October by Shahji Raja and
Asad-ul-Khawanin who had been sent ahead to secure the
frontiers against a rebellion of the Hindu princes.   Here
too came Shivappa Nayak with a contingent of 3,000 cavalry.
He was sent to keep watch on the Raja of Shrirangapatam
with more than 30,000 force.   Dadu Nayak, the Raja of
Harpanhalli, joined the army with a force of 30,000 horse
and 2,000 foot, Then came Husaini Ambar Khan, Jujhar
Rao, Abaji Ghatge, a brother of Kengc Nayak, Balaji (son
of Haybat Rao), the Desais of Lakmeshwar and Kopal.
The last two alone arc said to have brought 20,000 foot
with them.

Strengthened with the troops of so many Maratha and
Muslim chiefs and of the local Nayaks, the Bijapuri army
advanced like an irresistible sea. It was greeted at Shivaganga
in the Tumkur district by the envoy of Shriranga and the
ambassadors of the rulers of Madura, Ginji and Tanjore
who had revolted against the authority of Shriranga Rayal,
the Emperor of Vijayanagar. Thereupon the latter too opened
negotiations with the Nawab to request him to abstain from
invasion and to renounce his alliance with Golconda.

While the pourparlers of peace were going on, the Emperor forthwith marched against the rebellious Nayaks with three lakhs infantry, 12,000 horse and 100 elephants. The Nayak of Ginji was soon subdued, but the other two rulers offered a stubborn resistence.

The Nawab turned deaf ears to the terms of the Emperor's ambassador and demanded the immediate withdrawal of the invading army from the Nayak's country. Thereupon the ambassador conveyed to his master the preliminary condition of the peace, so that the Emperor was compelled against his will to return to his capital without punishing the rebels. The ambassador was permitted to return with the Bijapuri envoy Mulla Ahmad to his master for settling the terms of the treaty. The Nawab was anxious to keep the Brahmin envoy in his camp as a hostage, but through the intervention of Shahji he was allowed to go back to Vellore. The Nawab's army was encamped at the head of the Nayakamere Pass, some 28 miles from Vellore. It has been seen that the rulers of the southern principalities like Ginji, Madura and Tanjore, as well as the Nayaks of Harpanhalli and Ikkeri, were with the immense Bijapuri army consisting of Maratha levies and Muslim troops. Even then Shriranga decided not to submit like a coward, but to await the decision of the sword.

He organised the defence, fortified the passes and proceeded to oppose the advance of the Bijapuri army through Jagdeva's territory of the Baramahals in the Salem district. Shriranga had come up to the strong fort of Krishnadrug with an army of one lakh foot and 12,000 horse. The Nawab probably wanted to surprise the Rayal from the rear. In the meantime a furious battle was fought in January 1646 between the advance guards under Jagdeva, the Raja of Kaveripattan,[1] and the Bijapuri army under Shahji and Asad Khan. As the latter was away from the field, Shahji alone was in command of the small force. Though the main

1. Sh. Bh. XI. 40.

armies did not take any part in this battle, yet Jagdeva was defeated and obliged to take refuge in Krishnadrug, while the Emperor seems to have fallen back towards his capital.

The version of the Basatin-i-Salatin is just the opposite of what is recorded in the Muhammad Namah. It is said that Shahji was defeated, and the elephant on which he sat at the time of the battle and his bag and baggage were taken away by the enemy. On hearing of Shahji's defeat, Mustafa Khan despatched the heavy baggage to Bangalore and rapidly advanced to Shahji's assistance. It appears that the defeat was very crushing, because the premier at once wrote to the King for more troops. Thereupon Khan Muhammad and Malik Raihan were ordered to postpone the operations on the Gunji Kotah side and to immediately join Mustafa Khan with all their forces. It is said that Malik Raihan was unwilling with his exhausted troops to proceed to the assistance of the main army, but the king repeated his peremptory orders by presenting his own portrait to him. Then the Malik hastened to the premier's camp which was situated between Banikalur and the Masti[1] Pass. The version of the contemporary Muhammad Namah ought, however, to be preferred to that of the Basatin-i-Salatin which was compiled later on.

After the approach of the main army under the Nawab, a plan was made to subdue the whole country under Jagdeva. Krishnadrug, Virabhadra Durg, (the capital of Jagdeva), Deva Durg, Anandbar, Amravati, Gudiyatam, Waranjpur (Vrinchipuram), Ranpur, Taranpur (Tirupatur), Kaveripattan, Hasan Raidurg, Raidurg, Ratnagiri, Kanakgiri, Malgiri, Arjunkot, Dhalenkot and others were captured after stubborn resistance from the defenders, so that the whole territory was overrun in one year.

After annexing a large part of the Baramahals, the Bijapuri army marched for the reduction of Vellore. A furious battle was first fought on the plain before the walls of the capital. Therein Shahji, other Hindu Vazirs and Muslim

---

1. Masti Pass—30 miles E. of Bangalore,

S. 16.

lords played a distinguished part. Shahji backed by his Muslim colleague Asad Khan, commanded the right wing of the Bijapuri army. A tumultuous battle lasted for several hours. Sometimes the Muslims were hurled back, at others, the Hindus. All of a sudden the Vijayanagar General, Damalvar who was a very famous hero, fell upon the army of Shahji. In the onslaught General Asad Khan was wounded and dismounted from his steed. The army seemed to fall back, but it was rallied by Malik Raihan. The Vijayanagar General advanced on his elephant further to the place occupied by Mustafa Khan, but he was closely followed by Malik Raihan. The premier even thought of getting down from his elephant, but he was dissuaded from doing so by a Maratha Sardar Tembaji Saheb. Soon after, the forces under the Vijayanagar General Damalvar and Malik Raihan came to grip with each other. In this battle the Hindu forces were defeated and thus the whole Hindu army was dispersed after a terrible slaughter. It is said in the Muhammad Namah that 5,800 soldiers lay dead on the field. The General himself was wounded by Mustafa Khan with an arrow and thereafter he fled away with his army. Thereupon the Bijapurians invested the fort. After some resistance, the Rayal submitted and agreed to pay 50 lakh huns and 150 elephants as an indemnity, and the hostilities were temporarily suspended. The Nawab left Shahji and Asad Khan for the government of the conquered Karnatic and returned home laden with an immense booty and rarest presents. He was highly honoured by the King who marched up to the river Krishna to receive the victorious Premier.

20. Campaign against Ginji in 1648

Nawab Mustafa Khan was again appointed to the command of the Karnatic campaign to crush Shriranga. He started from Hasanabad, a suburb of Bijapur, on 12th January 1648. The Nawab was received on the way by Shahji and Asad Khan who had been left for the administration of the Karnatic. The Nawab, with the assistance of Shahji, achieved a unique victory by the capture of the strong forts of the Jangama pass. The presence of Shahji at the siege of Jangama is attested by a Firman of 11th January 1648 issued to Jaswant Rao Wadwe for going to Jangama Kanvi with his contingent and joining Maharaj Farzand Shahji Bhosle. He was exhorted to live in agreement and concord with the Maharaj and to remain loyal to the government.

Thus it is evident that by this time Shahji was conferred the high titles of ' Maharaj ' and ' Son of the King of Bijapur.' The full text of the Firman is given in the Appendix. This obviously shows that his services in the Karnatic had been very much appreciated by the Sultan.

It is true that the Muhammad Namah does not often refer to the achievements of Shahji. But it should not be ignored that this history was written by Zahur who was the protege of Nawab Mustafa Khan. He is thus expected to sing the encomiums of his patron in and out of season and to ignore all others, particularly those who were not of his patron's party. Shahji belonged to the opposite faction which had been instrumental in confining Mustafa Khan in the Belgaum Fort. It is evident that the services of other generals like Asad Khan are also not mentioned by the author of the Muhammad Namah. Similarly, this history is often silent on the part palyed by Golconda in these wars. Just as some English, Dutch and Portuguese documents supplement the account recorded in the Muhammad Namah, similarly the Shivabharat and Marathi sources are to be relied upon to fill up the gaps.

Having been urged by Tirumal Nayak of Madura, Mir Jumla advanced to the formidable fort of Ginji. Vijayaraghava Nayak, son of Raghunath Nayak of Tanjore, being panick-stricken by the approach of a large army, surrendered to the enemy. This Nayak " knew that he could not give pitched battle to an enemy, whose mere number had created so much terror; but, he could no longer count on his ally of Madura,

whom he had scandalously betrayed. Obliged to take sides,
he did what one would always do, under the influence of
terror; he decided on the most senseless and disastrous
step: he delivered himself up to the king of Golconda and
concluded with him a treaty by which he surrendered at
discretion." [1] Tirumal Nayak soon repented of his short-
sighted policy and desired to amend matters by having
recourse to an alliance with the Bijapur king who immediately
sent him an army of 17,000 horse for his assistance. With
this imposing cavalry and 30,000 infantry of his own, he
marched to relieve Ginji from the forces of Mir Jumla. But
the Muslim armies soon came to an understanding among
themselves. Tirumal Nayak, being deserted by his Muslim
friends, hurled himself with all his army into the fort of Ginji
for its defence. "The fortress, protected by its advantageous
position, was, besides, defended by good fortifications,
furnished with a strong artillery and by a numerous army,
provisioned for a considerable time; it could, accordingly
defy all the efforts of the besiegers. But soon disagreements
and divisions sprang up among these men (the besieged) so
diversified in nationality and manners. A revolt broke out
in the midst of the general confusion, the gates of the citadel
were thrown open to the enemy, who rushed into it and
delivered the town, the richest in all these countries, to
pillage. The booty was immense, consisting of silver, gold,
pearls, and precious stones of inestimable value." [2]

This account by father Proenza is supplemented by that
recorded in the Muhammad Namah and the Basatin-i-Salatin.

Finding it impregnable, Mir Jumla succeeded in securing
the assistance of the Bijapur army. Thereupon, Tirumal Nayak
of Madura deserted by his Muslim friends began to actively
help the besieged.   He also succeeded in fanning the flames of
enmity between Golconda and Bijapur, and the result of
his diplomacy was the raising of the siege by Mir Jumla. The

1. La Mission Du Madure III. P. 45.
2. La Mission Du Madure III. P. 46.

latter retired to make new acquisitions in the Kadappa district and to consolidate his previous conquests. Thus the Bijapuri army was left alone to conduct the siege. There was a further trouble ahead. The principal commanders like Shahji, Khairiyat Khan and Siddi Raihan were dissatisfied with Mustafa Khan, and their rebellion naturally prolonged the operations. Sometime after, Mustafa [1] himself succumbed to old age and died in harness there on 9th November 1648. The command passed on first to Malik Raihan, and then to Muzaffar–ud–din Khan–i–Khanan Khan Muhammad.[2] With the heroic assistance of Afzal Khan, the fort is said to have been ultimately reduced in December 1648.

Mir Jumla who had his camp at Gunji Kotah, taking advantage of the sudden death of Mustafa Khan and of the mutual discord of the generals of the Bijapuri army, called upon Malik Raihan to raise the siege. This is confirmed by the Muhammad Namah wherein it is said that the ungrateful Abdullah Shah whose forces had been defeated by the Rayal and who could not have won an inch of the Karnatik without Bijapuri support, had formed a secret alliance with the Rayal, and sent his general Mir Jumla to assist the Hindus in the siege of Ginji.

It appears that the King of Golconda was dissatisfied with the Bijapuri generals for violating the treaty. The two kings were to conjointly conquer the Hindu territory and to divide the booty in the proportion of two to one, i. e., two–thirds was to be taken by Adil Shah and one–third by Qutb Shah. The latter even complained to Shah Jahan against Bijapur for the unjust appropriation of the share due to him.[3]

---

1. The death of Mustafa to whom a part of Rajapur belonged was noticed by the English Factors in their letter of 31 Jan. 1649, O. C. 2115.

2. Basatin–i–Salatin makes no mention of this general. Under the adverse circumstances, the Malik had to retire from Ginji to Waswati, a place 14 miles from Vellore. There he waited the arrival: of the new commander–in–chief. Then both proceeded to renew the siege.

3. Sir J. Sarkar in Modern Review 1929 July No,

According to the Basatin-i-Salatin, Rup Nayak, the Raja of Ginji, was very proud and wealthy. His family had been in possession of the fort for seven hundred years. Being given to a licentious and luxurious life, he had neglected the affairs of his kingdom. As he was not helped by the neighbouring chiefs during the siege and because his provisions and fodder were exhausted, he was ultimately forced to surrender the fort to the Bijapurians on 28th December 1648. Besides the vast amounts of wealth plundered by the soldiers for themsleves, the Bijapuri army got hold of all the accumulated riches of the Ginji rulers. It amounted to four krores of huns or 20 krores of rupees in cash and jewels.

" The country which had nothing except idol worship and infidelity for thousands of centuries was illuminated with the light of Islam through the endeavours and good wishes of the King. The treasures, gems, jewels and other property worth four crores of huns was added to the imperial treasury. Mosques were erected in the cities which were full of temples and the preachers and criers were appointed in order to propagate the Muhammedan religion."[1]

All the Muslim army was not employed in reducing the fort of Ginji. It appears from the English Records that in this campaign the Bijapur King employed the well-known Pindaries for the wanton desolation and devastation of the land. This fact is worth noticing, since afterwards Shivaji followed in the footsteps of Muslim rulers in some of his policies. His system of plunder was surely more humane than the one that was used by the Bijapuri war-lords in the Karnatic.

" Nations who lye within two daies journey one of another with powerful armies, watching all advantage upon each other, yet both strive to make a prey of this miserable and distracted or divided people. These are the Gulcandah and the Vizapoore (Bijapur) Moores, the latter of which hath brought in 8,000 freebooters who receave noe pay but plunder what they can; whose incursions, roberies, and

1. Muhammad Namah, P. 126.

devastacions hath brought a desolacion on a great part of the country round about, specially the three prime cloth ports, Tevenapatam, Porto Novo, and Pullacherey (Pondichery) of which the two last are in a manner ruin'd, the other hardly preserveing itselfe in a poore condition with continueall presents."[1]

Flushed with the conquest of Ginji, the Muslim lords advanced into the territories of Madura and Tanjore. Both the craven–hearted Nayaks shut themselves up in inaccessible forests and allowed the enemy to plunder and devastate the country in the manner described above. Finally, they opened negotiations and submitted to the Muslims. Thus after subduing two powerful Nayaks, gathering incalculable treasures, and without losing a single soldier, the army returned to Bijapur.[2]

21. Cause of Shahji's imprisonment

The Marathi Bakhars and Basatin-i-Salatin are unanimous in attributing Shahji's arrest to the rebellious conduct of Shivaji. He had taken possession of some forts and territories, had killed several Bijapuri officers, had surprised the escort below the Bhor Ghat and captured the royal treasure which was being conveyed from Kalyan to Bijapur. Besides his conquest of Kalyan and the hill forts of Rajmachi, Lohgad etc. frowning the Ghats below, had highly incensed the King of Bijapur. It was naturally concluded that these disloyal acts must have been done by the young Shivaji with the advice and instigation of his father. Hence secret orders were issued to arrest Shahji.

There are many versions of the method of his imprisonment. (i) The Sabhasad records that a letter was written to Shahji directing him to keep his son under proper control. Thereupon the Maharaja replied that his son was no longer under his control and His Majesty might consequently deal with him in any manner he liked. This

1. O. C. 2085. E. F. 1646–1650. P. 215.
2. Nayaks of Madura, p. 266,

incident has been wrongly connected with the appointment of Afzal Khan to punish Shivaji, so that the Sabhasad makes no mention of the imprisonment and release of Shahji in 1649. (ii) The Chitragupta and Shiva Pratap Bakhars, though they make the details more spicy, commit the same mistake (Sabh. 12; Chitragupta 7; Shiva Pratap, 77). (iii) According to Chitnis (36–37), Shahji wrote a letter to Shivaji censuring his conduct and ordering him to go to Bijapur. Thereupon Shivaji sought the advice of his wife, Sai Bai Saheb as well as of his officers and nobles, and thereafter despatched curt replies to his father as well as the King that he was ready to take the consequence of his deeds, but could not be thus diverted from his course. The King did not believe the Raje. As he had harboured a suspicion in his heart against Shahji, he ordered Baji Ghorpade to arrest Shahji by any means and bring him to the metropolis from Trivapi near Tanjore. (iv) The Shiva Digvijaya (133–138) reproduces all the letters mutually sent by Shivaji, Shahji and the King. Shivaji is said to have consulted his mother, his officers, his wife and his inspiring Goddess Bhawani before sending replies to his father and the King. The latter deputed Baji Ghorpade and Sarjc (Sharza) Khan to persuade the Raje for fully controlling his son. The Nabob excused himself on the ground of his friendship with Shahji, but Ghorpade consented to carry out the order of the King to arrest Shahji. (v) The Muhammad Namah has a different story altogether. During the siege of Ginji some incidents happened which caused ill–will between the Nawab and Shahji. Instead of showing obedience to the premier and chief command, Shahji had the temerity to disavow his authority. Hence the Nawab thought out plans to arrest him.

" As the siege lingered on, Shahji Rajah who always changes sides like the dice of the gamblers, sent his chamberlain to the Nawab, requesting his permission to go to his own dominion, so that his soldiers may get some rest.

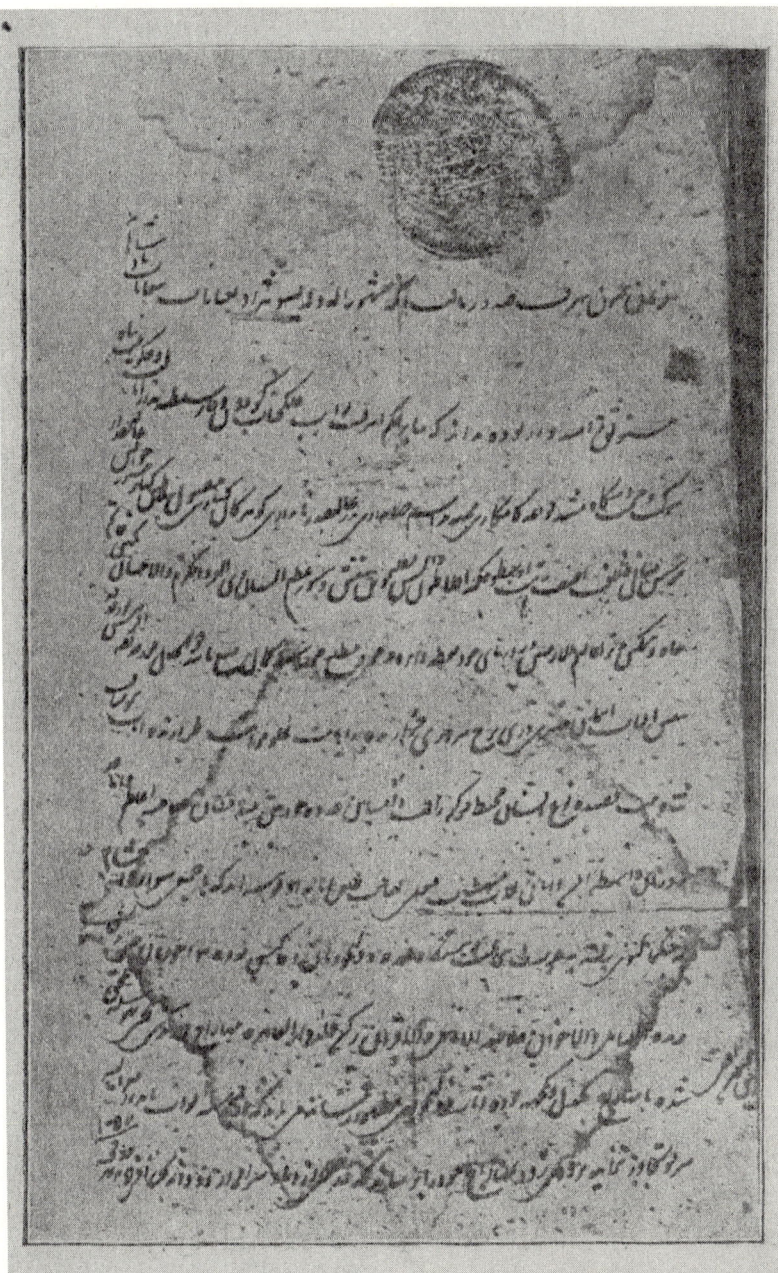

(3)   Yashwantrao Wadwe to Assist
Shahji Maharaj in the Karnatic.

(4)   Baji Ghorpade–A Martyr.

The Nawab replied that it amounted to creating disturbance if he were to break off at that critical time. Thereupon Shahji Raja again sent a word to him that in the camp grain was very dear and the soldiers could no longer put up with hardships and trouble, that under those circumstances there was no need of taking any permission and that he would leave for his country without any permission.

When the Nawab found that Shahji Raja was bent on kicking up a row, and through fox-like cunningness wished to mar the game, he used extreme prudence and skill and imprisoned him in such a manner that out of his ministerial property not a single *tasu* was lost, and all his wealth and property were taken into possession by the imperial authorities."

Sir J. Sarkar suggests that the arrest of Shahji was due to his disloyal intrigues. 'He was coquetting with the Rayal and Qutb Shah, and the latter sovereign divulged the fact to Adil Shah.' The evidence for suspecting Shahji's loyalty is to be seen in the fact that he allowed Venkayya Somaji, the ambassador of the Rayal, to return to his master against the wishes of the chief command, and secondly in a letter of 23rd December 1647 from Qutb Shah to his envoy at Bijapur that he had received a petition from Shahji Bhonsle, begging to be taken under his protection, but that he had then and repeatedly before this rejected Shahji's prayer and told him to serve Adil Shah. [1]

Sarkar's suspicion is based upon slender evidence. Let it not be forgotten that Shahji as Governor was a virtual king of the Karnatic, that he possessed large estates in the Karnatic and Maharashtra under Bijapuri jurisdiction, that he had enjoyed the unbroken confidence of his king for ten years without any evidence of a rupture between them, and that he was conferred the titles of Maharaj and the Son

1. Modern Review 1929, July No.

S. 17.

of the Sultan of Bijapur. It is unlikely that under such circumstances Shahji could have thought of leaving his personal and ancestral jagirs for an insecure service under Kutb Shah. The real cause of the rupture with Mustafa Khan seems to be his protest against the treacherous policy of the Khan in terminating his alliance with the puissant prince of Madura and making a common cause with Mir Jumla. It has been seen that the new treaty did not help Bijapur, because the Nayak of Madura made things hot for Muslims. Shahji's view of relieving Ginji from the siege of Mir Jumla with the assistance of the Nayak was justified. It is also possible that Mustafa Khan might have forestalled a strong Hindu League consisting of the Nayaks of Madura, Ginji, Tanjore, Mysore, Kaveripattan and Bednur, of Shriranga of Vijayanagar and of Shahji Raje against the Muslims. These seem to have been the causes of the rupture, and of the subsequent imprisonment of Shahji.

22. Release of Shahji

The account of Shahji's imprisonment being the same in the Basatin-i-Salatin and the Shiva Bharat, seems to be reliable, while the story of the Bakhars is quite contradictory. It has been said in the Shiva Bharat that one day early in the morning when the sun was about to peep out, Dilawar[1] Khan, Masud Khan, Ambar Khan, Rajahs of Adoni and Karnpur, Farhad Khan, Khairat Khan, Yaqut Khan, Azam Khan, Bahlol Khan, Malik Raihan Khan, Balal, son of Haybat Raja, Sidhoji, Mambaji Pawar, Mambaji Bhosla, and some other nobles, besieged the camp of Shahji. As his soldiers had kept awake that night, they had no idea of such a sudden attack and were unprepared, and so there was a great disorder and tumult in their camp. Masud Khan himself was commanding the forces. Then Khandoji, Ambaji, Manaji, Baji Raje

---

1. Basatin-i-Salatin gives the names of only three Sardars Baji Rao Ghorpade, Yashwant Rao Wadhwe, and Asad Khan.

Ghorpade, Yeshwant Rao Wadhwe, and others entered the camp of Shahji and thus awakened him. Shahji ordered all his nobles to be prepared. Then he rode on a powerful horse and attacked Baji Raje Ghorpade. His faithful nobles stood on all sides to protect him. Then a close fight began and Shahji exchanged blows with the Ghorpade, but finally he swooned, fell down wounded, and was arrested by the Ghorpade himself. The three thousand horse of Shahji soon dispersed, and much plunder was secured from the camp.

The traditional account according to which Shahji was invited by Baji Raje Ghorpade of Mudhol in his house for a banquet and was treacherously put under arrest, is obviously wrong. [2] No treachery or stratagem was at all practised by the Ghorpade. In obedience to the orders of his commander, like so many others, he too pursued Shahji and after a tough fight succeeded in capturing him. It has been seen that Yaswant Rao Wadhwe bore some enmity to Shahji and the Ghorpade too was not on good terms with him. Even near kinsmen like Mambaji and Trimbakji Bhosle were in the pursuing party, as were Sidhoji and Mambaji Pawar. Baji [3] Raje was really accompanied with seven Maratha Sardars.

The vast booty acquired in the fort of Jinji and Shahji were brought to Bijapur under the vigilant escort of Afzal Khan who was received with a great pomp in the Kalyan Mahal by the King. The Muhammad Namah thus relates the imperial treatment meted out to Shahji.

" Shahji Raja who was brought in chains was sent to the prison of example (ordinary confinement), and at this

2. This romance has been accepted without doubting its veracity by Kincaid, I. 142.

3. Kincaid (I, 142) is grossly wrong in asserting that ' the King (Adil Shah) had *recently conferred* the fief of Mudhol on Baji Ghorpade and he was now expected to show that he had deserved his promotion. ' Mudhol was conferred on Rana Bhairavsinha for the first time in 1398 and since then the grant used to be confirmed to each successor. Thus Mudhol had been in the possession of Baji's ancestors for 250 years and yet it is said by Kincaid to be ' *recently conferred* ' on Baji.

kind treatment of the King towards Shahji, the nobles and the residents of the city were surprised, because they thought that Shahji Raja deserved capital punishment and no favour in the form of a guard or watch. As he was put in confinement, they thought that he might be pardoned and liberated. Some of the councillors did not like his release in the least, because he was very cunning and resourceful. Another party were unanimous that to bestow liberty on that treacherous and reckless fellow would be tantamount to trampling the tail of a snake, or opening the knot of the tail of a scorpion with one's own hand with full knowledge (of) and after seeing clearly (the danger involved in the adventure). It is not the way of the wise to regard a a porcupine as a heap of mud and a wasp's abode as a fit pillow for the head.

The King, who was ever ready to pardon the crimes of the created beings, entrusted Shahji Raja with the instructions that if he would give up to the imperial authorities the strong fort of Kondwana (which fell into his son's hands through treachery after the death of Dadaji Kond Deva), with the forts of Kundarpi and Bangalore, he would be honoured with his former position.

Khan Ahmad Khan accordingly carried Shahji to his own house and kept him in confinement. Then he broached to him the glad tidings of the royal kindnesses and left no stone unturned in sympathising with him and soothing his heart. When Shahji saw that his black deeds had brought forth white flowers on account of the showers of royal favour, he agreed readily to obey implicitly. He sent letters to his two sons who were firmly seated in the above mentioned forts. "As soon as these few sentences reach you, you should deliver the forts of Kondwana, Bangalore and Kundarpi to the trusty agents of the king." They abided by this behest of their father immediately.

The King called Shahji Raja into his presence and honoured him with the robe of *Vizarat,* and restored to him his former country."

Even a cursory reading of this detailed account brings out the facts that (1) Shahji's arrest was not connected with the rebellion of Shivaji, as is asserted by the Bakhars; (2) that he was not thrown into any cell, but was kept as an honourable guest in the custody of a nobleman at Bijapur; (3) that there is no foundation in the tragic story relating that a wall was raised round the body of Shahji and he was threatened with death till his rebellious son Shivaji made himself over to the King; (4) that the intercession of Shah Jahan was not the cause of his release from the brick coffin; (5) that the services of Randulla and Murar Jugdeva for securing his release are not mentioned at all; (6) that none of his sons, Sambhaji or Ekoji, was in captivity with him at Bijapur, because Sambhaji defended Bangalore from the Bijapur forces and afterwards Shahji wrote letters to his sons to give up the forts to the Imperial officers; and lastly, (7) that the forts of Kondwana and Bangalore were taken back by the King probably to test the submission of Shahji, hence these were restored to him soon after his release. Some of these points require elucidation.

Had there been a grain of truth in the story of Shahji's confinement in a stone dungeon which was completely closed up except for a small aperture, the writers of Muhammad Namah and Salatin-i-Basatin on one side, and the authors of the Shiva Bharat, Shivabhushan and Radha Madhava Vilas Champu would have most romantically narrated it. Since all these works are silent on the point, it must be concluded that the event never happened.

Though a few letters passed between Shivaji and Prince Murad Baksh, the Bakhars have brought in the intercession of Shah Jahan who probably knew nothing of Shahji's imprisonment. Sir J. Sarkar is right in concluding that notwithstanding these promises the Mogul government did not probably in the end actually intercede for Shahji. None of the contemporary sources corroborate the evidence of the letters regarding Shah Jahan's intervention. (i) It is certain from Murad's letterrs, that a dress of honour was despatched to Shahji. Even this much favour must have had a great effect. The Sultan clearly saw that he could not long keep Shahji in captivity without incurring the wrath of the Emperor and furnishing him with an excuse to pounce upon his territory. (ii) Shahji's release without reconciliation would have sent him and his sons to the Mogul Court, where they would have been highly instrumental in conquering Bijapur. (iii) The death of Mustafa Khan who had personal grievances against the Raja, must have improved the matters. (iv) The affairs in the Karnatic too required a strong and an experienced governor to maintain law and order in the new conquests. (v) The crushing defeats inflicted by the sons of Shahji on the imperial forces should be considered as an effective cause of reconciliation. On the news of his father's arrest, Sambhaji strengthened the defences of Bangalore and prepared to fight the forces that advanced under Tanaji Dure, Vithal Gopal and Farhad Khan. Another army was despatched against Shivaji who had fortified Purandhar. As both the armies were routed by the undaunted brothers, Adil Shah thought of saving his prestige by securing the possession of Bangalore and Sinhagarh in lieu of Shahji's release.[1]

Sir J. Sarkar is wrong in asserting that Shahji was kept in prison along with his eldest son. (i) Neither the Persian histories like the Basatin-i-Salatin and Muhammad Namah, nor the Shiva Bharat and Jedhe Shakavali make any mention of the imprisonment of any of his sons. All these books would have taken special pleasure in mentioning that fact. (ii) Murad's letter should not be literally but metaphorically translated. His sons were to be released from anxiety and not from imprisonment. (iii) From Murad's letter it is clear that Shivaji requested him to secure the freedom of his father but not of his brothers. Hence Shahji was arrested alone and he was kept under surveillance at Bijapur and not

1, Sh Bh. XV 15-53.

in any prison. (iv) Shahji sent letters to his sons for delivering the forts.

The Bakhars are full of chronological confusion. Randulla Khan had died in 1643 [1] and Murar in 1635. Yet both these are said to have interceded with the King in favour of Shahji in 1648. Sarkar, following the Bakhars, has strangely written that ' it is therefore historically true that the release of Shahji was due to the friendly mediation of Sharzah Khan, and the bail of Randaula Khan, two leading nobles of Bijapur."[2]

23. Secret support to Swarajya

According to the Jedhe Chronology, Shahji was arrested with two of his chief secretaries. All the three were deported to Bijapur and kept in confinement there. After their release, Shahji gratefully thanked Kanhoji Naik Jedhe and Dadaji Krishna Lohokare for all the hardships of captivity and told them that he had been given a territory of twelve gaves (120 miles) and the province of Bangalore yielding 5 lacs of hons. As he was ordered to undertake an expedition into the Karnatic, he entrusted to them the guardianship of his son Shivaji who was in charge of Khedebare and Poona. As they wielded great power in the Mawals, they were to remain there with their forces and see that all the Mawal Deshmukhs submitted to him and carried out his orders. Should any Mogul or Adil Shahi army come against him, they were to be loyal to him and fight against the enemy. To seal their loyalty to each other's cause, Shahji and Jedhe took an oath to mutually support each other. Thereafter Shahji presented them both with dresses of honour and sent them to Shivaji with confidential letters. It is evident that Shahji soon expected hostilities against Shivaji from both the Moguls and the Bijapur ruler. To ward off the danger he gave his son two of his most influential and trusted friends for assistance.

1. P. S. S. 488; Kincaid I, 143; Rairi Bakhar.
2. Shivaji, p. 38.

24. Shahji and Baji Ghorpade

It has been seen that Baji Raje Ghorpade had taken a prominent part in arresting Shahji and hence their enmity had been deepened. Adil Shah councelled Shahji to be indulgent to Baji Raje, because he had done the deed under royal orders. To put an end to their quarrels, Ghorpade's jagir in the Karnatic was exchanged with Shahji's jagir in the Wai Parganna, so that the Ghorpades would have no cause to fear from Shahji who as Governor of the Karnatic might have troubled them.

25. The burning of Mudhol

Shahji could not forget and forgive the part played by Baji Ghorpade in arresting him. Hence he wrote to his son to be on the lookout for wreaking vengeance on him. The opportunity came only in 1661. The Savants of Savantvadi proposed to the Bijapur Court to co-operate with them in crushing Shivaji. Thereupon troops were sent under Baji Ghorpade and Bahlol Khan to assist the Savants. But before the coufederates could unite, Shivaji first swooped down upon Mudhol, entered the mansion at night, and killed Baji Raje. All his sons, wives, kith and kin whoever fell into his hands were executed. Terrible was the slaughter in the town. After extinguishing the whole family, he desolated the town and plundered the whole territory. Fortunately for Mudhol, one Rani with her son Maloji had gone to her father's house in the north. This young boy was brought back to Bijapur where the King conferred the old ancestral jagirs upon him. Maloji soon after distinguished himself in the service of Bijapur. There is no European document on the Mudhol tragedy, but we have first an important letter to Shahji from Shivaji himself (Appendix) and then the Adil Shahi Firman granted to Maloji wherein his father Baji is described to have died a martyr in the cause of the Kingdom.[1]

---

1. See Persian grant and its translation No 4.

26. Chronology

1623   P. D. Valle visited Ikkeri.

1631–33 Struggle between Timma Raja and the Emperor of Vijayanagar.

1637   Ikkeri captured. Indemnity taken from the ruler.

1638   Virabhadra of Ikkeri rebelled. Bijapur annexed Ikkeri and made the Nayak a vassal.
Sira conquered and given to Kenge Nayak. Bangalore captured and given to Shahji.
The ruler of Shrirangpatam defeated and compelled to give an indemnity.

1639   Basvapattan conquered by Bijapur. Several other towns were plundered.

1642   Accession of Shriranga.

1643   Ikkeri captured by Virabhadra.

1644   Ikkeri and Sagar conquered by Bijapur.

1645   Vellore saved from Mir Jumla.
Treaty between Rayal Shriranga and Rustam Zaman. Capture of Golconda territory. Shriranga defeats southern Nayaks. Mir Jumla captures Udagiri.

1646   Gumti fort captured by Bijapur. Shahji's victory over Jagdeva. Jagdeva's territory and the Kutb Shahi forts were captured by the Bijapur forces.
Vellore again besieged and captured.

1648   Mustafa Khan leads an expedition into the Karnatic. Shahji's victory at Jangam, Ginji invested.
Nayak of Tanjore surrendered to Mir Jumla.
Nayak of Madura invited Bijapur to take Ginji.
Bijapur and Golconda allied themselves against the Hindus. Shahji's threat to leave the siege and his arrest. Mustafa Khan died. Ginji finally fell.

1649   Shahji released.

1651   The Dutch obtained a grant of Tegnapatam from Mir Jumla.

S. 18.

CHAPTER V

SHAHJI IN THE KARNATIC (Cont.)

1. Power of Mir Jumla

The incarceration of Shahji, the fatal illness of Muhammad Adil Shah and the threatening attitude of the Moguls made the Bijapur Court suspend its activities in the Karnatic. On the other hand, Nabob Mir Jumla who had annexed a territory 300 miles long and 50 miles broad, containing many fortresses, strongholds, prosperous ports and rich mines and yeilding an annual revenue of 40 lakhs of hons, had become almost an independent king. He made peace with Shriranga and entered into correspondence with Adil Shah and Aurangzeb for holding this rich kingdom as a fief under their suzerainty. Thus instead of adopting an offensive policy, Mir Jumla was busy consolidating his position. In a letter of 17th January 1651 sent from Fort St. George to the Company, the power and position of this renowned general are thus described by Walter Littleton and Venkata Brahmani who had been sent as envoys to the Nabob.

" The whole kingdom of Gulcunda is governed by him of whome the people stand in feare and subjection unto as to the King himselfe. The revenues that hee yearly brings the King in, amounts unto twentye hundred thousand pagodaes. Alsoe he hath conquered and subjugated the major part of the kingdom of the Carnatta and is on election of all in a short tyme under his government it being the onely country you trade in for matter of all sortes of cloth. There is allsoe bezar, dyamonds, yron, steel, and saltpeter, of which he told us he could make and procure a great quantitie annually. The revenew that he hath taken from the Jentue in the aforesayd country is to the somme of fortie hundred thousand pagodaes per annum. Hee hath of his proper owne foure thousand horse, three hundred elephants, four or five hundred cammels.

and tenn thousand oxen, which transporteth his goods up to severall countryes as Gulcundah, Vizapore (Bijapur) and into dyvers partes of the Great Maguls country, with whome hee is in much favoure, the Great Magull himselfe esteeming and respecting him as a very near man unto him in all which place he hath alwaies his factors and merchants. Concerning forrain–negotiation hee hath trade to Pegue, Tennassaree, Acheen, Rackan (Arakan), Persia, Bengalla, Moka, Peruck, Maldeevaes, and Macassar. He hath ten vessells of his owne and intends to augument them makeing much preparatyon for building of more."[1]

2. Shahji's victory over Mir Jumla in 1651-52

The kings of Bijapur and Golconda could not agree with regard to the division of the Karnatic, hence a war broke out at the end of 1651. The rout of Mir Jumla is referred to in a Fort St. George letter of January 1652.

" Warrs being commenced betweene the Moors of Gulcondah and Vizapore, who, haveing shared this afflicted kingdome, are now bandying against each other, whilst the poore Jentue hopeing their mutuall destruction watches oppertunity to breake off his present miserable yoke. In the interim many bickerings have bin within two daies journey of this place and ' tis reported that the Nabob with his whole armey is besieged among the hills of Gulcondah whither hee retired for the more safety, by the Vizaporians; which hath soe distracted this country that wee could not adventure your monies abroad without too much hazard."[2]

There is no mention of Shahji in this despatch, but Jairama has given a vivid description of the crushing defeat sustained by Mir Jumla who was considered to be the richest grandee and the greatest general of his time. Such a proud and powerful noble was compelled to buy peace by paying down 6 or 9 lakh pagodas to Shahji. This brilliant victory exhibited his martial genius, spread his fame throughout India and immensely enhanced his prestige in the Bijapur Court.

1. O. C. 2199. 17 January 1651.
2. E. F. 1651-54. P. 99. O. C. 2246. January 1652.

This success gave a new vigour to the campaigns of Bijapur. Shahji and Ikhlas Khan advanced against Shriranga and defeated him at Jankal. Their forces captured the important fortress of Penugonda which had been the capital of Vijayanagar for many years.It was natural that the loss should have greatly alarmed the Hindu Rajas.

3. Shriranga in the field

It has been seen that Shriranga Rayal of Vijayanagar, having lost his eastern possessions and Penugonda in particular, had sought refuge in the territory of Mysore. After 1650, he was attempting to form a confederacy against the Muslim conquerors. The opportunity came to him when Prince Aurangzeb was appointed as Viceroy of the Deccan in 1653. He sent his agent Ramrao to the Prince for asking protection against the Deccani Sultans, but Aurangzeb did not like to save a Hindu King from the onslaughts of the Muslims. Shriranga was not disheartened by this disappointment. With the help of the Mysore army alone, he reconquered a part of his territory and even regained Vellore from the Bijapurians. The latter once more invested the fort, and after a long siege captured it. Then a treaty was concluded with the Rayal by which Chandragiri with the revenue of certain districts was left to him.[2] Even the Golconda army was repulsed by the Rayal, but he was soon betrayed by the treacherous Nayak of Madura who opened the passes to the combined Muslim armies against Mysore. [3] Shriranga was routed and compelled to seek refuge in the forests where he led a miserable life.

1. O. C. 2257. 12 February 1652. Radha Madhav Vilas Champu, pp. 92-93, 96.

2. Dutch Records, Transcripts, Series i, Vol. XIX, no. 550 (i). The issue of all this is told in a letter from Batavia of November 7, 1654 which states that the Bijapur general had, after a long siege, captured Vellore and concluded a treaty with the Raja by which Chandragiri was left to the latter, with the revenues of certain districts (ibid., no. 551).

3. The Nayaks of Madura, p. 267,

It appears that he lost even Chandragiri and Chingalpat to the forces of Golconda, and hence ultimately sought [1] the protection of Shivappa Nayak of Bednur. The latter gave him the government of Belur and Sakkarepatana, and even adventured to besiege Shrirangpatam in his behalf to punish the Raja for not espousing the cause of the Emperor. But in this war Shivappa was defeated. Hereafter the Emperor could not be restored to his eastern possessions which had finally fallen into the hands of the Muslims.

Proenza has truly remarked that the Emperor was made unhappy by the folly of his vassals, though his personal qualities rendered him worthy of a better fate. Even in this campaign large contributions were raised by the Muslim invaders from the short-sighted Nayaks of Madura and Tanjore, and the Khan-i-Khanan returned to Bijapur full of riches.

The war of the noses

Soon after the departure of the enemy, Kantirava Narasa Raja of Mysore poured forth his hordes into the kingdom of Madura for wreaking vengeance by plunder and devastation. The district of Satyamangalam fell into his hands, yet most barbaric outrages were perpetrated on the inhabitants. Trichnopoly, the capital of Madura, was saved only by the intrepidity of the Maravas. This war was characterized with an inhuman [2] cruelty and passionate revenge. Both the armies took delight in disfiguring the people by cutting off their noses. On account of its notorious barbarity in this respect, it is known as ' the War of the Noses.'

In the meantime, Shriranga was anxious to save the remnants of his Empire through the assistance of Aurangzeb. He offered him very tempting presents and a large tribute,

---

1. The Mysore Gaz. puts the flight of the Emperor to Belur in 1646, but it should be put in 1656 or so.

2. The Nayaks of Madura, p. 136 n.; J. H. Grose, A Voyage to the East Indies, p. 247; J. T. Wheeler, Madras in the Olden Time, I, p, 104.

and even promised to turn Muslim with all his relatives and dependents, provided he could save his remaining Kingdom from the Deccani Sultans. Aurangzeb sent his ambassador to give him protection, but really he was to extort presents from the Rayal and the Sultans. In fact, Shriranga was left to his own fate. 'This episode,' says Sarkar, 'proves that the Mogul Empire was only a thinly veiled system of brigandage.'[1]

Shriranga Rayal was not the man to be easily disheartened. He put up a most stubborn resistence to the advance of his enemies. Sphinx–like he rose up again and again from his ruins to face the Muslims. In November 1656 he was seen besieging Pulicat which was under Mir Jumla. It appears from the Dutch Records that Koneri Chetti, the general of Shriranga, who was carrying operations near Pulicat, betrayed his master and went over to T. Krishnappa, the lieutenant of Mir Jumla. Strengthened with this defection, the latter was able to score a victory[2] over Shriranga in September 1657. Later on, there was a war between the forces of Golconda and of Mir Jumla under T. Krishnappa for the possession of the Karnatic.[3]

4. Situation in the Deccan

For four years of 1654–58, there was no serious war in the Karnatic, because Golconda was first weakened by the revolt and defection of Mir Jumla and then sacked and devastated by the Moguls. The miseries of the people of the Karnatic and the result of the rebellion of Nabob Mir Jumla are depicted in a letter of 18th September 1654.

"It hath been no small miserye that this poore heatheen country hath suffered any tyme these ten years almost, since the Moores of Vizapore on one side and those of Gulcondah on the other side first made inroads upon it. And now, when wee hoped all would have beene put in some good posture of government, to continue still those miseries

1. Sarkar, Aurangzeb, I, p. 251; Ruqat-Alamgir. Pp. 150–57.
2. E. F, 1655-60, pp. 97–99.   3. E. F. 1655-60, p. 176.

(or rather to adde a greater burthen to it) our Nabob (Mir
Jumla) is lately up in armes against the King of Gulcondah
his master, whose commands hee slighted intending (soe
farre as is conceived) to keepe what part of the country
hee hath conquered to himselfe; which he can accomplish,
hee will soone bee as great a king as his master, and his
yearly revenew little inferriour [1] to it. What the issue to
these things wilbee the Almighty only knoweth; in the
meane tyme wee that live here amongst them shalbe sure
never to want troubles on every side." [2]

Similarly, Bijapur was in the agonies of a revolution
brought about by the death of Muhammad Adil Shah on
4th November 1656, the succession of Ali, a youth of 18
years, the revolt of many polygars in the Karnatic, and the
mutual discords among the courtiers corrupted as they were
with the gold of Aurangzeb. In 1657 the latter declared an
unjust war to annex the kingdom from the boy-king. The
impregnable fortresses of Bidar and Kalyani were captured,
and even Bijapur was invested. It would have soon fallen
into his hands, had he not been peremtorily called back
by Shah Jahan. Still the King of Bijapur agreed to pay an
indemnity of 1½ krores of rupees, to cede Bidar, Kalyani,
and also Parenda with all its territory, all the forts in the
Nizam Shahi Konkan, and the district of Wangi. This treaty
of 1657 very much reduced the power of Bijapur, though its
independence was not effected.

5. The last ten years of Shahji.

Shahji had regained the confidence of Muhammad Adil
Shah as is borne out by a Portuguese letter of 16 April 1654.

" The persons acceptable to the King Idalxa and according
to his belief loyal to him are Fatecan, Xagi (Shahji) and
Meliqne Acute[3] (Malik Yaqut)" ...

1. Mir Jumla continued to stay in the Karnatic up to July 1656. E. F,
1655-60, p. 91,
2, O. C, 2419, 18th September 1654.
3. Pissurlenkar, Shvaji, p, 33.

Shahji, as Governor of the Karnatic, was engaged in the difficult task of subduing the refractory Polygars during the revolutionary period. The polygar of Kanakgiri revolted against the authority of Bijapur. Thereupon Afzal Khan was sent from the capital and Sambhaji marched from Bangalore for the reduction of the rebel. During the siege operations Sambhaji was shot dead by a cannon-ball. Thereupon Shahji himself proceeded to take revenge of his son's death and brought the place and the polygar to submission.

He blamed Afzal Khan for not supporting his son, and thus their enmity was still more deepened.[1] In 1658 Ekoji was sent to capture the country round Shri Shail Malikarjuna. In his company was poet Jairama who has described the successful operations of this expendition.

The Nayak of Madura, Muttu Virappa, threw off the Muslim yoke by refusing to pay the tribute, fortifying Trichinopoly and by making vigorous preparations for resisting the Muslim armies. Shahji won over the Nayak of Tanjore to the side of Bijapur against Madura. The Adil Shahi troops rapidly advanced under Shahji and Mulla Mahammad up to the very gates of Trichinopoly, but being terrified by the preparations of the Nayak of Madura, they unexpectedly fell upon Tanjore itself on 19th March 1659. The fort was most heroically defended by the Kshatriya warriors called Rajas, and they preferred a glorious death to a dishonourable life. The victorious army of Shahji proceeded southward, captured Mannarkovil and Vallamkottai. This hill-fort situated on a steep rock with high ramparts and erected with incredible expense, labour and art, was the last refuge of the Nayak, but on the approach of the enemy, the coward ruler fled away to the

---

1. Radha-Madhav Vilas Champu, P. 93. Rajwade places Sambhaji's death in 1655. There is no confirmatory evidence. Sambhaji left a son whose grants of the years 1665 and 1666 are quoted by Wilks. After this nothing can be traced of his line.

Fort of Jinji.

Vellor Fort.

forests. 'The Muslims have already been for several months,' writes Proenza, ' in possession of this beautiful and fertile country, no one knows now what their ulterior designs are, whether they will establish themselves there, or will content themselves with collecting the riches they can find there.'[1]

Soon after a terrible famine and a fatal pestilence increased the mortality among the people and Bijapur forces. A second attempt to capture Trichinopoly failed, and hence Mulla retreated after receiving a moderate tribute from the Madura Nayak.

Muttu died soon after his victory and was succeeded by Chokanatha Nayak in 1660. This energetic prince reversed the policy of Tirumal and made preparations for the restoration of the Vijayanagar dynasty to its former glory and for the conquest of Ginge from Bijapur. A triple alliance was made among the Nayaks of Tanjore, Madura and Gingi. In 1662 the Madura Commander, Lingama Nayak led an army of 40,000 men to drive Shahji from Ginji, but the Madura ministers were so bought up by Shahji as to hatch a plot to dethrone the young Nayak. The Nayak of Tanjore was also separated from the alliance. Chokanatha still proved more than a match for them. One of the treacherous ministers was murdered, another blinded, but the third Lingama joined Shahji and brought him to invest Trichinopoly. Even the new commander of Chokanatha's army was corrupted by Shahji. Thereupon the young King, though betrayed a second time, boldly assumed the command of his forces. His boldness electrified the soldiers. They fought with the courage of despair. Shahji, seeing no chances of success, withdrew to Tanjore. After sometime, Chokanatha followed him there with a well-disciplined army of more than 70,000 warriors. Thereupon Shahji returned to Ginji and the Nayak of Tanjore made an abject surrender to the Madura ruler.

1. The Nayaks of Madura. P. 272,

S. 19.

6. Tegenapatam captured by Shahji (1661)

The people of Shahji laid siege to the town of Tegenapatam on 15th December 1660 with the result that the Dutch Company's business was at a standstill there, but the residents hoped nevertheless to have 200 bales of carpets ready for Batavia about the middle of February, 1662.

" We further note from the letter of Governor Pit written to Seylon (which we have already mentioned several times before) that *Sahagie's* men have looted the town Carcal a few days before the letter was closed and that they had robbed the inhabitants of not less than 1,700 pardaux. Although he was short of cash, the Governor has sent 3,000 pardaux to Negapatnam to pay the garrison there.

The war round the fort Tegenapatnam is finished and the fort has been delivered to Sahagie's men on the 4th February 1661, so that Tegenepatnam and the premises of the Company there are now under the command of Sahagie. This looks serious, but the Governor does not believe that he will trouble us, because he is aware that the Company can rely on the strong forces at Porto Novo, which would make his profits useless. It would be possible to transfer the trade to Poolesere (Phulchari or Pondichery), about 4 miles from Tegenapatnam, and to leave the premises at Tegenapatnam under the supervision of an assistant and 3 or 4 soldiers, but the merchants would not dare come out of fear for Sahagie; and Kistapaneyak, (Krishnappa Nayak) who is an upper-regent of Poolesere on behalf of Mir Jumla, would not be able to protect us against him, so that discharging cargo at Paelesere would only cause trouble to the Company, " [1]

7. Porto Novo taken by Shahji

By October 1661 Shahji was successful in capturing Porto Novo and it was made the base of his depredations into Tanjore.[2] Shahji's policy was to bring the port towns into his

1. Dagh-Register, 1661. P. 126 16 May 1661. Even in Aug. 1654 a Farman was obtained from the Sultan of Bijapur for Dutch privileges at Tegenapatam and the neighbouring ports. Hague Transcriptions, series I, Vol. 18, Nos. 550, 551, 556-7.

2. E. F. 1661-1664, pp. 50-51.

possession and thus carry the Bijapur flag to the extreme east. All those ports were under Mir Jumla before, but the desertion of that general to the Moguls created an interregnum, The King of Golconda claimed all the parts governed by Mir Jumla as his own, and hence sent his agents for ousting the men of the latter. On the other hand, Aurangzeb ordered Qutb Shah to recall his officers from the Karnatic. The latter were extremely loth to yield these rich towns. Qutb Shah was often rebuked and threatened for his double-dealing. It was only after Aurangzeb had firmly seated himself on the throne of Delhi that he could enforce the surrender of the Karnatic.[1] During this period of confusion, Shahji saw an opportunity to extend his power, and he siezed as many places as he could.

8. The capture of Tegenapatam and after

The details of the war with Madura and Tanjore are given in the following Dutch letters:—

" After spending a short time in his capital, the Neyck of Tansjouwer has left it again and has placed himself under the protection of the Nayak of Madura in the fortress of Siretenapalle (Trichinopoly). And after these two rulers had made an alliance, the commander Lingamaneyk has proceeded in the end of June with an army of 40 thousand footmen and 2000 horsemen to Sillenbron, 2 miles south of Porto Novo, where Shahgie was lying in camp and daily robbed the province of Tansjouwer. Before taking up the arms, Lingamaneyk tried to have a conference with him, but seeing that he was short of water, he drove him out from there and from several other castles into the interior. The robber therefore retired to his strong fortress of Arni. The young Amberchan or his tutor Antosie Plontele who is still staying in the capital Singier (Ginji) has promised to deliver the castle Arni to the Nayak of Madura, if Shahgie is driven out from there. If this could be done, the bigger part of the province Singier would be freed of the Visiapour Moors. The castle of Tegenepatnam which is also occupied

1. Sarkar, Aurangzeb I, pp. 146–47.

by Sahagie's men has so far been left alone by Lingamaneyk, because he had to follow up Sahagie closely. In the meantime he has written to Governor Pit that as soon as he has driven out Sahagie, he will send forces to Tegenepatnam to release the son of the Nayak of Tansjouwer and two other sons of two Gentu nobles who are being kept there as hostages by Sahagie's men. He promises that he will see to it that our people residing there will not be troubled by the soldiers.

On the other hand, the Governor is afraid that the Moors if they see an army marching against them will pilfer the premises of the Company, especially as they keep a "Champan" ready either to flee if necessary or to abduct the said hostages. Therefore the galleon "Tayoan" will remain for some time in front of Tegenepatnam to safeguard the capital which the Company has got there.

It is apparent that the Ruler of Tansjouwer when he will have completely recovered, will not drop his claim of the balance of the present, although he has not reminded Governor Pit since January last.

Mr. Ranvel Kistapaneyk, ex-regent of Paelesera, has joined *Sahagie*, but has afterwards left him again and has gone into the forest behind Tegenepatnam, however without joining either of the parties. Therefore the proposal made before to transfer the office of the Company from Tegenepatnam to Poelesera is automatically cancelled, For as long as the Jentus remain masters in the Sigier province and when they have taken the castle of Tegenepatnam, it is best that the residency remains at Tegenepatnam, especiatlly because there is no Government at Poelesera which could protect the Company against possible looting or violence from outside the town.

As soon as *Sahagie* had been driven back into the interior, people at once noticed more activity in the trade, at Tegenepatnam. The cloths have since been in better supply, On the other hand, the war between Lingamaneyk against Sahagie has caused such a panic in Porto Novo that the leading inhabitants of the country have fled and are staying on the ships, so that perhaps this year nothing will be sent from there to other places. Governor Pit has therefore not been asked yet for passports from Porto Novo to Malacca, Queda and Achin, except by Armocta Chitti for his ship which will sail to Malacca and which passport we shall give him, provided he first pays the Company the value of the goods taken from the stranded jollyboat which he had readily bought from the robbers. The said jolly-boat has got in the sand on the Colleroon riff so badly that nothing can be saved from her anymore. And of the fair things that have been saved, Sahagie would only give 56 pieces of canvas cover, some cooking pots and some lamps." [1]

9. The war between Shahji and Lingama Nayak

" The Commander Lingamaneyk, mentioned above, has not made so much progress against Sahagie, as was expected in the beginning. He and his army were led round the whole province of Singier by the cavalry of Sahagie, so that, not being able to pursue him close enough, he had returned in the end to take the castle of Tegenepatnam. But when he had approached to the ditch, Sahagie appeared with 8,000 horsemen and cut off the communications of his enemy, so that Lingamaneyk was forced to break up the siege and to resist Sahagie. But later on, on the 2nd September the two parties made an agreement that Sahagie would retain the countries which he has possessed before, viz., Porto Novo and Tegenapatnam till further orders from the king of Visiapore and that he would no longer do any damage in the countries of Tanasjouwer and Madura; and that he would release the son of the Neyk of Tansjouwer, provided the father would pay 50 thousand Rials. The Neyks of Tansjouwer and Madura who were displeased with this contract imprisoned Lingamaneyk in the castle Tritsienapille (Trichinopoly.) with the intentions of making further war against Sahagie. But after thinking matters over, the Neyk of Madura released him and gave him nice presents. The Neyk of Tansjouwer joined in this, the contract was confirmed and until further confirmation it was arranged that the Neyk of Tansjouwer would marry the daughter of Lingamaneyk and that Lingamaneyk would

1. Dagh-Register 1661. P. 320. 18 October 1661.

marry the sister of the Neyk. Whereupon Lingamaneyk
went to his master, the Neyk of Madura and left his servant
behind with 3000 men to receive the said 50 thousand Rials.
But afterwards he received a letter from Antosie Pontele
that Sahagie would not wait for the money any longer and had
therefore broken the contract. This meant that they were
again up against each other. Before Lingamaneyk had
come near the castle Tegenepatnam, the men from the
castle had been twice in Porto Novo, had looted the town
and driven the inhabitants into the country and dispersed
them. Seeing how many troubles the Company had to go
through in this heavy war, Governor Pit had ordered
the residents that they would embark with the valuable
merchantdise in the gallot Tayoan which was lying in the
roadstead for that purpose, and that if the troubles would
not have ceased on the 25th September they should go to
Palleacatte, leaving the premises for a short time under
protection of the Company's soldiers. But if peace had
been concluded, this would not been necessary. They had
already loaded some of the merchandise in the said Gallot,
but had unloaded it again. Sahagie is very much satisfied
that we have remained neutral in this affair." [1]

10. Bahlolkhan's raid in Tanjore

A brief account is recorded in a Dutch letter. "Balbulachan
keeps his Visiapore army ready to cross the river Colleron
into Tansiower. An advance of 2000 horsemen invaded
this country already and carried off many men and cattle,
but they were driven back over the said river by Lingamaneyk who is now commander-in-chief of the Neyck of
Tansiower. The Neyck of Madura is on the alert, but is
not much concerned over the difficulties of his neighbour.
And the trade of Tegenepatnam having been very bad for
the last 6 or 7 months and the merchants having left
the town during the siege in order not be robbed by
the chief of the Visiapores, who has taken the castle of
Tegenepatnam. " [2]

1. Dagh-Register 1661. P. 404. 30th November 1661.
2, „ „ 1663. P. 109. 31st March 1663.

11. War between Tanjore and Madura

The payment of the subsidy to Shahji gave rise to complications which ended in a war between the allies. The details of this war are to be found in the Dagh–Register.

" Let us start with Tegenaptnam. On page 147 we mentioned already that the Visiapore commander-in-chief had come to an agreement with the Neyk of Tansiower, whereby it was arranged that the Neyk should pay 300 thousand pardaux to the commander-in-chief. From the letter of 23rd March written by Governor Pit to Mr. Van Goens which we received along with the enclosures, it appears that the said commander-in-chief died and that his son called Nirnemya has succeeded him. The contract drawn up by the Neyks of Tansiower and Madura on one side and the Commander of the Visiapore on the other side provides for a payment of 9 lakhs pardaux, out of which the Neyk of Madura has to pay 6 and the Neyk of Tansiower 3. It further appears that a dispute had arisen between the castle–keepers of Tegenapatnam and Singier and that the one of Singier with 200 horsemen and 400 footmen raided and looted the town of Tegenapatnam about the middle of March, but that the quarters of the Company and the houses of the native merchants with whom the Company were doing business were left unharmed. It is further mentioned in the letter that the said Commander of Bisiapore seeing that the Neyks mentioned above were rather slow in paying off the tribute has turned back and has made an agreement with the robber Sahagie, whereby the place Tegenapatnam, Porto Novo and others will be delivered to Sahagie and that they will both turn their arms against the above–mentioned Neyks especially against the Neyk of Madura, The said contract with the Neyks has thereupon been broken and the castle Tritsenepilly, (Trichinopoly) being one of the bigger towns in the country of Madura is under siege. The Neyk of Madura shows much courage against the invaders, but the Neyk of Tansiower keeps idle and feeds the Visiapore army now and then with 40 or 50 thousand pardaux. In the meantime our residents in Tegenapatnam have received orders to be on the alert and the Company keeps a big (boat) ready to keep the silver, the money and valuables in safety. " [1]

" The Visiapore Commander, Babbulachan (Bahlol Khan) ordered by the King of Visiapore to make war in the country of Canara, has already proceeded there. " [2]

" In the province of Tansiower there is again a dispute going on between the Neyks of Tansiower and Madura about the payment of 500 thousand pardaux to the Commander of Visiapore, the Neyk of Madura pretending that he paid more than was due by him. As the Neyk of Tansiower is not willing to contribute anything, the Neyk of Madura has crossed the river Colleroon with a fairly big army and marched to the capital Tansiower. As regards the town and fortress of Nagapatnam, the Governor has made a proposal to reduce the defence-works." [3]

" In the sourthern districts everything remains as it is. The war between the Neyks of Tansiower and Madura is not yet finished and the first mentioned Neyk is being besieged in his capital by his enemy." [4]

" The Neyk of Tansjouwer has closed peace with the Neyk of Madura at the price of 500,000 pardeaux which is a big sum of money. And therefore he has asked the Company to lend him some money, offering to give some addeas or villages as security, but the Governor has declined it. The said Neyk had also asked for payment of the tax of the villages, as half the toll, etc. Although he asked 3,000 pagodas, the Governor has promised to pay 1,000 pagodas for the last 2 years, this being the bigger half, we fixed so high with a view to the present difficulties of the Neyk. The Governor has made a certain proposal to the Neyk regarding the town of Negapatam and if the Neyk agrees, he expects that the Company will get good accommodation and will also benefit otherwise, but he is of opinion that it will not come off. The merchants of the Company are now

1,   Dagh-Register 1663. P. 365. 31 July 1663.
2.   •   „   P. 447. 13 September 1663.
3.   „   „   1661. P. 433. 9th October 1663.
4.   „   „   P. 549, 14th November 1663.

idle there.   Lingamaneyk has joined the forces of the Madurese.   The regents in Tegenepatnam with whom we have got to deal, are not doing well.   Anatchan has thrice been deposed from the governorship and everytime he has been reinstated, but last time the deposition was final.   Our people had made a contract with him for 5 years for the lease of the revenues of the town Tegenepatnam at the price of 2,700 pardaux a year, but the next day he cancelled the contract again, because he had a dream foreboding evil, which dream proved to be quite true, because the king of Visiapour who was staying only 15 days journey from there, had deposed him for the third time." [1]

" The armies of Visiapore had almost completely chased the Neyck of Canara, but now they had concluded peace with him again." [2]

" The Neyk of Madura is at war with the Tenver, but it looks as if it will be over soon.   The country of Madura extends further than people would think.   The profit at Tuticurin amounts to 22, 916 guilders." [3]

" Ali Adelsiah, King of Visiapour, has invaded the country of Canara with his army and has already practically conquered it.   But being out mostly for booty, he has arranged with the Neyk that the conquered countries would be given back to him on condition that he would pay the said King 1, 500 thousand pagodes of 5 guilders each. And the said Majesty has therefore returned to Visiapour triumphantly in January last." [4]

" The advices from Canara mention that the Badrapaneyk has been poisoned and that his brother, a child of 8 years, has succeeded him.   On account of the lack of prestige big quarrels and feuds have started amongst the nobles, in which the Court merchant Narna Malse has been wounded." [5]

" It was further reported that the ruler of Visiapour came down to Canara again and that a few nobles at the Court of Bidnur had conspired to deliver the country to that ruler." [6]

1. Dagh-Register 1664. P. 154. 12 May 1664.
2.   „   „   „   P. 147. 12 May 1664.
3.   „   „   „   P. 205. 17 May 1664.
4.   „   „   „   P, 322. 13 August 1664.
5-6. „   „   „   P. 325. 13 August 1664.
S. 20.

12. Horrible consequences of the war

The country, however, terribly suffered from the cruelties committed by the Bijapurian army and the desolation universally wrought by them. Hundreds of people were sold as slaves by the Dutch, and thousands were carried away by famine and pestilence. The people could hardly get a breathing time when in 1663 the tide of Muslim deluge once more advanced under Vanamian, the most valiant captain of Ali Adil Shah, and laid siege to Trichinopoly.

" The general of the enemy tried at first to frighten the king by his threats and show of power; seeing that he gained nothing by these methods, he successively delivered several attacks, and was constantly repulsed with loss by the artillery of the fort. But, by his attacks, he destroyed all the suburbs. After making fruitless attempts against the citadel, the besiegers broke out on the country, devastated the harvest, burnt the villages, and captured the inhabitants to be made slaves. It is impossible to describe the scenes of horror which then enveloped this unhappy country. The Indian nobility, thinking it infamy to fall into the hands of these despicable beings, did not fear to seek refuge in death, less frightful, in their eyes, than such a dishonour. A large number, after slaying their women and children, plunged the sword into their own bodies and fell on their corpses. Entire populations were seen resorting to this tragic death. In other villages the inhabitants gathered together in several houses, to which they set fire and perished in the flames."[1]

The result of the conquest and occupation of the country by Bijapur is recorded by an eye-witness in these words:—

" But nothing can equal the cruelties which the Muhammadans employ in the government of Gingi; expression fails me to recount the atrocities which I have seen with my eyes; and if I were to describe them, truth would be incredible. To the present horror are added the fears of what is to happen; for it is announced that Idel Khan sends a strong army to raise the contributions, which the Nayaks had promised, by force.[2]

1. The Nayaks of Madura. P. 276.
2.   „   „   „   „   P. 279.

13. Second rebellion and imprisonment of Shahji

From the Dagh-Register it appears that Shahji made an effort of becoming independent in the Karnatic in 1659-60.

" The Neyk of Tansjouwer had returned to his capital Tansjouwer, and had demanded the remaining donation from our men residing at Negapatnam, but they courteously refused. Afterwards news arrived that the Neyks of Madure, Tansjouwer and Lingamaneyk had concluded a treaty with the rebellious chiefs of Visiapour, Sahagie and Anthosie Pantoelooe (Antoji Pantole), to help each other against any force from outside. So that he (the Nayak of Tanjore) will probably grow to be stronger." [1]

It appears that the extraordinary success of his son in despatching Afzal Khan and a large part of his army to the other world, created the belief in Shahji that the Adil Shahi Kingdom was drawing to its end and that he could sound its death-knell by first declaring his independence in the Karnatic and then by capturing the metropolis itself. Thus both Shivaji and Shahji were to lead their armies for the siege of Bijapur. Revington's letter from Kolhapur to the Company dated 10th December 1659, contains the significant news that " One months tyme more will, wee believe, put an end to his trouble; for Sevagyes father, Shawjee, that lyes to the southward is expected within eight dayes with his army consisting of 17, 000 men, and then they intend for Vizapore (Bijapur), the King and Queenes residence, whose strength consists onely in men and they are not above 10, 000 souldyers; so that in all probability the kingdome will be lost." [2] Though Shahji was not successful in invading Bijapur, he seems to have maintained his independence up to 1663, as is evident from the two succeeding documents.

" The Neyks of Madura and Tansjouwer and the commander *Sahagie*, Antosie Pantele and Lingamaneyk have

---

1. Dagh-Register 1661. P. 40.
2. Shivaji The Great Vol. 1, 53.

met to conclude an offensive and defensive contract, which is a serious thing to us. And therefore the Governor has excused the intended visit of the Masulepatnam settlement. But afterwards the Governor was informed that the contract mentioned above had been cancelled and that the Neyks had secretly conferred to attack Sahagie." [1]

It appears that Bahlol Khan of Bankapur was deputed by the King to put down the rebellion of Shahji and to take possession of the countries conquered by him. The latter was to be dislodged from his strongholds of Arni and Bangalore.

" The said residents further advice that the Neyk of Tansiower had come to an agreement with Balbulachan, the commander-in-chief of Visiapore whereby he promised to pay 300 thousand pardaux. And the said commander-in chief will now proceed to the fortresses Arny and Wingeloer (Bangalore) against the rebel Sahagie." [2]

An astute diplomat like Shahji won over the Bijapur commander to his side. The King was fear-stricken at the approach of Shaista Khan's army and left his capital for taking refuge in Bancapur. At such a critical time both Shahji and Bahlol Khan were to be pardoned for their crimes of treason, but when they came to wait upon the king, they were arrested and put in chains.

This rebellion of Shahji is confirmed by an English letter of 20th July 1663 sent from Goa. Bahlol Khan and Shahji were both imprisoned near Bancapur. ' This Jassud (spy) sweares before he came out of Bunckapore he saw irons put on Bussall Ckan and Shagee (Shahji) but taken off of the latter in two dayes: who is now with the King without any command.' [3] The detailed account is given on P. 95 of Part II of this volume. Shahji seems to have been won over by the King and restored to the Governorship of the Karnatic. While he was luckily restored to his

---

1. Dagh-Register 1661. P. 126. 16 May 1661.
2.   ,,   ,,   1663. P. 147, 11 April 1663.
3. Shivaji The Great, Vol. I, 95.

former dignities and estates, Bahlol Khan was murdered by order of the King. The Maharaja did not live long to peacefully enjoy the vicerolyalty of the kingdom of the Karnatic. In 1664 he joined the Bijapur army for assisting it in reducing some refractory polygars in the Shimoga District. He had a serious fall from his horse while he was hunting near Basvapatan on the bank of the Tungbhadra. Here on 23 January 1664 at the age of 63 an active and useful life was suddenly cut short.[1] At his death he governed a territory which included at least Bangalore, Balapur, Kolar, Nandi, Basvapatan, Arni, Gingi, Tegenapatam, Huskota, and Porto Novo in Tanjore. In all these places he was succeeded by his youngest son Vyankoji as Jagirdar and Governor. The latter was also the fortunate possessor of the personal property of his father in the Karnatic. In a few years by his valour and diplomacy he added the kingdom of Tanjore to his possessions.

14. Shivaji, an independent King

Shahji's dream of the establishment of Swarajya by his son was realized before his death and it was fortunate that he himself was the instrument of putting a seal upon his independence. The young king Ali was much distressed by the lightning blows dealt by Shivaji in the Konkan, by the rebellion of his father Shahji and of Bhadrappa Nayak of Bednur, and the insurgence of the Muslim lords like Siddi Jauhar, Siddi Yaqut, Siddi Masud and Bahlol Khan. The rebellion of all these nobles was put down after much bloodshed, but Shivaji was too strong for Ali. In that situation he was mortally afraid of Aurangzeb who was sure to find one excuse or another for pouncing upon Bijapur. To bring peace to the distracted land, a secret treaty was made with Shivaji by which his independence was acknowledged by the Bijapur

1. Jedhe Ch.

King, the whole country of Konkan[1] and a long strip of territory in the Deccan were ceded to him, and his ambassador, was permitted to stay at the capital. Shivaji agreed not to molest Bijapur any more. The Marathi chronicles record that he was to be given an annual subsidy of seven lakh huns. The Dutch Diary gives a different version: "Siwasi has made a present to His Majesty of 30 thousand pagodas, 2 elephants and 80 beautiful horses. He asked thereby to slacken the war against him a little. He advised the king with many persuasive words to revolt against the Mogol and offered him 30 thousand pagodas yearly if he would do that. They say that a more close and secret alliance has been made between those two rulers. And many say that the king cannot go on pretending any longer and that he would rather draw sword against Eurengxeeb than against Siwasi."[2] Shivaji was no longer a jagirdar of Bijapur, but an independent sovereign who, on a basis of equality, entered into a compact with his erstwhile suzerain.

15. Interview of father and son

The Bakhars assert that Shahji was deputed by Ali Adil Shah to confirm the treaty and counsel his son to keep peace in the Kingdom. Shahji had not visited his jagir and worshipped his family gods for the last twenty-five years. He jumped at the opportunity afforded him by his sovereign to see with his own eyes the work of the wonderful

1. This term is confirmed by a Rajapur letter of 6th February 1663 to Surat (Shivaji The Great Vol. I, p. 150; Basatin-i-Salatin, p. 302). Tal Konkan was given to Shivaji before August 1661. P. S. S. No. 857. This treaty is said to be concluded in 1662, but it is most unlikely Shivaji surprised Shaista Khan on 5th April and by the middle of that month he started for the conquest of Kudal and Vingurla. He is not expected to declare war after a few months of the conclusion of the treaty. I should prefer the end of 1663 as the time of the treaty.

2. Shivaji The Great, Vol. I, pp. 115-16.

Fort of Daulatabad

Fort of Burhanpur

Interview of Father and Son

exploits of his famous son.[1]   He proceeded to Poona with
his second wife Tukabai and her son Vyankoji. On the
way he visited the sacred places of pilgrimage like Tuljapur,
Shingnapur, Pandharpur and Jejuri. At the last place he
was received by his son with great humility and royal
pomp. We are told that Shivaji prostrated himself at Shahji's
feet, that he held his father's slippers in his hands and
walked by the side of the palanquin wherein Shahji was
being taken to Shivaji's camp, and that in the levee
subsequently held, the father was seated on the divan,
but the son stood reverently with folded hands and frequently
asked forgiveness for the troubles given by him to his
father. Moved with emotion at the touching scenes of
filial love, humility and reverence, Shahji joyfully praised
the glorious deeds of his son and showered blessings upon
him for his future success. The four months of the
rainy season were spent in a round of festivities at Poona.
Then Shahji was taken to all the important fortresses
like Sinhagad, Purandhar, Rajgad, Rairi, Torna, Pratapgad,
Panhala, Vishalgad, Rangna. The experienced general and
ripe administrator like Shahji advised Shivaji to select
Rairi as his capital. This high hill surrounded on every side
by a sea of mountains, bids defiance to all the world.
From the top of this everlasting mountain he could challenge
the Empires of Bijapur and Delhi and say— " this rock shall
fly from its base as soon as I." [2]

"Shahji, highly gratified, returned to Bijapur, the bearer
of presents from Shivajee to the King, and, what strengthens

---

1. Sh. Dig. 200-204; Takakhav, 204-212.

It is worth noticing that the Basatin-i-Salatin, Shivabharat, Jedhe
Chronology, Jedhe Karina, Tarikh-i-Shivaji, Rairi, 91 Q. Bakhar, do not
mention the fact of Shahji's visit to his son in 1663. We must wait for a
confirmatory evidence of the statement of the Bakhars. Shahji's visit is tradi-
tionally placed in 1662. Then Chakan and Poona were in the hands of
Shaistakhan, and Shivaji was engaged in a life and death struggle with him.
Hence 1663 has been preferred by me.

2. Shivaji The Great Vol. II, pp. 1-2.

the supposition of Shajee's having been the mediator,
hostilities from that time were suspended between Sivajee
and Beejapoor during the life of Shahjee; nor, when they
were renewed, was Sivajee the aggressor."[1]

16. Shahji at Bangalore

The prosperous city of Bangalore was defended by a
deep moat, strong ramparts, and high towers adorned
with numerous cannon, and was well-guarded by a large
army.   The capital presented a very beautiful sight with
its stately mansions, lofty and superb temples, lovely groves
and green bowers in its exquisitely laid gardens, numerous
tanks, broad streets and everflowing fountains. The painted
walls in the palaces were designed with wonderous art.
Such a poetic description savours of exaggeration, yet it is
literally true of modern Bangalore, the Paris of India, and
may give us a real picture of the city under its popular
ruler Kemp Gauda and under an experienced administrator
like Shahji.[2] It was the capital of the Bijapur Karnatic
for a generation under Shahji.

Living in such a charming place, the Raja used to spend
his time in hunting, military exercises, in visiting armouries
and magazines, in reviewing troops, in singing, dancing
and flirting with beautiful damsels; nay, even in visiting
Sadhus, studying books aud performing meditative practices.
Both Shahji and Shah Jahan gave themselves up to a life
of ease, amusement, even of voluptuous luxury after 1637,
though each of them had led a very hard and sturdy life
before that year.

17. Shahji's work in the Karnatic

Shahji was appointed to govern the districts subdued
by the Bijapur forces in Karnatic and Dravida, named

---

1. G. Duff. P. 85.
2. Sh. Bh.; Mysore and Coorg Gaz. Pp. 21-22.

Bijapurian Karnatic. His jagir included Bangalore,[1] Kolar,[2] Hoskota,[3] Dod–Ballapur,[4] and Sira.[5] Each one of these places had been the residence of a ruling Nayak. Shahji used to stay sometimes at Ballapur and sometimes at Kolar.

Though in the beginning of this conquest, fanaticism was shown by the Muslim commanders in demolishing temples and building mosques in their places,[6] the

1. Kemp Gauda founded Bangalore in 1537, and his son of the same name gained possession of the Magadi country and Savandurga.

2. More prominent were the Sugatur–nad Prabhus, who usually had the name Tamme–Gauda. Their territory included a great part of the Kolar District, and they founded Hoskote. For his aid in defeating the Mussalman attack on Penugonda, the chief received the title of Chikka-Rayal, and his possessions were extended from Anekal to Punganur. The inscriptions of the Sugatur Prabhus date from 1451 to 1693. When Kolar and Hoskote were taken by the Bijapur army, the chief retired to Anekal, but was expelled when this place was taken by Haider Ali. Shahji bestowed the Punganur district upon Chikka Rayal Timme Gauda in place of Kolar, the charge of which he committed to his own son Sambhaji, on the death of whom, his son Soorut Singh managed Kolar, and subsequently it formed part of the territories of Venkoji or Eccoji.

3. Hosa-Kota, ' new fort, ' so called to distinguish it from Kolar was built about 1595, by Timme Gauda, the chief of Sugatur, who had recently settled at Kolar and obtained from the Penugonda sovereign the title of Chikka Rayal. (Mysore, Vol. II, p. 68.)

4. Malla Baire Gauda of Devanhalli founded Ballapur. With the help of the Vijayanagar Emperor, he speedily subdued the neighbouring country, so that this principality yielded a revenue of a lakh of pagodas. His descendants continued to rule this dominion until it was reduced by the Bijapur army. (Mysore, Vol. II, p. 68.)

5. The foundation of the town and fort is attributed to Rangappa Nayak, the chief of Rantnagiri. Before the fort was completed, Sira and its dependencies were conquered by Randulla Khan. One Malik Husen who was appointed governor, completed the fort and enclosed the town with mud walls. Malik Riban was Subadar from 1638 to 1650 (Mysore, Vol. II, p. 198.)

6. After the capture of Basavapatna the town of Sante Bennur was taken by the Mussalman forces of Bijapur, under Randulla Khan, who destroyed the temple and erected in its place a mosque of very large dimensions. Hanumappa Nayak who had been forced to retire to Tarikere and Kaldurga, was greatly incensed at this, and watching his opportunity planned a night attack, in which he put to death the Muhammadan Governor, and desecrated the mosque with the blood of hogs, pulling out a stone from the wall of each compartment. (Mysore, Vol. II, p. 469.)

S. 21.

inconoclastic spirit was definitely checked by the appointment
of Shahji as Governor of the Karnatic. On the other
hand, he became the champion of the Hindu Rajas,[1]
of Hindu supremacy and of Hindu culture and literature.
Then Marathi became the court language and Marathas
were appointed as revenue clerks and collectors. Thus
Shahji, during the long viceroyalty extending over one
generation, Marathaized the Kanarese population. The
administrative system set up by him was faithfully followed
by his successors in those parts. To sum up, he was the
founder of Greater Maharashtra in the Karnatic.

18. Policy of consolidation

Shahji followed a most remarkable policy of conciliation
and consolidation. While he took possession of the capital
town of every dispossessed chief and administered the
revenues of each principality through his own agents, he
granted the ousted chief an estate in some less productive
part of his territory. This resulted in bringing under
cultivation and attracting population to the more neglected
tracts of the country. Thus Basavapattan and its possessions
being retained, Tarikere was given to the polygar; Bangalore
was taken, but Magadi was left to Kempa Gauda. Similarly,
Hoskota was taken and Anekal granted; Kolar was captured
but Punganur returned; Sira was taken and Ratnagiri[2] was
retained with the chief. Thus all the ruling Hindu families
were continued in existence, and yet these were bound by
ties of gratitude to Shahji.

19. The Maratha revenue system in the Karnatic

The Bijapurian Karnatic was distributed into *parganas*
Each of these districts was devided into *samats, tarafs.
mauge,* and *mujare* Jamadars or collectors were appointed.

---

1. Sh. Bh. XI. 7; XV. 9.
2. Mysore Gazetteer, Vol. I, p. 359.

for each pargana. "In the time of the Rayals, the accountants had been called *Samprati*, but the Mahrattas introduced the different offices of Deshpande, Deshkulkarni, Sar-Nad-Gaud, Deshmukh and Kanungo, by whom the accounts of the country were kept; they also appointed Sheristedars to all the parganas. When jagirs were granted to the Killedars and Mansubdars by the Sarkar, the revenue accounts of the districts for the last years were previously examined, and the new revenue rated annually on the jagir to be granted. In fixing the revenue thus established, the inams or free gift lands, land customs, &c., were discontinued or deducted, and the net revenue, more or less than the former, ascertained by means of the Jamadars.

The Deshkulkarni was to write the *kaulpatta*, the contract or lease for the revenue; the Deshpande was to sign it in Mahratti characters at the bottom of the paper; the Deshmukh, Kanungo and Sar-Nad-Gaud were also to add their signatures to the written deed, and the Amildar finally to seal it. The particular accounts of the parganas were kept as follows: The Shanbhog was to keep the written accounts of the mauje or village, the Deshkulkarni to keep the accounts of the samats, the Deshpande the accounts of the parganas, and the Kanungo to sign the *patte* or revenue agreements. He was also to keep a written register of the revenue of the district, to be delivered to the Sarkar. It was the duty of the Deshmukhi and Sar-Nad-Gaud to control and inspect all accounts, and report them to their superiors; they were also to inquire and report generally on all affairs, and the settlement of the district." [1]

"The accounts of all kinds were accidently kept in Kannada, but after the Mahratta chiefs attained power in the Carnatic, many Deshasts or natives of their countries followed them, who introduced their language and written characters into the public accounts. Even in the samsthans of the Palegars, where the revenue and military accounts had been kept in Kannada alone, some of them beginning

1. Mysore Gazetteer, Vol. I, pp. 588-589.

then to entertain large bodies of horse, employed Mahratta accountants to check the pay accounts in that language for the satisfaction of the horsemen of that nation. After the Moguls came into the country and established the Suba of Sira, the Persian language came into use." [1]

20. A view of Shahji's life

The salient features of the political career of Shahji are now summarized to enable the reader to have a clear view of the same. In 1621 Shahji captured Poona from the Bijapur officer and obtained the Mokasa of Poona and Shirwal from Malik Amber. After the desertion of his father-in-law Jadhavrao, Shahji and the other Bhosles were the great feudal lords left in the Nizam Shahi State. This is clear from the list of officers who took part in the battle of Bhatwadi in 1624. Shahji distinguished himself in this battle, while his younger brother was killed in an action. He must have then held a high position, because he manfully maintained his independence in his jagir against all the power of Malik Amber in 1625. The Bijapur Court conferred upon Shahji the rare titles of Sarlashkar and Maharaj. He was employed in the conquest of the Karnatic and in putting down the rebellion of the chief of Phaltan. After his return to the Nizam Shahi service, we find him as the Subedar and Commandant of the most important fortress of Parenda in 1630. When he joined the Moguls in this year, he was given the dignity of 5,000 horse and even his cousins were made commanders of 2,000 horse. He was granted the estate of Fateh Khan, the prime minister of the Nizam Shahi Kingdom. After deserting the Moguls, he remained a petty independent ruler. With his own forces he assisted Randulla Khan in conquering Daulatabad. Then he became the King-maker or the actual ruler of the Nizam Shahi State for three years. Even Shah Jahan after hurling vast hordes against Shahji found it impracticable to subdue him, till he had completely

1. Mysore Gazetteer, Vol. I, pp. 589-590,

brought under him the Golconda and Bijapur Kingdoms. Then the allied forces of Bijapur and Delhi hunted out Shahji from all places and finally compelled him to surrender himself and his puppet-king at Mahuli. It was one of the terms of the treaty that this great man must be given to Bijapur, because in the Mogul service he would have been an effective instrument for the conquest of the Deccan, just as afterwards Mir Jumla was the cause of the conquest of Golconda in 1656. Such a ripe administrator, shrewd statesman and a wealthy lord could not but be taken into the rank of the highest nobility in Bijapur. There is evidence of Basatin-i-Salatin (p. 254) that Shahji was appointed to a high post in the Bijapur army.

As Shahji Raje had won over the confidence of the commander-in-chief Randulla Khan by his achievements, he was appointed Governor of the Karnatic and given a very big jagir there. It is said that the General carried on the administration with the advice of Shahji. Similarly, after the death of Randulla Khan, each successive general who went for the conquest of the Karnatic, naturally followed the advice and policy of Shahji,[1] the man on the spot. He continued to fill this post up to his imprisonment in 1648 and even after his release up to his death in 1664. He used to stay at Bangalore, Kolar, or Ballapur and had Nandi as his summer captial in the Karnatic.

In the war with Shriranga Rayal near Vellore we find him commanding the right wing of the Bijapur army with Asad Khan as his assistant.

In a legal document bearing the seal of the Sultan, Shahji is addressed as Farzand (Son) and Maharaj.[2] Both these honours which were conferred on him by Bijapur are confirmed by another Royal Firman issud to the revenue officer of Poona on 7 September 1649.

1. Sh. Bh. XI, pp. 8-10.
2. See B. I. S. M. Quarterly, Vol. X, No. 3, p. 131. In a document of November 1654, he is addressed as Maharaj.

In 1659 when he commanded the campaign into Tanjore, Mulla Muhammad was his second-in-command. In 1653 he was one of the three greatest lords of Bijapur; so also in 1659 he is described as being of the same rank as Rustam-i-Zaman and Bahlol Khan. From 1661 he is named as the commander-in-chief of the Bijapur forces in the Karnatic. He attempted to set up an independent kingdom in the south during 1659-1663, but the result is not clear from the available sources. His policy, diplomacy and wars so mortally weakened the Tanjore state that it fell an easy prey into the hands of his son Vyankoji. His successors continued to enjoy the fruits of Shahji's labours for generations. In fact, Shahji deserves to be styled the founder of the Maratha rule in Southern India, as his famous son, Shivaji, proved to be the founder of the Maratha Empire in India.

21. Shahji, the inspirer of Shivaji

Shahji ought to be given the full credit for bringing about favourable circumstances for a successful rebellion of his son against the foreign rule. We should not be put on a wrong scent by believing the words of this subtle statesman which he is said to have written to the Bijapur Court that his young son was a rebel against his authority, and that he be severely dealt with by the King in any way which was thought desirable. The following points ought to be kept in view:—

(1) Shahji failed twice in 1630 and 1633-36 in establishing an independent kingdom. He played the role of a king-maker and a real ruler. As such he measured swords with Adil Shah and Shah Jahan.

(2) Shivaji was sent to look after the Poona jagir with Dadoji Kond Deva and other veteran statesmen. They were entrusted with the insuperable task of defending the estate from the encroachment of the Moguls and Bijapurians.

(3) When Shivaji was a mere boy, Chakan was captured by his officers and men who were in name under the boy

Shivarai. This offensive could not have been taken by him without the consent of his father.

(4) The real cause of the arrest of Shahji in 1648 is said by the author of the Shiva Bharat to be his ambition to establish an independent Kingdom in the Karnatic. Mustafa Khan was deputed by the King to imprison Shahji on the basis of this suspicion.

(5) After his release from captivity in 1649, Shahji entered into a sacred alliance with Kanhoji Naik Jedhe which the latter solemnly observed even at the risk of his jagir. Jedhe and Lohokare were to bring all the Mawal Deshmukhs under the authority of Shivaji and to repel the invasions of the Adil Shahi and Mogul forces on Poona. We will be justified in concluding that all the Maval Deshmukhs of the Konkan were to be subdued after 1649, and that this work was really undertaken by Shivaji under the orders of his father.

(6) Rataji Rupaji Yadav — Deshmukh of Aund, and Vangoji Mudhoji Nimbalkar of Phaltan rebelled against the Bijapur Kingdom. They took the fort of Karad and plundered the rich districts round about. It is confirmed by Jedhe who was requested by Nimbalkar to help him. This Jedhe, being in the service of Shivaji, could now and then goad him to rebellion. It is said by him that after the rebellion of Vangoji Mudhoji Nimbalkar, Shivaji revolted against the King. The attempt to establish Swarajya is called rebellion in contemporary Marathi letters. The European and Muslim writers, one and all, looked upon the attempts of Shivaji to throw off the foreign yoke as a rebellion against the established government. He has been frequently called, ' the arch rebel of the Deccan. '

(7) In 1662-63 Shahji became the mediator between his son and the Bijapur King for concluding a treaty between them. By this subtle act he safeguarded the interests of Shivaji and protected the tender plant of Hindu Swarajya.

(8) Chitnis supplies us with another proof. It is said

that Shahji had taken a vow to donate a golden idol worth
one lakh of rupees to the temple at Jejuri for the fulfilment
of Shivaji's mission of founding an independent Kingdom,
of protecting gods, cows and Brahmins and of establishing
the ancient religion. Shahji got a beautiful figure made in
the Karnatic and presented it to the temple on the brilliant
susccess of his son.

(9) Then, Gagabhat who as the most eminent scholar
of his age, performed the installation rites of Shivaji, calls
Shahji 'the new incarnation of the duties of the military
class' for protecting the weak and destroying the wicked.
(Shivaraj-prashasti)

(10) Even at the close of his life, Shahji tried his best
for some three years to throw off the Adil Shahi yoke and
govern the Karnatic as an independent King; but even
this time he could not realize his ambitious dreams. It is
thus evident that a life full of romantic adventures,
extraordinary fortitude, wisdom and foresight, and distinguished
with statesmanship and generalship of a high order, could
not but serve as an illustrious example to Shivaji. He had
indeed a rich inheritance and a powerful incentive from his
father for establishing Hindwi Swarajya.

22. Chronology

1651   War between Mir Jumla and Bijapur. Mir Jumla
        defeated by the Bijapurians.
1652   Peace between Mir Jumla and Bijapur.
1653   Aurangzeb came as Viceroy to Burhanpur in October
        and to Daulatabad in November.
1654   Vellore captured and lost by Shriranga, and treaty with
        Bijapur. Mir Jumla rebelled against Golconda.
1655   Golconda army defeated by Shriranga but the latter
        was ultimately routed.
        The war of the Noses between Mysore and Madura.
1656   Pulicat besieged by Shriranga. Mahammad Adil Shah
        died on 4th November and Ali II succeeded.

1657   Shriranga defeated by the lieutenant of Mir Jumla.
       Aurangzeb declared war against Bijapur. A treaty
       between Ali and Aurangzeb.

1658   Shahji invaded Madura and Trichinopoly.

1659   Shahji suddenly entered into the territory of Tanjore,
       and captured its capital and other important towns.
       Shahi rebelled and marched to the north to join
       Shivaji.

1660   Second siege of Trichinopoly failed.   Treaty with
       Madura.

1661   Triple alliance of the rulers of Madura, Tanjore and
       Jinji.
       Tegenapatam and Porto Novo captured by Shahji.

1662-3 War between Shahji and the allies.   The former
       ultimately   driven   from   Madura   and   Tanjore.
       Tegenapatam besieged by Lingama, but relieved by
       Shahji.   Treaty   concluded   between   Shahji   and
       Lingama, but it was finally disregarded.   A Bijapur
       army under Bahlol Khan raided Tanjore.
       Bahlol Khan marched against Shahji to expel him
       from Arni and Bangalore.
       War between Tanjore and Madura, concluded by the
       payment of an indemnity by Tanjore.
       Bahlol Khan and Shahji made a common cause
       against the King.   Both of them were imprisoned.
       Bahlol Khan was murdered, but Shahji was restored
       to his governorship.   Shahji brought about a
       reconciliation between Shivaji and the Bijapur State.

1664   Bednur conquered, but restored to its ruler.
       Succession disputes at Bednur and the interference
       of Bijapur in them.
       Death of Shahji.

S. 22.

APPENDICES

APPENDIX I

(See p. 1 of this Part)

Imperfections of the Bakhars

The distinguished historian Rajwade submitted the Marathi Bakhars to a scathing criticism some thiry years back. He summarized his conclusions in Marathi on pp. 67-69, 105-107, 133-239 of Vol. IV of the ' Sources of the History of the Marathas. ' Sir J. Sarkar has done the same thing in a general manner. In spite of this, he frequently relies upon the Rairi Bakhar and Tarikh-i-Shivaji. A recent attempt has been made by Mr. V. S. Vakaskar of Baroda to defend this group of Bakhars. In this section I have consequently selected a few passages relating to the life of Shahji alone and shown their unreliability. [1]

The 91 qalmi Bakhar, the Short Chronicle of the Maratha Empire, and Tarikh-i-Shivaji (History of Shivaji in Persian) are related to each other. The last two are based upon the first one. Moreover, there are three different recensions of the 91 qalmi Bakhar:— the one printed by Rajwade, the other by Parasnis and the third used by Forrest for translation into English. All these *six* works supplement each other, but they contain only a few grains of truth buried under the debris of myths and fables. Facts have been jumbled up in such a manner that truth has been murdered, chronology sacrificed and history mutilated. We can scarcely rely on these for the history of Shivaji's ancestors, the life-story of Shahji or the early career of Shivaji.

---

1. Vakaskar, Shivachhatrapatichi 91 Qalmi Bakhar; Sahvichar, Oct. 1931.

Section 1:– Babaji Bhosla was a Patil of the village of Hingni Berdi and Devalgaon in the district of Poona, but his sons being dissatisfied with their homes, emigrated to the village of Elora. They supported themselves by agriculture and then went to Sindkhed for service under Jadhavrao. They were appointed door-keepers at 5 huns per month each.

The 91 Bakhar does not go beyond Babaji; it gives no real cause for the emigration of his sons to Elora, nor any explanation why Elora was selected for their residence. The whole story is made up to show the low origin of Maloji and his phenomenal rise through divine grace. We have seen that the contemporary sources present an entirely different picture. Pp. 50–53 supra.

Section ? :– It is said that Jadhavrao had no son.

He had several sons and grandsons. The names of Raghuji, Dattaji, Achaloji, Bahadurji are known from several sources. P. 80.

Sections 3–5:– relate the story of the Rangpanchami Holi festivities from the antics of Shahji and Jijabai who were only 5 and 3 years old to the discovery of a large treasure by Maloji.

The baselessness of these events has been shown on pp. 58–60.

Sections 6–7:– The two brothers asked the help of Jagpal Nimbalkar who was already making depredations in the Nizam's territory. They were given two thousand horse. With a force of three thousand horse, the brothers proceeded to Daula-

One need not explode the ugliness of this baseless story. Maloji did not need three thousand horse for putting two dead hogs in a mosque at night. After this childish act had been done, the brave Maloji was so mortally afraid of the royal wrath that he returned with tabad and threw two hogs in a mosque and tied a letter to each of them. Having performed this deed, they returned to Phaltan.

post-haste to Phaltan. Then it is simply incredible that the King should have been so much unnerved and fear-stricken at this incident that, instead of punishing Maloji, he should have sent for Jadhavrao from Sindkhed and asked him to pacify the evil-doers. The whole story is no better than a fable to amuse the children.

Sections 8-9:-All the three, Maloji, Vithoji and Shahji were granted the ranks of 12,000 horse each, so that they became the equals of Jadhavrao and the marriage was celebrated at Daulatabad in 1603-4.

It is most unlikely that favours should have been shown to the rebels, that the highest lords including Jadhavrao himself should have been sent to receive the two brothers who, three years before, were mere door-keepers of Jadhavrao, and that each of the three should have been given the highest rank in the nobility. Secondly, Daulatabad was not the capital of the Nizam Shahi at that time. The royal family took refuge first in Ausa and then in Parenda up to 1610. P. 60.

Section 11:- When Shahji reached the age of 25 years, both his father and uncle died. Soon after he had his first son who was named Sambhaji. In that year Nizam Shah Bahiri died leaving two

(1) Shahji is said to have been born in 1594 and to have become a minister in 1619/20 after the death of Nizam Shah. The latter died in 1627 and not in 1619. Hence if Shahji was really 25 years old at the death

sons who were seven years old. Sabaji Anant recommended Shahji for the post of prime ministership, and the Begums conferred the post on him and entrusted the care of their princes to Shahji.

of Nizam Shah, he must have been born in 1602, the year assigned by me on an altogether independent evidence. P. 58.

(2) In Sh. Dig. (65-66) it is said that sometime before his death, Amber requested the Bijapur Court to return Shahji or to lend the services of Sabaji. The latter is represented to have introduced all the financial reforms for which Amber is so well-known. If Sabaji came to Daulatabad in 1625-6, he could not have made Shahji Vazir in 1619.

(3) Shahji was in the Bijapur service from 1625 to 1628 and thus came to Daulatabad two years after the demise of Nizam Shah. Pp. 68-70.

(4) The Muslim chronicles do not name Sabaji as the Karbhari before or after the demise of Nizam Shah.

Thus this whole section is a concoction.

Section 12:- The rise of Shahji to the post of prime ministership and the ceremony of performing obeisance to him in the open court annoyed Jadhavrao. So the

Jadhavrao left the Nizam Shahi service in 1621 and returned to it in 1630, four years after the death of Murtiza Nizam Shah. He was soon murdered there. It was Fatch

latter with a few other Sardars' went over to the Moguls and brought the Mogul army under Mir Jumla to conquer Daulatabad.

Khan and not Shahji who was then the Chief Minister. Hence there was no occasion for Jadhavrao being offended with Shahji. The Bakhars place the desertion of Jadhavrao some six or seven years after it had actually taken place. Pp. 62,79.

Sections 13–14:— When Jadhavrao and Mir Jumla advanced against Daulatabad, Shahji with the royal family took refuge in the impregnable fort of Mahuli. The invaders hotly pursued the Raja and laid siege to the fort. For six months the siege continued. Shahji suffered much hardship and hence he opened negotiations with the Bijapur Court for being taken up in service there.² Having obtained a Kaul, he escaped from the fort with his wife and son. His wife, being pregnant, could not go far on horseback. She was left with 100 horsemen to look after herself. Jadhavrao soon arrived at the scene

In 1626 Jadhavrao was no doubt in the Mogul service, but there is no mention in Persian or English sources of the siege of Mahuli. No authentic history speaks of Mir Jumla as commander of the Mogul forces in 1626–27.

1. The same story is repeated in Sh. Dig. (Pp. 45–46). It names Shirke and Mahadik among the rebellious Sardars.

2. Sh. Dig. (48–49) has the same version. There is some extra information. Asharam Khoja entered into a plot with the Begams against Shahji. Naro Trimal and Mazumdar Hanmante were sent as vakils or envoys of Shahji.

and moved by the appeals of his followers and of his daughter, sent her to Shivneri which was in the possession of Shahji.

Section 16:—Shahji left the fort of Mahuli and went to Bijapur. There he waited upon Sultan Sikander Shah. He was given the command of 12,000 troops and a jagir in the Karnatic. Mir Jumla, failing to seize the Raja, returned disappointed to Delhi.

Even the name of the Bijapur King is not known, nor is the name of the Mogul Commander. How can we rely on such a history for true details? Sane's edition mentions the command of 10,000 horse being given to Shahji.

Section 17:— This section is full of the most eggregious blunders and the most unreliable fables. It is said that after Shahji's departure from Mahuli and the raising of the siege by the Moguls, the Nizam Shahi royalty was brought to Daulatabad by Sabaji Anant. He was asked by the Begums to find out a most suitable man for being the prime minister. The Pandit was one day going through a street and

Malik Amber was serving the Nizam Shahi State from the time of Chand Bibi and he died in May 1626, while Shahji is said to have left Mahuli in the beginning of 1627. Thus these Bakhars allege that Amber began service in the Nizam Shahi State one year after his own death and that too in the wonderful manner described in the 91 Q. Bakhar. He is represented to have again defeated Mir Jumla near Asirgarh. [1]

1. Sh. Dig. (P. 55). Mir Jumla was reprimanded by the Emperor for finishing the war without the complete conquest of the Nizam Shahi State. Hence he again returned with a resolve to capture Daulatabad this time. Further on Pp. 56–58, Amber is represented to have defeated Mir Jumla once more and even Prince Aurangzeb himself. These are fibs and not historic truths.

he accidentally came across a Fakir lying on the ground. By looking at the beggar for some time, he found out that he would be a most capable minister. So he was given a bath, brought before the Begums, and appointed prime minister. The beggar was no other than Malik Amber who had been a servant of Changiz Khan, a minister of the king of Bijapur.

Sections 18–19:– It is said that Malik Amber proceeded against Bijapur, but was defeated and pursued up to the bank of the Bhima. Though the river was in flood, it gave way to Amber's troops, but again rose high at the approach of the pursuing army. Thus the saintly character of Amber has been proved.

The Malik was never defeated near Bijapur. He burnt down the suburb ef Nauraspur and raided the territory to his heart's content in 1624. P. 66.

In Sane's Bakhar it is said that Malik Amber dispersed the Bijapur army at Bhatwadi; at that time Sahaji went to the Karnatic [1] and that on

The battle was fought in 1624, the weighing ceremony took place in 1633 and Shahji was sent to the Karnatic in 1637. These three different

1. Sh. Dig. (Pp. 59-60) has the following:—Malik Amber and Jadhav raided Poona, etc. Shahji bravely fought in defence. Finally, he defeated both the aaid generals, and pursued them for four Koses. He could not go further on occount of the floods. They encamped at Koregaon on the Bhima. On the day of the solar eclipse, Murari went to Nangar Gaon (Tulapur) and performed the weighing ceremony. The way of weighing the elephant was told by Shahji. In reward for this service, Shahji was made Sursubha of the Karnatic. His son Sambhaji was already there.

his return from this battle, Murari performed the weighing ceremony.

Section 20:—Poona is said to be the stronghold of the robber chief, Martand Deo. Murari plundered the town, razed it to the ground and caused its soil to be ploughed by asses. As the country was greatly desolated, Murari conferred the whole tract from the frontier of Poona and the fort of Chakan to that of Wai, Sarwai (Shirwal), Supa and Indapur as jagir on Shahji after the weighing ceremony at Tulapur. According to Sane's edition, even Junner fort was included in Shahji's jagir.

Kond Deva, the Kulkarni of Hangni Berdi was appointed Karbhari and he was asked to look after Jijabai and Shivaji.

Section 21:— (1) Shahji made a resolution never to see Jijabai or his son Shivaji, and he consequently married Tukabai, daughter of one

events have been jumbled up into one by the chronicle.

The weighing ceremony took place in 1633 and Shivaji and his mother are represented to have come to Poona in that year, but it is not borne out by other chronicles. Shahji was in the grip of difficulties and could never have hazarded to place his family at Poona in 1633. Murari was sent against Shahji who had revolted after his father-in-law's murder in 1630, to expel him from Poona. After the burning of the place by Murari, Shahji returned to Shivneri and took shelter with its ruler. Three years after, Murari was sent to help Shahji against the Moguls and to revive the Nizam Shahi monarchy. It was during this expedition that the weighing ceremony was performed. But the 91 Q. Bakhar has made a mess of both these expeditions and added the unreliable news that Murari conferred a jagir upon Shahji.

(1 According to the Sh. Dig., Shahji married Tukabai at Bijapur in 1549 Shaka (1627) before Shivaji was born. It means a difference of more than

Mohite after Shivaji was placed under Dadaji Konddeva.

(2) Sultan Sikandar died in the year when Shahji sent a present to Dadaji Konddeva for his exemplary honesty. Both Murari Jagadev and Shahji were then at Bijapur.

(3) Later on Murari was put to death by order of the Begums.[1]

(4) Soon afterwards the Begums sent a large army against Daulatabad. They were met at Bhatari by Malik Amber.

ten years. The same chronicle (Pp. 53,62) says that Sambhaji was born at Daulatabad in 1545 Shaka (1622 A. D.) and he was killed at the age of eight at Kanakgiri. This statement is wrong, because Shahji left off the service of Bijapur in 1628 and returned to Daulatabad. He again joined Bijapur service in 1637. 91 Q. Bakhar (sect. 21) says that after the death of Sambhaji, his son Umaji Raja who had married a daughter of the house of Jintikar continued to fight with the Polygar.

(2) Even the name of the king of Bijapur is not known to the author. It was Muhammad Shah and not Sikandar Shah. He died in 1656, Malik Amber in 1626 and Murari in 1635. Yet the latter two are said to have been living after 1656.

(3) Murari was put to death by order of Muhammad Shah in 1635, and not by his Begums after 21 years.

(4) The battle of Bhatavadi was fought in 1624 and yet the event is placed after 1656.

---

1. Sh. Dig. (P. 72) has the same anachronism that Murari was disgraced and put to death by the Begums, inspite of his becoming a Sanyasi and renouncing the world.

Section 22:– It is said that after the death of Murari, Shahji established himself in the Karnatic, assisted the Nayak of Madura, killed Vijayaraghava, captured Tanjore and appointed his son Venkoji to rule the country.

After the conquest of Ginji the Muslims entered Tanjore and wrought incalcuable havoc, but were finally repelled up to Ginji. Shahji was a prisoner at Kanakgiri and hence could have no part in plundering Tanjore. Vijayaraghava died in 1674, ten years after the death of Shahji. Tanjore was conquered by Ekoji in that year. Therefore Shahji had no hand in the conquest of Tanjore. [1]

Section 23:– 1) Malik Amber and Sabaji died in that year at Daulatabad. Shah Jahan lost no time in sending Aurangzeb.

(2) Shah Jahan sent Aurangzeb and Mir Jumla to the Deccan.

(3) The object was to conquer Daulatabad which they soon captured.

(4) Aurangzeb is said to have changed the name of Khirki to Aurangabad in 1653.

(5) Aurangzeb is said to have been defeated by the Bijapuri forces and to have

(1) Malik Amber died in May 1626. Shah Jahan had not come to the throne till Jan. 1628, yet he is said to be sending Aurangzeb to conquer Daulatabad.

(2) Prince Aurangzeb was appointed Viceroy of the Deccan on 14th July 1636 and continued in that office for eight years up to 28th May 1644. Mir Jumla was not with him. That General was then in the Golconda service.

(3) Daulatabad had already been captured by the Moguls in 1633.

(4 It was in his first vice-

---

1. History of the Nayaks of Madura, pp. 130, 165-70.

returned to Aurangabad where he stayed for some years in administering the affairs of the Deccan.

royalty that this change was made and not in 1653.

(5) He led his army into the Bijapur territory in February 1657, conquered the most impregnable forts of Bidar and Kalyani, so that Bijapur was forced to sue for peace. Aurangzeb was soon called back to the north on account of the severe illness of Shah Jahan.

To ascribe the composition of this Bakhar to 1685 is an aggregious blunder.[1] It is incredible that the author writing this history of Shivaji only five years after his death, should not know the elementary facts of his life. He places the death of Afzal Khan in 1652 and the Karnatic expedition before the coronation in 1673 (Pp. 147/150, 154). We are told that Raigad was made capital before the death of Chandrarao More, i. e. in 1654 (P. 57). Shahji is said to have been seized by Baji Ghorpade after the death of Afzal Khan, and to be released from imprisonment (say in 1661) through the intercession of Randulla Khan who had died in 1643 (P. 116). He is represented to be living at the time of the imprisonment of Shivaji at Agra (P. 101). It is asserted that the Raja performed the coronation ceremony soon after his release from Agra (P. 105). The Mogul offensive of 1669-72 is placed *after* the desertion of Sambhaji in 1679 (P. 110). Shivaji is said to have gone on an expedition to chastise Shivappa of Bednur when Rajaram was born. Shivappa was murdered in 1662 and Rajaram was born in 1670. Yet the two events are made synchronous (P. 112). Finally, the author reveals the time of the composition of the Bakhar when he says that the

1, Vakaskar, Shivachhatrapatichi 91 Q. Bakhar, p. 2. The references to pages in this para are to 1939 edition of this book,

two sons of Ekoji died without any issue, but Tukoji the youngest son, had one issue 'whose descendants *are still* reigning at Tanjore' (P. 45). So the Bakhar might have been written in the reign of Pratapsingh ' (1739–1763) and not in 1685.

Thus it is evident that the 91 Q. Bakhar and the other five chronicles dependent upon it are full of anachronisms, inconsistencies and improbabilities, and hence their accounts are mostly incorrect and unreliable.

APPENDIX II

(See p. 37 supra)

Shivaji's Ancestry.

A geneological tree of the ancestors of Shivaji was prepared after much ¸research by order of Raja Pratapsinhji of Satara. Therein the order of names is as under:—

Pratapsen, Suhagsinha, Samarsinha, Lakshmansinha, Rajansinha, Dilipsinha, Sinhaji, Bhosaji, Deorajaji, Indrasenaji, Shubhakrishnaji, Rupasinhaji, Bhumindraji, (Ba)paji, Barhadji, Khelaji, Karnasinha, Sambhaji, Babaji Maharaj, Maloji, Shahji Maharaj, Shivaji Maharaj.

In this geneology based on the information supplied by the Bhats, Lakshmansinha has been shown as the son of Samarsinha. But Ratnasinha or Ratnasi was really the son and successor of Samarsi, and he and his wife Padmini laid down their lives in defending Chittor from the Muslim hosts. Lakshmansinha belonged to a different branch and was not a descendant of Samarsi or Samarsinha.

Even the ancestors of Samarsinha are wrongly given in the Satara geneology. From the four inscriptions of the Vikram Era 1330, '342, 1496 and 1517, used by Gauri Shankar Ojha, it appears that Padmasinha, Jayasinha, Tejsinha and Samars. iha were the successive ancestors of Ratnasi.

1. K. R. Subramanian, Maratha Rajas of Tanjore, Madras, 1928.

Mr. Ojha has constructed the following geneology of the two branches of the solar dynasty on the basis of inscriptions. [1]

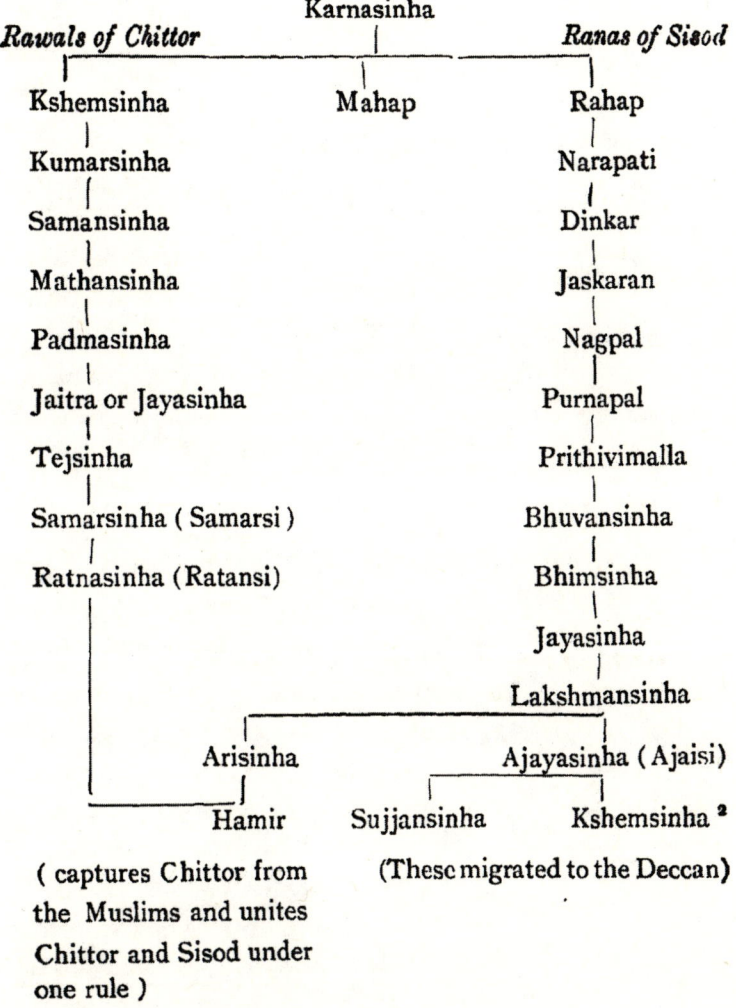

Karnasinha

Rawals of Chittor *Ranas of Sisod*

Kshemsinha	Mahap	Rahap
Kumarsinha		Narapati
Samansinha		Dinkar
Mathansinha		Jaskaran
Padmasinha		Nagpal
Jaitra or Jayasinha		Purnapal
Tejsinha		Prithivimalla
Samarsinha (Samarsi)		Bhuvansinha
Ratnasinha (Ratansi)		Bhimsinha
		Jayasinha
		Lakshmansinha

Arisinha   Ajayasinha (Ajaisi)

Hamir   Sujjansinha   Kshemsinha [2]

(captures Chittor from   (These migrated to the Deccan)
the Muslims and unites
Chittor and Sisod under
one rule)

1. The History of Rajputana, Vol. I, pp. 441, 522.

2. In the Mudhol Bakhar his name is Ajab Sinha, He is said to have committed suicide.

S. 24.

The geneological trees of Shivaji's ancestors

*1. Kolhapur Durbar 2. Tod   3. Chitnis and 4. Stone inscrip-
                           Satara Museum   tion of
                                            Tanjore*

1. Kolhapur Durbar	2. Tod	3. Chitnis and Satara Museum	4. Stone inscription of Tanjore
1. Lakshmnsinha died 1303	1. Ajeysi	1. Lakshmansinha	1. Yekoji
2. Sajjansinha came to Sondavada in 1310	2. Sujunsi	2. Sajjansinhaji	2. Sharbhji came to the South
3. Dilipsinha	3. Duleepji	3. Dilipsinhaji	3. Mahasen
4. Shivaji	4. Seoji	4. Sinhaji	4. Ekashiva
5. Bhosaji	5. Bhoraji	5. Bhosaji	5. Ramchandra
6. Devarajji	6. Deoraj	6. Devarajji came into the South in 1415	6. Bhimarai
7. Ugrasen	7. Oogursen	7. Indrasenji	7. Ekoji
8. Mahulaji	8. Mahoolji	8. Shubhakrishna	8. Varah
9. Kheloji	9. Khailooji	9. Rupasinhaji	9. Ekoji
10. Janakoji	10. Junkoji	10. Bhumindraji	10. Brahmaji
11. Sambhaji	11. Suttooji	11. Dhapaji	11. Shahji
12. Babaji	12. Sambaji	12. Barbataji	12. Ambaji-Revavu
13. Maloji	13. Sevaji	13. Khelakarna or Kheloji	13. Parasoji
14. Shahji		14. Karnasinha or Jaykarna	14. Babaji-Revavu
15. Shivaji		15. Sambhaji	15. Maloji-Uma
		16. Babaji	16. Shahji
		17. Maloji	17. Ekoji
		18. Shahji	

Jintikar[1] Bhonsle of Gwalior gives the names of only six ancestors:—Bakhataji came into the south; then followed Nagoji (Sh. 1379), Vyankoji, Babaji, Vithoji (Sh. 1430), Maloji, Shahji.

The geneology given in the Tanjore Inscription is hopelessly wrong and worthless. The geneological trees of Kolhapur and Chitnis are wrong in skipping over Ajaysinha or Ajaisi, the son of Lukhamsi (Lakshman Sinha) and the father of Sujjansinha. Both are incorrect in having the 4th descendant as Shivaji and Sinhaji. In the Sanad, he is called Sidhaji. The 7th descendant is called by Chitnis Indrasen. The Mudhol Bakhar (P. 88) says that Indrasen was known as Ugrasen for the terror that he struck in the hearts of his enemies. He was also known as Ugra Sinha. But we should stick to Ugrasen only, as this name is found in the Sanads. The names from the 8th degree are different in all the four trees, but the last three names of Babaji, Maloji and Shahji are the same in all the five geneologies. The names of these immediate ancestors of Shivaji are borne out by various documents. The intermediate names must remain doubtful till some genuine grants and letters can throw light on them. The correct geneology is given below:—

1. Jintikar Bhosles are descendants of Shahji —

Shahji
|
Sambhaji
|
Umaji Raje (B. 25th Nov, 1654.)
|
Parsoji (adopted),
|
Jintikars of Gwalior.

Mr. M. G. Dongre has given two more geneologies prepared by Mr. Bhide and Rao Bahadur Sane, but they are of no value. (The Geneological Tree of the Bhonsla Family. Pp. 5-6.) The geneological tree preserved in the Satara Museum is identical with the one given by Chitnis in his chronicle. Ibid.

True ancestry of Shivaji

On the basis of Sanads

- Lakshmansinha
- Ajayasinha
- Sujjansinha   departed for the South in
- Dilipsinha   about 1320 A. D.
- Sidhoji
- Bhairoji or Bhosaji
- Devarajji
- Ugrasen
- Shubhakrishna

Tentative

- Rupsinha
- Bhumendraji
- Dhopaji
- Barhatji
- Kheloji [1]. It is incredible that the author of the Shahi Makrand writing about the ancestry of his patron Shahji in 1650 should have committed any mistake in naming his immediate ancestors.
- Parsoji

Documents

- Babaji
- Maloji
- Shahji
- Shivaji

The Senior Branch of the Bhosles of Mudhol

Ugrasen
Karansing } Sanad 5
Bhimsing

Kheloji.	Sanad 6
Kheloji	Sanads 7–8
Maloji	Sanad 9

1. These have been preferred to the names given in other geneologies. In the Bhosal Vanshavali Parsoji is said to be the father of Babaji.

$$\left.\begin{array}{l}\text{Abhaising}\\\text{Karansing}\\\text{Cholraj}\end{array}\right\}\ \text{Sanad 10}$$

Pilaji   Sanad 11

Pratapsinha   Sanad 11

Bajiraje   Sanad 19

Maloji   Sanad 22

(See p. 56 supra.)

APPENDIX III

The Bhosles are Rajputs

The Kshatriya origin of the family of Shivaji has been proved from the sanads. A few other contemporary evidences may be mentioned here:—

1. *Shiva Bharat* I. 41–42; II. 59; XXIV. 74. Maloji and Shahji are described as belonging to the Solar dynasty.

2. *Parnal Parvatgrahan Akhyan* gives Sisodia as the family of Shivaji.

3. *Sabhasad* (P. 82): Pure Kshatriya Sisodia family of the north.

4. *Bhushan's Shivaraj*: Maloji is born of the best Kshattriya Solar family of the Sisodias. 5–6 couplets.

5. *Shahji*   calls himself a Rajput in a letter addressed to the King of Bijapur. Doc. 710 in P. S. S.

6. *Bhundhela Memoirs*. Scott's History of the Dekkan, p. 4:– Sisodia Rajputs.

7. *Khafi Khan*: Descended from the Ranas of Chittor.

8. *Ramchandrapant's Royal Edict*: Describes Shivaji as an ornament of the Kshattriyas.

9. *Radha-Madhav-Vilas Champu*: This book was written by Jayaram between 1654–58 and its testimony is most trustworthy.

Shahji Bhosla descended from Sisodia Rajputs-pp. 257, 268, 269, 270.

That he belongs to the solar dynasty, is mentioned on pages 267, 269.

10. *Gaurishankar—Ojha*: in his History of Rajputana Vol. II, 514 on the basis of Rajput sources traces the Bhosles to the Sisodias

11. *An English letter*: of 28th November 1659 describes Sevagy "a great Rashpoote." Shivaji Vol. I. P. 54; Nos. 20, 24 of P. S. S.

12. *An English letter*: of 10th December 1659:— Rashpootes are differentiated from other Hindus. Shivaji Vol. I. P. 51.

13. *Tod's Rajasthan* Vol. I. gives the geneological tree of Shivaji wherein Ajeysi or Ajayasinha is the founder of this new branch. (Pp. 225, 288. Madras Edition 1873).

14. *Russel's Castes and Tribes* of C. P. Vol. IV. P. 200:—

" In 1836 Mr. Enthoven states the Sesodia Rana of Udepur, the head of the purest Rajput houses, was satisfied from the inquiries conducted by an agent that the Bhonsles and certain other families had a right to be recognized as Rajputs. "

15. *A letter of the Maharana of Udepur*:

This result of the enquiry is to be had in the two letters published in the Sidhanta Vijaya by Mr. Dongre. There is a letter from the Maharana of Udepur and another from the Royal Priest Amreshwar of Udepur to Maharaj Shri Pratapsinha of Satara. Therein it is said that " you are our near kindred. No difference regarding matters of that and this place is to be kept in mind. Originally we are one."

16. *Historical Sketch of the Native States of India* by Col. G. B.
    Malleson (1875). Pp. 254–255:—

> " According to Maratha tradition Shivaji
> claimed descent from that branch of the
> Royal Family of Udaipur, which reigned
> in Dongarpur. One of the disinherited
> sons of the thirteenth ruler of that family
> left his father's house for Bijapur, entered
> the services of the king of that place,
> and was recompensed for his services by
> the grant of the district of Mudhol
> comprising eighty-four villages and the
> title of Raja. This man who was called
> Sujunshi had four sons, from the youngest
> of whom, Sugaji, Sivaji claims to be
> directly descended. "

17. *Historical Sketch of the Princes of India by Clunes.* P. 130:—

> " One of the latter, named Sujansee, came
> to the Deccan and entered the service of
> the king of Bijapur, who conferred upon
> him the district of Moodhul comprising 84
> villages with the title of Rajah. Sujunsee
> had four sons; Bajee Raja, in whose line
> descended the Mudholkar Estate; the
> second died without family; from Wolubsye
> is Ghorpuray of Kapsi; Sugajee, the youngest,
> had a son named Bhosajee, from whom are
> derived all the Bhonslays.[1] He had ten sons,
> the eldest settled at Deoolgaor, near Patus,
> the Patel of which Maloojee Raja, was an
> active partisan under the king of Ahmednagar,
> and had a jahageer conferred upon him,

---

[1] Even the very name ' Bhosla' is indicative of the origin of the dynasty,
as it is an abbreviation of Bhaswatkula on the authority of the *'Shahendra Vilasam,*
and *Sangita Saramritam.* In an other couplet he is described as a descendant
of Rama and his successors. The *Sahitya Manjusha* tells us that Shivaji belonged to the Kaushika gotra. Maloji is called an ornament of the Solar race in
the *Sangita Makranda* (Shivaji Nibandhavali I, p. 33). Bhosla can be a deriva-
tion ot 'Bhaswatkula' on the analogy of Deva-Kula= Devula, the 't' being
dropped as in Pratipada=Padwa. Then Bhasa- ula= Bhasola= Bhosala.

which descended to his son Shahajee, afterwards a principal Maratha leader, under the Bijapoor dynasty. He acquired, in the Jahagir, nearly the whole of what now forms the Collectorship of Poona, together with the part of the territory now under Satara and it was in these valleys that his son, Shivaji, matured his plan of Hindu independent sovereignty."

There are many inaccuracies in this account, yet the central fact of Shivaji's Rajput origin is undisputed.

APPENDIX IV

(See p. 47 supra.)

Mudhol Sanads

No. 6.   Kheloji confirmed in his jagirs and titles

" Our exalted and holy mind has been convinced of the fact that Raja Kheloji Bahadur Ghorpade, the son of Raja Bhimasing and the grandson of Raja Karnasing Ghorpade, has acquired Mudhol and its surrounding 84 villages and the Forts in the Pargana of Ben (Wai) and the Mansab and the title by his most arduous, whole-hearted and excellent services in the Royal cause during the Bahamani Rule. We have confirmed the same Jagir, Mansab and the ancient title of Raja Kheloji Bahadur Ghorpade and have made him ' Sarfaraz '. Following in the wake of his father, grand-father and ancestors, therefore, he should serve faithfully and arduously for the welfare of this Dowlat, and retaining Mansab, Jagir and Forts should enjoy them, so that he may be eligible for promotion in future.   896 A. H." 1491 A. D.

No. 7.   Seal of Kasim Bareed

After wishing the welfare of Raja Kheloji Ghorpade the one in the enjoyment of Royal favour:— At present some evil-doers have started quarrels and are now showing eagerness to fight, so have done damage to the foundation of the Empire. So, at this juncture, the presence of one who has stood the test by trustworthiness and valour at the capital is highly desirable. Hence immediately on receipt of this you should be present at the capital with the troops under your command and be expectant of royal favours. Dated the 13th day of Safar Hijri year 901 = 1496 A. D.

No. 8. Seal of Sultan Mahmud Bahamani

Raja Kheloji Ghorpade, the one expectant of Royal favour, is hereby informed that due to the cropping up of certain matters in our empire the attendance at Court of the well-wishers like you is necessary. Hence you should report yourself immediately on receipt of this and get the benefit of our Imperial audience. The forces under your command should accompany you; it is necessary. Your House has stood the test for reliability in this ancient Bahamani Empire. Hence further explanation on this subject is here superfluous. Dated 22nd Rajab Hijri 896—31 May 1491.

No. 9. Firman of Ismail Adil Shah to Maloji

This auspicious Firman is issued to Raja Maloji Ghorpade-highly distinguished for valour, one ever ready to risk his life, the leader of the brave, the chosen wielder of the sword, the pearl in the ocean of distinction, a jewel set in the ring of victory, the weapon to destroy the shield of the enemy, the thrower of the lasso on the parapet of victory and fame, the unparalleled in valour and strength, the foremost in the battlefield of unwavering loyalty, the fully devoted well-wisher, the chief and brilliant gem in the crown of the Imperial grace, one closely acquainted · with heavenly Government and enjoying the fullest confidence, one ready to risk his own life-to Raja Maloji Ghorpade Bahadur; that after the massacre of Kamalkhan of unripe mind, Amir Kasim Barid overstepped the boundary of dignity at the

S. 25.

assistance of Nizamshah, Kutubshah and Imadshah, and advanced with an army towards our territory, as a result of which he had to take part in the tremendous fight at Allapur in the neighbourhood of Bijapur. It can only be compared with the deluge. On this critical occasion your father fell on the field after working havoc in the ranks of the enemies and left a name of valour and bravery on the page of time. When on the banks of Krishna in the action against Timraj of Vigayanagar's army, we had to slightly withdraw our army, owing to the numerical superiority of the enemy, when the ways of safety to the river-crossing were blockaded from all directions, we were very uneasy at the situation, on that occasion you, the treasure of our confidence, without the least regard for your life, by thousands of repeated rushes at the enemy, relieved us from the life-destroying whirlpool and escorted us to the shores of safety. For this grand deed praises were showered on you from both heaven and earth. It was a great exploit by which you have been brought to the Imperial notice that you in return for your exploit have made yourself deserving of a great many royal favours. It was opened to our luminous mind that you the faithful have your devoted mind reduced among your equals on account of the formality of " Kurnish " and " Zamin Bosi; " so we have excused you from the labour of this formality. Because to sacrifice one's own self and to risk one's own life are quite different from formalities. It is unjust to burden faithful persons with customary and formal services. The chamberlains of the Court are informed of the fact that they should not trouble you with these obligations, so that you should strive for the prosperity of the Empire with a happy mind and a satisfied heart. In addition to this we have given you permission to use two Morchels. Dated 928 Hijri = 1522 A. D.

No. 10.   Firman of Ali Adilshah to Cholraj

The following Firman is issued by Ali Adilshah to Cholraj, the son of Karnasing and grandson of Akhaising:-

All the valour and bravery exhibited by your forefathers in the great war, and their endless exertions in the destruction of the enemy, have come under our holy observation. On the said critical occasion your father Karnasing gave up his life only after slaughtering a great many of the enemies, and thus enlisted his name in the roll of the valiant and faithful heroes of the world. Keeping in mind all these services and valour, we have bestowed on you the Jagir of Mudhol including the eighty four villages, and the tracts round about Raibag, Hukeri, and the forts and forty villages situated in the Paragana of Ben (Wai), which have been continued to this day in your family from ancient times, along with Pargana Torgal. And we have conferred on you the rank of the " Commander of Seven Thousand " and for the expenses of the armies at Mudhol you are granted villages near " Kallur ". So you should always keep yourself in possession of these grants, authority, Jagir, villages and forts, and exert yourself to the utmost in the service of this Kingdom. You should also know that herein lies your welfare. Dated Hijari year 972— 1564 A. D.

No. 11. Firman of Ibrahim Shah to Pratapsinha

This devoted servant of God came to learn on this occasion through petition from Sardars of this (Gadi) Kingdom and the defenders of this Empire that Raja Cholraj Ghorpade's son, Raja Pilaji Ghorpade, after discharging the duties of the Royal service, faithfully and whole-heartedly went to the other world as God willed. His son Pratapsinha Ghorpade is exerting himself arduously in the service in place of his father and is brave and faithful. Remembering the claims of his father's services, the grant of Kasaba Mudhol and 84 villages and his father's Mansab of 7000 and Jagirs have been recognised and confirmed upon him and he is thus honoured. Following the path of his ancestors, he should be dutiful, faithful, honest and ardent in service and should enjoy the Mansab and Jagir and other Royal favours. He should realize that in our gratification lies his welfare. Dated 11 Rabilaval 1007 A. H.—1598 A. D.[1]

APPENDIX V

(See p. 76 supra)

The English Records on Khan Jahan

Shah Jahan came to Burhanpur in the beginning of the year 1630 to put down the rebellion of his Viceroy, Khan Jahan Lodhi, and to reconquer the parts of the Nizamshahi State which were ceded back by the Viceroy without the order of the Emperor. During his stay of two years in the Deccan, he rooted out the rebellion, overawed the Deccan kingdoms, and had the satisfaction to see that his rebellious Viceroy was despatched to the other world. These events have been referred to in the following contemporary English letters:

"The Country is in peace and quietness, and the King in Barampore (Burhanpur), intending a warre against the Deccannees. "[1]

"Our project against Damon and Diu is growne cold; wee doubt through sinister informaciouns of this Governoor, inclined more to the Portugall then to us, as we gather by some passages between them. Yett is the King now in Brampore, and (it is) said hee will fall uppon the Rajaes of Mullier and Abnagar, bordering uppon Damon; whoe, although they pay him yearely tribute and acknowledgement of homage were never truly subdued nor will surrender their fortresses or castles into the Kings hands, as hee hath required. These brought into subjeccion, itt is likely hee will bee doing with the Portugalls country about ‚Damon or Bassein,. though the cittie and cittadell of Damon ittselfe bee not pregnable without forces by sea, to keepe them from succor

Mulhier and Daman threatened.

---

1. No. 11 of Mudhol Mss.
2. O. C. 1306. Swally Marine. 13 April 1630.

and releife.   Others say hee will fall into Decan, pretending
a conquest of that country; which is likeliest.   Soe soone as
the raines are past, wee shall see what are his   intents.
His owne country is in peace and quietness, and for ought
wee understand likely soe to continue, having pollitickly
wrought his owne securitie by cutting off all the blood
royall, without leaving any butt his owne sonnes that canne
lay claime to his crowne; and then impoverishing his amrawes
or nobles by taking from them all their treasure and livings,
allowing noe more then will maintaine them barely in an
ordinary state." [1]

" Wee can expect noe lovely vend thereof, especially
by reason of the present warrs with Decan, which wee hope
are now drawing to their period by the subtill contrivance
of Assuff Chaun, the great favorite, who with a powerfull
armye is gon out with pretended show to
Asaf Khan in   effect that by force which betwixt him and the
the Deccan.   great ambrawas of that councell they intend to
performe by an underhand composition of peace, thereby to
save (as much as in them lyes) the honour of the King, who
shalbee made beleeve that his power, and not his secret
pollicie, shall have brought to passe soe great a victory
aymed at. " [2]

" Will now wait for better markets, in view of the
expected termination of the wars in the Deccan. "[3]

" The King still prosecutes his warrs with Decan, and
hath lately atcheived a petty victory against Ckaun Jehaun. "[4]

A direfull famine and a continuous war in the Deccan
have put a stop to trade in 1630.

" This direfull tyme of dearth and the Kings continued
warrs with the Decans disjoyned all trade out of frame; the
Famine in 1630.   former calamitie haveing fild the waies with
desperate multitudes, who, setting their lives
att nought, care not what they enterprize soe they may but
purchase meanes for feeding, and will not dispence with the

1.   O. C. 1306. Swally Marine. 13 April 1630,
2.   Surat Factory Outward Letter Bk. Vol. I, P. 74. 12 Nov. 1630
3.   Ibid. Vol. I. P. 103. Surat to Ahmadabad, 30 Nov. 1630
4.   Ibid. Vol. I. P. 112. Surat to Masulipatam. 3 Dec. 1630

nakedest passenger not soe much as our poore pattamars with letters, who, if not murthered on the way, doe seldome escape unryfled and thereby our advises often miscarried on the other side. The warrs with Decan haveing stopped up all passages, and accustomed conflewence of marchants to and from those parts are intercepted whereby the vend, not only of your currall (whose greatest expence is in Decan) wilbe hindered, but likewise your fraight and customes in Persia much lessened by the want of those finer goods out of Decan, in whose liew your ships are only fraught with these of groser quallitie." [1]

"The king being now resolved (or at least likely) to continew his residence in that place, for it seemes he prosecutes the warrs with Decan." [2]

The letter of 10th June 1631 gives an account of the heroic death of Khan Jahan Lodhi, of the triple alliance of the Deccan States against Shah Jahan and of the expected invasion of a pretender for the throne of Delhi.

"The warrs with Decan are yett still contynued, but with slowe mocion and small successe or performance. Ckaun Jehaune, in his flight from thence towards

Honourable death of Khan Jahan.

his owne countrey being interrupted in his passage and persued by Abdela Ckaun with advantage of nomber, encountered the terrour of his desperate fortunes and with admirable courage preffred an honourable death (which the marks of 15 wounds well testified) before that life that must have suffred the scorne and contempt of his persecutors, and so finished his daies amongst the thickest of his enemyes fighting. The Kinge nevertheles desists not in his aymes against

Triple alliance of Deccan kings.

Decan, whose three kings are now strongly confederated which before were partely devided. And in the interim Balsuneber, the sonne of Jehaunguires brother, who of the bloud royall being the only man that surviveth, and having formerly conveyed

1. O. C. 1335. Surat to Company, 31 December 1630.
2. O. C. 1342. From Surat. 23 February 1631.

himselfe into the Tartarian territoryes is there linckt in
matrimony with the King of (blank) his
A pretender for Delhi throne. daughter and assisted by his father in lawe
both with men and moneys, layes clayme to
Cabull, Multan, and all those parts towards Lahore; which
is thought will begett a peace with the Decans and divert the
thoughts of this kinge that wave. "[1]

The war in the Deccan was coming to an end, but
the calamities resulting from the famine were intensified.

"The warre with Decan is at a pawse and a peace now in
treaty, though the armies on neither side dismissed, (and?)
the King still in Brampore; which preventing the supplies
of corne to these parts from those others of
Famine and pestilences. greater plenty, and the raynes hereabout
having falen superfluously, which with bad
government is cause of the highest extreame of scarcity,
wheate and rice being rissen to $2\frac{1}{2}$ sere for a mamoodee,
butter at a seare and a quarter, a hen at 4 or 5 Ma
(moodees) and rare it is to see one; and to aflict the
more, not a family throughout either here or Broach
that hath not been vissited with agues, feavours, and
pestilentiall diseases. God avert these judgements from us,
and give us strength to suffer His chastisements
with patience."[2]

"This base Kinge contynueth ungratefully his warrs on
Decan and prosecuteth them most wilfully, tho the famine
and their good successe hath hitherto
The war continued in 1632. made him much the looser. Now lately he
hath sent Asaph Caun upon them (against
his will) with 40 or 50,000 horse which will be to little
purpose. The Shawe his embassadour is dispeeded from
Brampore, where the Kinge is; and (as is reported) the
Governor of Agra beares him company as embassadour
back again."[3]

"The King, being in Brampore, hath taken up 800
camells of ours. You must prevent the comying out of

1. F. R. Surat Vol. 34. P. 3. Surat to Persia. 10 June 1631.
2. O. C. No. 1374. Surat to Bantam. 8 September 1631.
3. O. C. No. 1416. Surat to Persia, 23 January 1632.

such as Capt. Quaile is; at home you may look to the security he hath given to the King."[1]

The cessation of war in the Deccan is referred to in several letters. One of these is important in mentioning the name of Raja Chhatrasall of Bundi who owed some money to the English for purchasing tapestry.

"Nothing is said here about Saif Khan; but it is supposed that the King will winter at Ahmadabad, 'and so hee may bee ecclipsed by the greater light."[2]

"Newes at present is that the Mogull and the Kinge of this place hath concluded a peace, and that the Mogull hath sent out his firemen to have his armies returned back."[3]

"Steel is so much dearer, owing to the Deccan wars and the difficulty of transportation, that its price is nearly the same as in England; they have sent patterns of different sorts and, if these are approved, they hope, by the time they receive fresh instructions, to find it cheaper here or to procure it from Dabhol, which is nearer to the spring head from whence it is derived."[4]

"The Kinge is yett at Dowlattabad (Daulatabad), from whence it is not yett divulged whether (i. e. wither) he will remove to winter. Mandoo is the likliest place; some say Amadavad. 'Had almost resolved to visit him at either place, carrying thither some Persian horses, scarlet and violet broadcloth, and some China Commodities,) with confidence to have at least received the debt owinge by Cuttor Saile (Chhatrasai) for the tapestrie belonging to Sir Francis Craine, and to have setled our businesse in India according to the conveniencie of the present times."[5]

"Here is writeing from Vizapore (Bijapur) that the Mogull hath concluded a peace with the Kinge of this country and that his army is returned back."[6]

1. O. C. No. 1428. Surat to Company. 24 April 1632.

2. F. R, Surat, Vol. LXXXIV part iii, p. 80. Surat to Ahmadabad. 27 February 1636.

3. F. R. Surat, Vol. I, P. 454. Dabhol to Surat. 20 April 1636.

4-5. O. C. 1558. Surat to the Company. 28 April 1636.

6. F. R. Surat, Vol. I. P. 631. Dabhol to Surat. 19 May 1638.

Bijapur Kings.

Shahjahan on his Peacock Throne.

" In return he has promised that, if Chhatarsal fails to pay, his wakil in the royal camp shall be imprisoned. Hopes to receive the royal farman in four or five days: it 'wants but the Kings choop' (stamp : Hindi. Chhap). " [1]

APPENDIX VI

(See p. 77 supra)

Composition of Shah Jahan's army in 1630

The first was commanded by Schaast Chan (Shaista Khan), the Son of Assaph-Chan, and consisted of several Regiments, to wit, that of Schaast–Chan, which was of five thousand Horse.   5000

That of his Father consisting of
five thousand Horse, all Rasboutes.   5000

Sadoch Chan.	3000
Myrsa Sedt Madaffer,	3000
Giasar Chan.	2500
Seid Jaffer.	2000
Jafter Chan.	2100
Mahmud Chan.	1000
Alawerdi Chan.	1000
Sasdel–Chan Badary.	2000
Myrsa–Seer–Seid.	700
Baaker–Chan.	500

Whereto were added besides, four thousand six hundred Mansebdars, in several loose Companies.

The Second Body, under the Command of Eradet-Chan, consisted of the following Regiments.

That of Erade-Chan, of	4000
Rau–Donda (Ram Dhonda)	1000
Dorcadas (Durgadas)	1200
Kerous.	1200

---

1. F. R. Surat, Vol. I. P. 647. Royal Camp at Narbada to Surat. 25 August 1636.

S. 26.

Ram Tschend Harran (Ram Chand Hada) 1200
Mustapha-Chan. 1000
Jakout-Chan (Yakut Khan). 2000
Killously. 3000
Sidi Fakir. 1000
Eca Berkendas. 1000
Jogi-Rasgi, the Son of Lala Berting 7000
Teluk-Tschaud (Trilokchand). 400
Jakoet-Beg (Yakut Beg) 400
Three other Lords commanded each two hundred
                                        Horse............ 600
Aganour, Chabonecan, Babouchan,
Seid-Camel, Sidiali, and Sadaed-Chan, each
five hundred Horse. 3000
So that this Body consisted of 28,000

The third Body, under the Command of Raja Gedsing,
consisted of the following Regiments:

Raja-Gedsing (Jaisinha). 3000
Raja-Bideldas.. 3000
Oderam (Uderam) 3000
Raja-Biemsor   (Bhimsen) 2000
Madosing, Son of Ram Rattung (Madhusinha)... 1000
Raja-Ros-Assou. 1000
Badouria Raja-Bhozo (Bhoj)........................ 1000
Raja-Kristensing (Krishnasinha) 1000
Raja-Sour. 1000
Raja-Chettersing (Chhatrasinha) 500
Wauroup. 500
Raja-Odasing (Udai Sinha).......................... 5000
And under several other Rajas 4500

That Brigade, which was about the Kings Person at
Barampour, and to be as it were a Reserve, consisted of one
and forty thousand Horse; to wit,

Haddis and Berken-Dasse............................ 15,000
Asaf Chan. 5000
Rauratti. 4000

Wasir-Chan.	3000
Mobat-Chan.	3000
Godia Abdul Hessen.	3000
Astel-Chan.	2000
Serdar-Chan.	2005
Raja—Jessing.	2000
Feddey-Chan (Fidh Khan)	1000
Jaffer.	1000
Mockly-Chan.	1000
Serif-Chan.	1000
Seid-Chan.	1000
Amiral.	1000
Raja Ramdas.	1000
Tork Taes-Chan.	1000
Mier Jemla	1000
Myrsa Abdulac	500
Muhmud-Chan	500
Myrsa Maant Cher	500
Ghawaes–Chan.	1000
Moried-Chan.	1000

And under the Command of several other Lords, of their quality, whom they call Ommeraudes........ 10,000

The total of the Horse[1]............................ 62,500

APPENDIX VII

(See p. 85 supra)

The Dutch records on the extinction of the Nizam Shahi

" The said Mogul further intended to make war with the Decan to bring this country under his obedience and had left with his army for Barampour." [2]

"Further that His Majesty had proceeded with a mighty army from Agra to Doltabath, where he still stayed. There was no certainty yet what the object was, but there

---

1. Mandelslo's Travels into the E. Indies. Pp. 39–40.
2. Dagh - Register 1636. P. 50.

were rumours that the king had already taken possession of the countries of the kings of Golconda and Vissapour without striking a blow and had sent his governors there as viceroys and had given the said kings a pension."[1]

"From Danou the six Portuguese galleons (together having 230 big guns and 1700 men amongst which many were ill) went to *Bombaij,* in order to spend the winter there and to watch the movements of the Mogol. They were afraid that he might attack their fortresses in Bassijn and Chaul, because he kept a big army in those districts and they were also afraid that we might make an alliance with the Mogol.

The Mogol still stays in Doltabath and has three armies in the field, viz. two sent to Visiapore to attack that state from two sides and to bring it to his obedience, and another army sent to the Deccan to make his youngest son (whom he has made governor there) take possession of that country. The King of Golconda has willingly submitted to the Mogol giving a big present, and remains in his kingdom. The King of Visiapore has also offered this, but Sja Jean would not accept any reasonable conditions and detained tbe Visiapore ambassador. In the meantime the King of Visiapore had also come into the field with a mighty army, had but to fight one of the Mogol's armies, killed many and had taken 6 or 7 Mogol leaders as prisoners to Visiapour."[2]

"The great Mogol still stays in Doltabat and there are persistent rumours that he has made a contract with the King of Visiapour, whereby the latter would pay him 50, 00,000 ropias in gold and jewels, but this has not been confirmed." (Dagh-Register 1636. P. 273.)

The merchandise and spices had not been sold since September, on account of the unsafe roads between Golconda and Berampour, which were continually occupied by the Mogul and had not yet been opened; and they remained warehoused, although there were plenty of merchants in Masilipatan with much money who would not probably buy if the roads and by-roads were open.

1. Tagh-Register 1636. P. 114.
2. do.   do.   1636. P. 250.

The king of Colconda, from whom the Mogul king of Industan had asked a tribute of 900,000 pagodas, had already paid to His Majesty 500,000 pagodas, viz. 300,000 in cash and 200,000 in diamonds.[1]

"The two vessels had tested the river *Dabul* and found it to be 18 fathoms deep when coming in at half tide, and 6,7 or 8 fathoms further up, and they found it capable of sheltering a thousand ships without seeing the sea."[2]

"In the Guserat Districts no particular changes had occured. The king has defeated the rebellious ragie's Jougerat, has conquered the whole of his country and has subdued the whole of Deccan. He has appointed his son viceroy in Dolatabath, has received big tributes from the kings of Golconda and Visiapour, from the defeated ragie Sjougerat and from Deccan, allogether amounting to about 200 lakhs of 100,000 rupees per lakh. He set out victorious from Doltabath to Mandu and from there to Agra."[3]

"*In Dabul*, which had been such a flourishing place but had suffered severely from epidemics and had declined very much as a mercantile town, Mr. Van Twist could not find merchants, who could buy such a big cargo as he had brought or even part of it, and he therefore sent the ship and the yacht back to Goa with some cows and other refreshments for strengthening the fleet."[4]

APPENDIX VIII

(See p. 136 supra)

Shivaji's letter to Shahji

"In your last letter you wrote to me as follows:—

Far from helping the cause of his faith, Baji Ghorpade of Mudhol became party to the insidious schemes of the Mahomedans and Turks, and by foul and treacherous means

---

1. Dagh-Register 1631-1634. P. 241.
2. Dagh-Register. 1637. P. 75.
3. Ibid P. 106.
4. Ibid P. 254.

he brought us to Bijapur. What terrible danger faced us there, you well know. It seems that the Almighty has in his infinite wisdom decided to carry out your aspirations, to establish the Maratha power and protect the Hindu religion. Therefore it was that the peril was averted.

At present, inspired by malignant motives, Khawas Khan has marched against you, and ready to serve him Baji Ghorpade of Mudhol and Lakham Savant and Khem Savant are with him. May God Shankar (Shiva) and Goddess Bhavani grant success to you.

Now it is our desire that we should be fully revenged upon them and as we are fortunate to have such an obedient son, ready to carry out the wishes of his father, we command you to do this work. Baji Ghorpade has gone ahead to Mudhol with his men."

On hearing this from you, we went with an army to Mudhol, left the territory in ruin and took his thanas (garrisons). On learning this, Baji Ghorpade gave battle to us, in which he with other notable men fell. It was a great battle. We marched up and down the country and plundered it. Our gain on this occasion was enormous. We then proclaimed peace and brought the territory under our control. At this time Khawas Khan was coming upon us. With our army we fell upon him, defeating him and turning him back sad and despondent to Bijapur. Our next work was to crush the Savants. Fort after fort came into our possession. On we went, completely devastating their territory. They ceased to receive help from Goa, but the killedars of Phonda fought for them. By means of explosives, we blew up one of the bastions of the fort. Thus we became masters of their territory.

We next turned our arms aga..sr the Portuguese and took a part of their territory. They sued for peace and presented us with guns. The Savants could no longer consider themselves safe in Portuguese territory. For they sent one Pitambar as their Vakil to us. "We are," they pleaded, "likewise the descendants of the house of Bhosle and you ought to care for our interests. You should take half the revenue of our possession and the other half we shall

devote to the expenses of our troops with which we shall serve
you. Their requests are granted. Thus it is by your blessings
that everything ended as you desired and I have great pleasure
in submitting this account to you.[1]

APPENDIX IX

Ruling Dynasties of the Deccan

(1) The Bahmani Kings

Year of accession		Year of accession	
1347	Ala-ud-din Bahmani 1.	1435	Ala-ud-din II.
1358	Muhammad I.	1457	Humayun Shah Zalim.
1375	Mujahid Shah.	1461	Nizam Shah
1378	Daud ,,	1463	Muhammad Shah
1378	Mahmud ,,	1482	Mahmud ,, II.
1397	Ghiyas-ud-din.	1518	Ahmad ,, II.
1397	Shams-ud-din	1520	Ala-ud-din III.
1397	Firoz Shah	1522	Wali-Ullah Shah.
1422	Ahmad ,, I.	1526	Kalim Ullah ,,

(2) The Adil Shahs of Bijapur

Year		Year	
1490	Yusuf Adil Shah	1580	Ibrahim Adil Shah II.
1510	Ismail ,, ,,	1627	Muhammad Adil Shah
1534	Malu ., ,,	1656	Ali Adil Shah II.
1535	Ibrahim ,, ,, I.	1673-86	Sikandar Adil
1557	Ali Adil Shah I.		Shah.

(3) The Nizam Shahs of Ahmadnagar

Year		Year	
1490	Ahmad Shah	1595	Ibrahim Shah
1508	Burhan Shah I.	1595	Ahmad ,, II.
1553	Hussain Shah	1596	Bahadur ,,
1565	Murtaza ,,	1600	Murtaza ,, II
1588	Miran ,,	1631-33	Hussain Shah II
1589	Ismail ,,	1633-36	Murtaza N. Shah
1590	Burhan ,, II.		III.

1. A History of the Maratha People, Kincaid and Parasnis, Vol. I, P. 178.

(4) The Qutb Shahs of Golconda

1512	Quli Qutb Shah	1580 Muhmammad Quli Shah
1543	Jamshid ,,	1612 Muhammad Shah
1550	Subhan Quli ,,	1626 Abdullah ,,
1550	Ibrahim ,,	1672–87 Abul Hassan Shah

(5) The Rulers of Ikkeri-Bednur

1.	Chaudappa Nayak, son of Hulibailu Basappa		1499-1513
2.	Sadasiva ,, son of 1......	......	1513-1545
3.	Sankanna ,, I, son of 2......	......	1545-1558
4.	Sankanna ,, II, younger brother of 3.		1558-1570
5.	Ramaraja ,, son of 3.	.....	1570-1582
6.	Venkappa ,, I, younger brother of 5. ..		1582-1629
7.	Virbhadra ,, grandson of 6, and son of Bhadrappa Nayak.		1629-1645
8.	Sivappa ,, grandson of 4, and son of Siddappa Nayak.............		1645-1660
9.	Venkatappa ,, II, younger brother of 8.......		1660-1661
10.	Bhadrappa ,, son of 8.	...	1661-1663
11.	Somasekhara ,, I, younger brother of 10.		1663-1671
12.	Channamaji, * widow of 11......................		1671-1697

* Mysore and Coorg. P. 157. Mysore Gaz. II. P. 432; Sarkar observes that Shivappa ruled from 1618 to 1662. He is wrong in the light of this genealogy. Several English letters mention Shivappa living in 1662. (Pp. 82, 83, 95, 99. Shivaji the Great Vol. I.) Ventappa (Venkatappa) is said to rule for one year in this genealogy, but from the Dagh-Register he appears to have reigned for two years. Ali Adil Shah really advanced against Bhadrappa and not Shivappa. I too have mentioned the latter on the basis of the English letters. The Dutch documents reproduced on pages 99-100 of Vol. I clearly state that Ali Adil Shah advanced against Bhadrappa. It is confirmed by the Basatin-i-Salatin. Pp. 299-300. Cf. Mysore Gaz. P. 434. This Bhadrappa was succeeded by his brother Somasekhara in 1663 and the latter by Channamaji in 1671.

(1) THE DEED OF PARTITION.

Raja Sahajee Bhonsla recently represented to the lofty Court that the grandson of Cholraj Raja, Prataprao Ghorpade Bahadur, has by force withheld his half share from ancient times in the Mudhol Jagir, the townships of Pargana Ben and the forts therein and the possessions in Karad; also no share is given to Rao Malojee, the grandson of Vallabhsing. But he has given a share to Mansing and Ambaji in the villages of Mudhol, hence his (Shahaji's) own share and that of Malojee, the grandson of Vallabhsing, be granted by the holy Sarkar. This representation has been considered by our holy Great Mind and our attention has been drawn to it, for it is a matter of our Imperial policy to see that the requirements of this honest and obedient ancient house are provided for; this has ever been our policy in accordance to which the following agreeable Firman is issued: Raja Prataprao, the grandson of Raja Cholraj, should feel himself satisfied with Mudhol with the 84 Moujas (towns or villages) and the Pargana of Torgal and half the township of the family possessions of Karnatak and Karad and the command and rank of 7,000. Raja Sahajee should have half the villages of Pargana Ben and 26 townships of Karad and half the family possessions in the Karnatik as his portions with the rank and command of 5,000, and Malojee, the son of Bhairavasing, the son of Valabhsingh, has been granted 30 villages in the neighbourhood of Vijayanagar with the command of 2,000. Separate Sanads have been issued. From this all the members of the family should be satisfied

with the liberal grants conferred and they should be all
attention to the welfare of the ever-increasing Empire
and the services pertaining to it

Dated 1047 Shuhur = 1056 A.H. or 19th August 1646 A.D.

(2) BAJI GHORPADE MADE VAZIR AND COMMANDER OF 7000. NO MORE PARTITION.

Bismillah-ir-Rahiman-ir-Rahim
Shaheddin Muhammad Ibrahim.

Rao Raje Bajirao Bahadur, Officer Commanding,
being under Royal favour should note this that at the
present juncture your father the repository of our confidence was killed on account of the intrigues of some
of our courtiers. This has worked upon our mind and
has created great inconvenience. Your ancestors have
been faithfully serving the Empire regardless of the
amount of trouble since the time of the Bahamani
Badashahs to this present day, and your family has ever
been enjoying our trust and confidence. Hence being
aware of the fact that you are deserving our Royal favour,
the rank of the Commander of 7,000 with 7,000 horse
and all the territory held in connection with it and the
half share of the Jagir in the Karnatik and Ben Pargana
that was continued in your branch has been as in olden
times granted and continued to you; along with it you
are also invested with the office of a Vazir. Henceforth
to avoid disputes in future no Jahgirs will be granted to
any of your kinsmen or partners adjoining to or in the
neighbourhood of Anagundi (Vijayanagar) and Kampli

where your Jagirs are situated. You should be pleased
with Royal favour and be diligent to your duties.

19 Shaban al-muazzam San Saba and Khamsen
and Alaf. (Shuhur 1057). [1]

(Banda Sultan Muhammad)

(3) YASHWANTRAO WADWE TO ASSIST SHAHJI MAHARAJ IN THE KARNATIC.

The auspicious farman has acquired the honour of
being issued that Mashhur-ud-Dawla (famous in the
Sovereignty) Yashawantarao, being strengthened and
hopeful by the extremeless imperial kindnesses, may
know that the Nawab with (a court worthy of the angles)
the thresholds as high as the sky-having the Magnani-
mity of the sky, pivot of the kingdom, the asylum
of authority and rule, the support of glory and
grandeur, strengthener of the regulations of success,
establisher of the customs of kingship, highly honoured
moon of fame, gem of the mine of prosperity, accepted by
the great Sultans, famous amongst the respected nobles,
strengthener of the foundations of Caliphate, possessor
of the rank of Asaf, wisdom of Aristotle, reason of
Plato, insight of Ptolemy, distinguished prime minister,
honoured, generous and obliger, the gem of the ring of
position and pomp, a statesman of the climes of the earths,
a pearl of the ocean of liberality, centre of the circle of
existence, the place of the rising of the sun of perfec-
tion, source of the help of All-Glory, Cultivator of the

1. It means 1067 A. H, or 23 May 1657 A. D,

garden (?) of creation, light of theso cket of sight, sun of the sky of greatness, star of the zodiacal sign of greatness, hoister of the banners of the exaltation of ranks, decorator of the signs (?) or the dignity of eulogies, the best couplet of the ode of mankind, the centre of the circle of kindness and obligation (?), model for the exalted nobles, the purest and best among the great and renowed persons of the age, means of safety and peace, gracious and high–titled Nawab Khan Baba has written to him that he should go to the Jangmakanvi pass (?) with a party of soldiers and followers, join the support of honour and bravery, the chief of the faithful well–wishers, model for the well-meaning loyal persons, the best amongst the tribes and brethren, the purest and best amongst the peers and contemporaries, pillar of the powerful government, Maharaj, our son (?) Shahji Bhonsla, and being sincere and harmonious with the Maharaj, should give expression to the signs of loyalty. It is incumbent upon him not to trespass the order of the above-mentioned eminent Nawab to the extent of a hair-tip even. He should betake himself to the Maharaj very quickly and in this he should think that his honour will be increased. Written on 25th Zu-hijjeh, 1057 A. H. (11th January 1648 A. D.)

(4) BAJI GHORPADE--A MARTYR.

In the name of the compassionate and merciful God. The Kingdom belongs to God.

An ink seal as follows.

Najaf Shah, a devoted servant of the valiant king Ali, the son of Sultan Muhammad Shah.

(This) auspicious (royal) farman (has) obtained the

honour of being issued (to) the one possessed of bravery and heroism, Maloji Raja Bahadur Ghorpaday of the Adil Shahi. From (one of) the months of the year one thousand and sixty-eight of Shuhur san (1068 Shuhur= 1668 A. D.), (upto) this time it has become manifest in the exalted court of the asylum of the world as follows:—Your father Baji Raja Ghorpaday of the Adil Shahi, possessed of bravery and heroism, with (good) faith of heart (sincerity) served the special (? noble) and illustrious Sarkar bearing the marks of bounty, for many days. And a dispute and fight also took place between the supreme (and) most holy Sarkar and *Shivaji Raja Bhonsle; in the fight your father having displayed gallantry and heroism and self-sacrifice, and having (thus proved himself) useful in every respect to the most holy Sarkar, died like a martyr.* In former times there was a Jagir held by him. For these reasons, we, having shown you perfect kindness, (and) having been pleased to direct our attention to the former services, *have exempted (you) from service and* have been pleased to confer (on you) five parganas:-(namely) Mudhol, Jamgay, Dohulesar, Macheknur and Lokapur; (in) all five parganas *as Inam,* the grant being (made) by the presence (which) is full of light and which affords protection to the people by way of Royal favour and excess of kingly kindness, i. e., we have been pleased *to give the same (as) Inam (to you) in perpetuity.* It is proper that you and your children and grand children (from) back to back (i. e. generation to generation), having taken (said) Inam in your possession, should remain pleased. Accordingly, for each of the five parganas, a separate stringent farman has been caused to be given ' Written on the 15th day of Jamadi-ul-akhir in the holy Hijri year 1081. (20th October 1670 A. D.)

(Seals follow)

---

1. The Rajasaheb of Mudhol has all these five Firmans with him.

INDEX OF PLACES

SUBJECT INDEX